PREDICATE TRANSFORMER SEMANTICS

Cambridge Tracts in Theoretical Computer Science

Managing Editor   Professor C.J. van Rijsbergen,
Department of Computing Science, University of Glasgow

Editorial Board

S. Abramsky, Department of Computing Science, Imperial College of Science
and Technology
P.H. Aczel, Department of Computer Science, University of Manchester
J.W. de Bakker, Centrum voor Wiskunde en Informatica, Amsterdam
J.A. Goguen, Programming Research Group, University of Oxford
J.V. Tucker, Department of Mathematics and Computer Science,
University College of Swansea

Titles in the series

PREDICATE TRANSFORMER SEMANTICS

ERNEST G. MANES
Department of Mathematics
University of Massachusetts at Amherst

PUBLISHED BY THE PRESS SYNDICATE OF THE UNIVERSITY OF CAMBRIDGE
The Pitt Building, Trumpington Street, Cambridge, United Kingdom

CAMBRIDGE UNIVERSITY PRESS
The Edinburgh Building, Cambridge CB2 2RU, UK
40 West 20th Street, New York NY 10011–4211, USA
477 Williamstown Road, Port Melbourne, VIC 3207, Australia
Ruiz de Alarcón 13, 28014 Madrid, Spain
Dock House, The Waterfront, Cape Town 8001, South Africa

http://www.cambridge.org

First published 1992
First paperback edition 2004

A catalogue record for this book is available from the British Library

ISBN 0 521 42036 9 hardback
ISBN 0 521 61610 7 paperback

"...I view Elgot's work as but a first chapter of a theory of iteration and fixed points of which we will see many more future chapters from many hands, alas, without Cal's criticism and guidance."

Dana S. Scott

TABLE OF CONTENTS

PREFACE

The founding paper [Pratt 1976] on dynamic logic begins as follows:

> "This paper deals with logics of programs. The objective is
> to formalize a notion of program description and to give both plausible
> (semantic) and effective (syntactic) criteria for the notion of truth
> of a description. A novel feature of this treatment is the development
> of the mathematics underlying Floyd-Hoare axiom systems independently
> of such systems."

This book continues study of such mathematics with particular emphasis on semantic frameworks. We intend for these frameworks to be flexible, relying on no particular concept of state. Ultimately, extensions of the theory are to address at least program semantics, operating systems, concurrent processes and distributed networks; but the accomplishments of the foundational core herein are modest.

We shall be concerned with a category-theoretic foundation. One possible paradigm is that a morphism is the behaviour of a program. Composition of morphisms models program-chaining. An implementation of a programming language must provide a definite category in which to assign morphisms to programs. We shall also require that high-level specifications about programs map, as well, to true-false assertions about the corresponding interpreted programs.

Our semantic frameworks are categories satisfying certain axioms, that is, are models of the first-order theory of categories. Composition is the only primitive operation. Such models are strongly typed in that two morphisms cannot be composed unless the target of the first coincides exactly with the source of the second. Other program constructs must be expressed in terms of composition; that this can be done is tribute to the unusual expressiveness of category theory as has been increasingly documented since the seminal founding paper by Sammy Eilenberg and Saunders Mac Lane in 1945. This greatly minimizes the assumptions about programming languages which need to be made up front. Whether the end justifies the means we must leave for you the reader to judge.

INTRODUCTION

A few preliminaries are in order. Generally we shall compose morphisms left to right,

$$X \xrightarrow{\alpha} Y, \ Y \xrightarrow{\beta} Z \ \mapsto \ X \xrightarrow{\alpha\beta} Z \ .$$

We often indicate the application of function f on argument x by xf rather than $f(x)$ but there are exceptions when convention warrants, e.g., $\mathcal{C}(X,Y)$ for the set of $\mathcal{C}$-morphisms from X to Y rather than $(X,Y)\mathcal{C}$.

Assumptions on the reader's preparation in category theory are modest. A list of "must" topics (listed in order of need from the beginning of Section 1) would be

- Commutative diagrams.
- Isomorphisms.
- Coproducts. Denote by $< \alpha_1,...,\alpha_m >$ the unique morphism from an m-component coproduct which is α_i when restricted to the ith coproduct injection.
- Functors. In particular, the functor $\mathcal{C}(X,-)$ from $\mathcal{C}$ to the category **Set** of sets and total functions which assigns to Y the set $\mathcal{C}(X,Y)$ of $\mathcal{C}$-morphisms.
- Natural transformations of functors.
- Products. Denote by $[\alpha_1,...,\alpha_n]$ the unique morphism from an m-component product which is α_j when followed by the jth product projection.
- Initial and terminal objects.
- Duality. $\mathcal{C}^{op}$ denotes the opposite category of $\mathcal{C}$.

Tangential mention is also made of

- Products of categories.
- Diagram categories.

Many basic definitions will also appear in this introduction.

Quite a few books on categories have been written. [Mitchell 1965] is in keeping with the historical origins of Boolean categories as discussed below. In this vein we also suggest [Freyd 1964] for its charisma and accessible style (but beware the Chaucerian dialect). For those who are not uncomfortable with examples and motivation from the mathematical mainstream there is [Mac Lane 1971]. There are also beginning texts on categories intended for computer scientists: [Arbib and Manes 1975], [Asperti and Longo 1991], [Barr and Wells 1990] and [Rydeheard and Burstall 1988]. Any one of these books goes far beyond the needs of this one.

Two very basic examples of semantic frameworks will be mentioned often so let us establish symbols for them. Denote by **Pfn** the category whose objects are sets and whose morphisms are partial functions, with composition as usual. This is the most standard deterministic category for program behaviour. The corresponding standard nondeterministic one is **Mfn**, the category whose objects are sets and whose morphisms are multi-valued functions, that is, if $\alpha : X \longrightarrow Y$ in **Mfn**, $x\alpha$ is a subset of Y. The definition of the composition $\alpha\beta$ is a familiar one, namely $z \in x\alpha\beta \Leftrightarrow z \in y\beta$ for some $y \in x\alpha$. In both of these categories the coproduct $X + Y$ is constructed as the disjoint union of the sets X, Y. Thus it is natural to interpret a morphism $\alpha : Z \longrightarrow X + Y$ as "making a choice". In **Pfn**, if $z\alpha$ is defined the choice is to map it into exactly one of X, Y; in **Mfn** one can also choose both. Another important construction in these categories is associated with a morphism $\alpha : X \longrightarrow Y$ and a "predicate" $Q \subset Y$. The "weakest liberal precondition" for postcondition Q, or $[\alpha]Q$ in the notation of dynamic logic, is given respectively in **Pfn**, **Mfn** by

$$[\alpha]Q = \{x \in X : x\alpha \in Q \text{ or } x\alpha \text{ is undefined}\}$$

$$[\alpha]Q = \{x \in X : x\alpha \subset Q\} .$$

In both categories, there is a unique morphism β such that the square

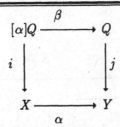

is a pullback, where i, j are inclusion functions. We strongly recommend that the reader first master these categorical constructions in **Pfn** and **Mfn** since they underlie the entire approach to be developed.

Preliminaries aside, which categories are to be studied in this book? Let us say at the outset that an active community continues research into category-theoretic models of semantics and while it is too early to predict which axioms are of long-term interest, it is fairly clear that no one approach can expect to be definative even for specific existing programming languages let alone for those around the corner. Elegant categories have been proposed by [Carboni and Walters 1987], [Curien and Obtulowicz 1989], [DiPaola and Heller 1987], [Longo and Moggi 1984] and [Robinson and Rosolini 1988]; these have a tensor product with product-like qualities, motivated in part by program semantics but also by basic recursive function theory and other concerns. Closer in spirit to our approach are the distributive categories investigated by the Sydney Category Seminar in early 1990 (see [Cockett 1990, 1991], [Cockett and Fukushima 1991]) and we shall provide an interface between these and Boolean categories in Part IV. What distinguishes our approach is a primal emphasis on finite coproducts; indeed, that is the title of Part I of the book.

It was [Elgot 1975] who emphasized that a category with finite coproducts is a compositional semantic model for the synthesis of straight-through networks. An m–input, n–output network is represented by a morphism of form

$$X_1 + \cdots + X_m \xrightarrow{\quad\alpha\quad} Y_1 + \cdots + Y_n \;.$$

Consider, for example, the network shown on the next page.

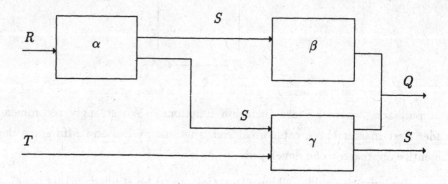

Here, $\alpha : R \longrightarrow S+S$, $\beta : S \longrightarrow Q$, $\gamma : S+T \longrightarrow Q+S$.   Thus if $t \oplus u$ is defined as in 2.5 below, we may form

$$R+T \xrightarrow{\quad \alpha \oplus id_T \quad} S+S+T$$

$$S+S+T \xrightarrow{\quad < \beta, \gamma > \quad} Q+Q+S$$

$$Q+Q \xrightarrow{\quad < id_Q, id_Q > \quad} Q$$

Then the semantics of the entire network is the composition

$$R+T \xrightarrow{\quad (\alpha \oplus id_T) < \beta, \gamma > (< id_Q, id_Q > \oplus id_S) \quad} Q+S \ .$$

Notice that, by categorical duality, using products instead of coproducts yields an equivalent abstract theory. But Elgot was thinking of the fundamental categories of Section 1 in which coproduct is disjoint union of sets whereas products, if they exist, may be hard to interpret and not semantically relevant. Notice that the general network morphism $\alpha : X_1 + \cdots + X_m \longrightarrow Y_1 + \cdots + Y_n$ decomposes, by the coproduct property, into $< \alpha_1, ..., \alpha_m >$ with $\alpha_i : X_i \longrightarrow Y_1 + \cdots + Y_n$ the behaviour if we allow only the ith input line; that $< \alpha_1, \cdots, \alpha_m >$ is tantamount to α reflects reality in basic computational frameworks.

Elgot chose to work with "algebraic theories" in the sense of [Lawvere 1963] rather than arbitrary categories with finite coproducts. This decision much affected subsequent work by many although we feel that this restriction is neither helpful nor necessary. (And it may not be too late! Much of the algebraic theories work in semantics requires only minor overhaul to be valid for more general categories.) We now define algebraic theories; our definition is equivalent to Lawvere's and clarifies how these categories stand in relation to general categories with finite coproducts. An *algebraic theory* is a category $\mathcal{A}$ whose objects are the natural numbers $0, 1, 2, \ldots$ and such that there exists a category $\mathcal{C}$ and an object D of $\mathcal{C}$ whose finite copowers exist (we write the copower $D + \cdots + D$ (n times) as $n \cdot D$) such that $\mathcal{A}(m,n) = \mathcal{C}(m \cdot D, n \cdot D)$, composition and identities being as in $\mathcal{C}$. Such $\mathcal{A}$ is equivalent to the full subcategory of all $m \cdot D$ (one must choose a specific copower for each m —see [Mitchell 1965, II.10] for a discussion of equivalence of categories) and has finite coproducts in particular, coproduct corresponding to integer addition. To understand the appeal of this approach, consider our analysis already given for the network above. In defining $\alpha \oplus id_Z$ we associate the coproduct $Y + Y + Z$ as $(Y + Y) + Z$. Yet the next moment, in defining $<\beta, \gamma>$, the association is $Y + (Y + Z)$. In reality, the composition $(\alpha \oplus id_Z) < \beta, \gamma >$ should be written $(\alpha \oplus id_Z)\psi < \beta, \gamma >$ where ψ is the canonical isomorphism from $(Y + Y) + Z$ to $Y + (Y + Z)$. In an algebraic theory with $Y = p$, $Z = q$, $(Y + Y) + Z = Y + (Y + Z) = 2p + q$. This tidiness is appealing, though it is ironic that the more precise notation of algebraic theories has made papers that use it unnecessarily inaccessible (and here I paraphrase the remarks of a leading practitioner at a recent conference.) Our preference is to stay within the categorical mainstream which entails some sophistication with unmentioned isomorphisms. While this is an art which takes some practice, we feel that the advantages are worth the effort.

In Section 2 we consider general choice operators $\star$ on X, these being object-indexed families $\star_Y : \mathcal{C}(X,Y) \times \mathcal{C}(X,Y) \longrightarrow \mathcal{C}(X,Y)$ with the property that for all morphisms $\gamma : Y \longrightarrow Z$, $(\alpha \star \beta)\gamma = \alpha\gamma \star \beta\gamma$, reflecting the property that "the choice is made before anything else". In fact it is proved that if there exists a copower $X + X$ with coproduct injections i, j then

$$\alpha \star \beta \;=\; X \xrightarrow{\;\; i \star j \;\;} X + X \xrightarrow{\;\; <\alpha, \beta> \;\;} Y$$

which shows that the choice *is* made (via $i \star j$) before α, β interact. This supports the "disjoint union" interpretation of $X + X$. We also use coproducts to define deterministic morphisms (in the sense of Dijkstra) and show that if $\alpha \star \beta = \beta \star \alpha$ and

$\alpha \star \alpha = \alpha$ then $i \star j$ is necessarily nondeterministic unless X is trivial. If-then-else is an example of a choice operator. We characterize it in terms of a polymorphism property which asserts that "a transformation of if-then-else specifications effects a transformation of the if-then-else's themselves".

In Section 3 we consider iteration in a category with finite coproducts. Again following [Elgot 1975] we view iteration as a function of form $\xi : X \longrightarrow X + Y \mapsto \xi^{\dagger}$ $: X \longrightarrow Y$. The heuristic meaning of $\xi^{\dagger}$, realized in concrete cases, is that it obtains from ξ on input x by continuing to apply ξ and collecting all outputs in Y (at most one in the deterministic case **Pfn** and a subset of Y for **Mfn**.) Elgot observed that the fundamental fixed point equation for iteration is easily expressed:

$$X \xrightarrow{\quad \xi^{\dagger} \quad} Y \;\; = \;\; X \xrightarrow{\quad \xi \quad} X + Y \xrightarrow{\quad < \xi^{\dagger}, id_Y > \quad} Y$$

Using special properties of an algebraic theory, Elgot defined a subclass of "ideal" morphisms (rough meaning: time delay > 0) and required a unique solution of the fixed point equation when ξ is ideal. This initial attempt was not a very general model, excluding even **Pfn**.

Settling on a set of axioms for $\xi^{\dagger}$ is problematic. Consider the algebraic theory $\mathbf{Mat}_R$ (described more generally in **1.4** below) for R the semiring of subsets of X^*, X^* being the set of all words on the alphabet X. Here a morphism from m to n is an m–row, n–column matrix with entries in R and composition is matrix multiplication. For $A \subset X^*$, its Kleene-$*$ is hopefully describable in terms of a suitable iterate $(-)^{\dagger}$ as $([A \; \Lambda]$ $: 1 \longrightarrow 1 + 1)^{\dagger}$ where $\Lambda \in X^*$ is the empty word. Thus general first-order axioms on $(-)^{\dagger}$ would give a first-order axiomatization of regular algebra, not a trivial undertaking as is clear from [Conway 1971]. Indeed, first-order axioms for the algebra of regular events have only recently been claimed in two independent preprints [Bloom and Ésik 1991], [Kozen 1990]. Bloom's approach is a specialization of the axioms presented in Section 3, which evolve from the efforts of many contributors. The original definition was explored by many (see [Bloom 1982, 1982a].) The unrestricted polymorphic axiom of **3.11** dates to [Arbib and Manes 1978] who proved **3.13**: the usual iterate in **Pfn** is the only polymorphic one satisfying Elgot's equation. But the most significant milestone was the introduction of "iteration theories" (as opposed to iterative theories) in [Bloom, Elgot and Wright 1980]. Here $\xi^{\dagger}$ was defined for all ξ. The axioms for iteration theories were refined by [Ésik 1980] and [Ştefănescu 1987]. A particularly elegant achievement is the "pairing axiom" **3.16**, first isolated by [Bloom, Ginali and Rutledge 1977], an equation which expands $< \xi, \theta >$[†]. As is seen from the exposition in Section 3, the pairing axiom captures both the "one-variable-at-a-time" method of finding the least fixed point of a system of fixed point equations and the formula, familiar in regular algebra, for the Kleene-∗ of a matrix of regular sets. At this stage, some concensus seems to have been reached that the pairing axiom as well as the "parameter axiom" and "left zero axiom" of **3.17-18** should be included. Bloom and Ésik include a fourth axiom which they call the "commutative identity". They have provided a wealth of evidence that the consequences of the four axioms are satisfactory and their theory excludes no important examples as far as we know. A stronger axiom (it directly implies the commutative identity) is a restricted form of the polymorphic axiom, and we follow [Ştefănescu 1987] in making this our fourth axiom. We restrict polymorphism to the "pure maps" in our definition of polymorphic iterate in **3.26**; these will also be discussed later in this introduction. Polymorphic axioms are much easier to understand than the horrendous commutative identity and only artificial examples are known to support any claim that the polymorphic version is too strong. We note, however, that because all the Bloom-Ésik axioms are equations they can argue that only equational logic is needed for the proof theory of first-order iteration. Most of Section 3 is concerned with an expository motivation for the iteration axioms as well as the establishment of some basic examples. The material on the lax Kleene-∗ there is adapted from [Manes 1988, Section 4].

Part II presents the main innovation of this book, the concept of a Boolean category. We pause to discuss, albeit but briefly, some of the influences that led to this idea. We begin with, of all things, algebraic topology. This is a science which maps information about a geometric space into a diagram in the category of abelian groups wherein geometric features are studied with a calculus of pluses and minuses which is easy to work with. This calculus is formalized by a first-order language of so called exact sequences. The basic process loses geometric information. To do better, techniques from algebraic topology and homological algebra called for the replacement of the category of abelian groups with more highly structured categories in which a single object could be a sheaf of compact abelian groups, an infinite two-dimensional diagram of abelian groups, or worse. It was clear from the tedium of giving what seemed to be the same proofs over and over to establish the language of exact sequences in these new categories that there had to be axioms for a category of "abelian groups" from which the fundamental results followed. The result was *abelian categories*. The fundamental theorem of that subject is the metatheorem that a sentence in the language of exact sequences is universally valid in all abelian categories providing it holds in the category of modules over a ring, a mild extension of abelian groups where direct verification is easy. See [Freyd 1964] and [Mitchell 1965] for very readable expositions.

The framework we develop respects the following table of rough analogies.

Algebraic Topology	Program Semantics
geometric object	program
abelian category	Boolean category
exact sequence	Hoare assertion
category of modules	**Mfn**

The last analogy refers to (the Boolean category version of) Kozen's metatheorem 11.15 that Hoare assertions valid in the standard nondeterministic frame are universally valid in all Boolean categories.

More striking, however, is the fact that direct imitation of the structure of abelian categories led to the forerunners of Boolean categories and that, even when all is said and done, the Boolean category axioms are orthogonal to those for abelian categories in that they constrain the same types of construction but with different requirements —no nontrivial Boolean category can be abelian. The first forerunner is the "partially-additive categories" which I was priviliged to develop jointly with Michael Arbib a decade ago. See [Manes and Arbib 1986] for an expository introduction. We will now motivate this idea and, along the way, we will set down some useful definitions and take a look at abelian categories.

Consider the network $\alpha : X_1 + \cdots + X_m \longrightarrow Y_1 + \cdots + Y_n$. In a category with "empty morphisms" $0 : X \longrightarrow Y$ (that is, a family of zero morphisms as will shortly be defined) we may define "projections" $\rho_j : X_1 + \cdots + X_m \longrightarrow X_j$ in terms of the Kronecker-deltas $\delta_{ij} : X_i \longrightarrow Y_j$ which are 0 if $i \neq j$ and the identity morphism $X_i \longrightarrow X_i$ if $i = j$ by $\rho_j = \ <\delta_{1j}, ..., \delta_{mj}>$. If we define $\alpha_j = \alpha \rho_j$ then $\alpha = [\alpha_1, ..., \alpha_n]$ is an "output line decomposition" of α. Indeed, in **Pfn** and **Mfn** we have $x\alpha = \bigcup x\alpha_i$ (where the union has at most one element in the partial functions case.) In general, such decompositions express a network as the sum of its paths, an idea crucial in applications which needed to be made explicit in semantic models. (We make the same point in connection with an equational axiomatization of if-then-else in Section 14.) We sought, then, axioms on a category that allowed "zero morphisms" and "sums". But these problems had already been solved in the framework of abelian categories. Despite crucial differences, the needed constructions will be so similar that there is no loss of efficiency in pausing now for the definitions required to understand the abelian category axioms. We need them anyway!

A *family of zero morphisms* in a category C is an assignment of a distinguished morphism $0_{XY} : X \longrightarrow Y$ for each pair X, Y of C–objects; these are subject to the equations

$$W \xrightarrow{\alpha} X \xrightarrow{0_{XY}} Y \xrightarrow{\beta} Z \;=\; W \xrightarrow{0_{WZ}} Z$$

for all α, β. At most one such family can exist: if $\perp_{XY}$ were another, $\perp_{XY} = \perp_{XY} 0_{XY} = 0_{XY}$. If there exists a *zero object* —an object Z which is simultaneously initial and terminal so that there exists a unique morphism $X \longrightarrow Z$ and a unique morphism $Z \longrightarrow Y$ for every X, Y— then $0_{XY} = X \longrightarrow Z \longrightarrow Y$ provides a family of zero morphisms. As already noted, **Pfn** and **Mfn** have zero morphisms via empty functions, but **Set** does not have a family of zero morphisms.

Let C be a category with zero morphisms. For $\alpha : X \longrightarrow Y$, a *kernel* of α is a morphism $i : K \longrightarrow X$ satisfying firstly that $i\alpha = 0_{KY}$ and secondly that given another such $j : L \longrightarrow X$ with $j\alpha = 0_{LY}$ there exists unique $\psi : L \longrightarrow K$ with $\psi i = j$. Dually, a *cokernel of* α is $\rho : Y \longrightarrow C$ with $\alpha\rho = 0$ and universal with that property. We write these $Ker(\alpha)$, $Cok(\alpha)$ respectively. These constructions, when they exist, are unique up to unique isomorphism because of their respective universal properties. We say a morphism i *is a kernel* if $i = Ker(\alpha)$ for some α. It is clear from the universal property that if i is a kernel than i is a *monomorphism* (or *is mono*), that is, if $ti = ui$ then $t = u$. Dually, if ρ is a cokernel, ρ is an *epimorphism* (or *is epi*) if $\rho t = \rho u \Rightarrow t = u$. In the category of abelian groups, $Ker(\alpha)$ is the inclusion morphism of the subset $\{x \in X : x\alpha = 0\}$ and $Cok(\alpha)$ is the canonical projection $Y \longrightarrow Y/Im(\alpha)$ where $Im(\alpha) = \{x\alpha : x \in X\}$. In **Pfn**, $Ker(\alpha)$ is the inclusion of $\{x \in X : x\alpha \text{ is not defined}\}$ whereas $Cok(\alpha)$ is $\rho : Y \longrightarrow C$ where $C = \bigcup \{x\alpha : x \in X\}$ and ρ is defined by $x\rho = x$ if $x \in C$, $x\rho$ undefined otherwise. Similar formulas work in **Mfn** replacing "$x\alpha$ is not defined" with "$x\alpha = \emptyset$". (Note: the kernel of **6.5** and the cokernel of **13.3** will extend the current definitions to certain categories which may not have zero morphisms.)

Given two monomorphisms $i : P \longrightarrow X$, $i_1 : P_1 \longrightarrow X$ with the same codomain X, say that $i \leq i_1$ if there exists $\psi : P \longrightarrow P_1$ with $\psi i_1 = i$; note that such ψ is unique because i_1 is mono. It is routinely checked that this relation is reflexive and transitive. It follows from generalities about posets that antisymmetry forms an equivalence relation $i \sim i_1 \Leftrightarrow i \leq i_1 \wedge i_1 \leq i$ whose equivalence classes form a poset under the well-defined relation $[i] \leq [i_1] \Leftrightarrow i \leq i_1$. This is called the poset of *subobjects of* X which we shall denote by $Sub(X)$. In **Set**, $i \sim i_1 \Leftrightarrow i, i_1$ have the same image so that $Sub(X)$ is isomorphic to the Boolean algebra of subsets of X. Exactly the same is true in **Pfn**. In **Mfn**, however, there are monomorphisms which are not represented by the inclusion of a subset, e.g. take $P = \{a, b\}$, $X = \{x, y, z\}$ and define $i : P \longrightarrow X$ by $a \mapsto \{x, y\}$, $b \mapsto \{z\}$. We leave the verification to the reader.

The definition of an abelian category can now be given: A category is *abelian* if it has a zero object 0, binary coproducts $X + Y$, binary products $X \times Y$, if every morphism has a kernel and a cokernel and if every monomorphism is a kernel and every epimorphism is a cokernel. These are extremely simple axioms and it is immediate not only that the category of abelian groups or indeed the modules over any ring is abelian but also that the dual of an abelian category is abelian, that a category of functors to an abelian category is abelian and so forth. How has the objective of creating zeroes and sums been realized? The zero part is obvious via the zero object. It can also be shown that the set of morphisms between two objects forms an abelian group with the zero morphism as group zero and that composition on either side distributes over addition. It is hard to imagine how so much structure can be derived from such simple axioms. Having come this far, we outline some of the constructions in [Freyd 1964] for an abelian category $\mathcal{A}$. First of all, $Sub(X)$ is a lattice. Given monomorphisms $i : P \longrightarrow X$, $j : Q \longrightarrow X$, construct $\theta : X \longrightarrow C = Cok(i)$ and let $Cok(j\theta) = \tau : C \longrightarrow D$. Then $P \bigcap Q = Ker(j\theta)$, $P \bigcup Q = Ker(\theta\tau)$. It is a standard theorem that a category is finitely complete if it has finite products and equalizers. Since $\mathcal{A}$ has finite products, we need only show that the equalizer $eq(\alpha, \beta)$ of $\alpha, \beta : X \longrightarrow Y$ exists. In many familiar categories, this is constructed on the set on which α, β agree and we can do the same here by intersecting the "graphs": set $E = ([id_X, \alpha] : X \longrightarrow X \times Y) \bigcap ([id_X, \beta] : X \longrightarrow X \times Y)$. Then the desired equalizer is $t : E \longrightarrow X$ where t is the common path $E \longrightarrow X \times Y$ followed by the X–projection. Dually, $\mathcal{A}$ is finitely co-complete. Continuing, it is clear from the universal properties of $X+Y$, $X \times Y$ that there are two bijective correspondences of form

$$X+Y \xrightarrow{\quad \alpha \quad} X \times Y \quad \leftrightarrow \quad \begin{bmatrix} a & b \\ c & d \end{bmatrix}$$

with $a: X \longrightarrow X$, $b: X \longrightarrow Y$, $c: Y \longrightarrow X$, $d: Y \longrightarrow Y$, two because we can build the matrix either by rows or by columns; but in fact these bijections are easily seen to coincide. Setting $a = id_X$, $b = 0_{XY}$, $c = 0_{XX}$, $d = id_Y$ gives an "identity matrix" $I : X+Y \longrightarrow X \times Y$. It is not hard to show that $Ker(I) = 0$, $Cok(I) = 0$. It is harder to prove, but true, that in an abelian category, if $Ker(\alpha) = 0$ and $Cok(\alpha) = 0$ then α is an isomorphism. Thus in an abelian category, given two objects X, Y, there is a single object $X \oplus Y$ and a diagram

$$X \underset{\rho}{\overset{i}{\rightleftarrows}} X \oplus Y \underset{\theta}{\overset{j}{\leftrightarrows}} Y$$

such that i, j gives a coproduct and ρ, θ gives a product. Let us call this a *biproduct system* (a special case of the "coproduct systems" to be considered in **7.10** below.) For example, in the category of abelian groups, let $X \oplus Y$ be the usual product group $X \times Y$ and let $xi = (x, 0)$, $yj = (0, y)$, $(x, y)\rho = x$, $(x, y)\theta = y$. Given $\alpha_X : X \longrightarrow Z$, $\alpha_Y : Y \longrightarrow Z$ the unique $\alpha : X \oplus Y \longrightarrow Z$ with $i\alpha = \alpha_X$, $j\alpha = \alpha_Y$ is given by $(x, y)\alpha = x\alpha_X + y\alpha_Y$. The sum $x(\alpha+\beta) = x\alpha + x\beta$ of group homomorphisms is an instance of the following binary operation on $\mathcal{A}(X, Y)$ for any abelian $\mathcal{A}$: given $\alpha, \beta : X \longrightarrow Y$, define their *sum* by

$$\alpha+\beta \quad = \quad X \xrightarrow{\quad [\alpha, \beta] \quad} Y \oplus Y \xrightarrow{\quad <id_Y, id_Y> \quad} Y \ .$$

The proof that $\mathcal{A}(X, Y)$ is an abelian monoid with 0_{XY} as unit is not too hard. To prove it's even a group, one examines for given $\alpha : X \longrightarrow Y$ the matrix

$$X \oplus Y \xrightarrow{\begin{bmatrix} id & \alpha \\ 0 & id \end{bmatrix}} X \oplus Y$$

and verifies that it has 0 kernel and cokernel and so is an isomorphism. But it is easy to see that the inverse must have the form

$$\begin{bmatrix} id & \beta \\ 0 & id \end{bmatrix}$$

with $\alpha + \beta = 0$ as desired.

Now let us return to the issue of zeroes and sums in program semantics. A straight-through network is to be the sum of its paths and, while we are at it, an iterate should be the (infinite) sum of its components, the n-th component being "exactly n times around the loop". For intuition let's examine **Mfn**. If we define the well-known *converse* of $\alpha : X \longrightarrow Y$ to be $\breve{\alpha} : Y \longrightarrow X$ given by $x \in y\breve{\alpha} \Leftrightarrow y \in x\alpha$, then $X \mapsto X$, $\alpha \mapsto \breve{\alpha}$ is an isomorphism of categories **Mfn** $\cong$ **Mfn**^{op} where the latter denotes the dual (or opposite) category. Thus if $X \oplus Y$ is the disjoint union $X + Y$ with inclusions i, j it follows that

$$X \underset{\breve{i}}{\overset{i}{\rightleftarrows}} X \oplus Y \underset{\breve{j}}{\overset{j}{\leftrightarrows}} Y$$

is a biproduct system. (**Mfn** is not abelian; the example above of a mono not a subset is also not a kernel since kernel = subset is easily checked. Dually, epi need not entail cokernel. The other axioms do hold.) As is well-known [Mitchell 1965] one does not need $\mathcal{A}$ to be abelian to get $\mathcal{A}(X, Y)$ an abelian monoid. The availability of the biproduct systems $Y \oplus Y$ which define sums is enough for this and we have that in **Mfn**. The formula $\alpha + \beta = [\alpha, \beta] <id_Y, id_Y>$ above indeed produces $\alpha \bigcup \beta$. A morphism $\alpha : X \longrightarrow Y \oplus Z$ satisfies $\alpha = \alpha_Y in_Y + \alpha_Z in_Z$ (with in_Y, in_Z the coproduct injections of $Y \oplus Z$ and $\alpha_Y = \alpha\rho_Y$, $\alpha_Z = \alpha\rho_Z$ if ρ_Y, ρ_Z are the product projections.) This indeed represents α as the sum of its paths. Further, if $\xi : X \longrightarrow X + Y$ so that $\xi = \xi_X in_X + \xi_Y in_Y$,

$$\xi^{\dagger} = \sum_{n=0}^{\infty} (\xi_X)^n \xi_Y$$

produces the least-fixed-point iterate of ξ. Note that **Mfn** has infinite biproducts too (which the category of abelian groups does not!) because of the strong self-duality which allows the converses of coproduct injections to be product projections. Indeed

$$\sum \alpha_n = X \xrightarrow{\ [\alpha_n]\ } \overset{\infty}{\underset{n=0}{\oplus}} Y \xrightarrow{\ <(id_Y)>\ } Y$$

produces $\bigcup \alpha_n$.

But **Pfn** is an important example too. To be sure we are onto something we must explain how the abelian category intuition motivates constructions there. Well, **Pfn** has disjoint unions and coproducts. In fact **Pfn** also has products. If $X \times Y$ denotes the usual **Set**–product, $X \times Y + X + Y$ underlies the product in **Pfn**. We leave the details to the reader since this product is a red herring whose only role is to demonstrate that **Pfn** does not have biproduct systems. But even so, the coproduct is sufficiently like a product for our needs. We don't need a converse operator to define the coproduct "projections"; define $\rho_X = <id_X, 0> : X + Y \longrightarrow X$, and $\rho_Y = <0, id_Y>$ similarly. (This gives the same projections as before in **Mfn**.) In order for these to give a product, two conditions must hold. First, ρ_X, ρ_Y would have to be *jointly monic*, that is, must satisfy that for all $\alpha, \beta : W \longrightarrow X + Y$, if $\alpha \rho_X = \beta \rho_X$ and $\alpha \rho_Y = \beta \rho_Y$ then $\alpha = \beta$. This is the uniqueness part of the universal property of the product, and it is routinely seen that it is true in **Pfn**. What fails is the existence part, i.e. given arbitrary $\alpha : W \longrightarrow X$ and $\beta : W \longrightarrow Y$ there exists $F : W \longrightarrow X + Y$ with $F\rho_X = \alpha$ and $F\rho_Y = \beta$. Now let $X = Y$. Then given $\alpha, \beta : W \longrightarrow X$ as above, *if* such F exists we say that α, β are *summable* and then, since such F is unique, we may define their *sum* as before by $\alpha + \beta = F <id_Y, id_Y>$. A similar definition applies to any (not necessarily finite) family of partial functions $X \longrightarrow Y$. One checks that a family is summable if and only if its domains are pairwise disjoint whence the sum is the union. The sum-of-paths and iteration constructions given for **Mfn** work correctly in **Pfn** as well.

These considerations lead to the *preadditive categories* studied in Section 7. Simply put, these have binary coproducts and a zero object and are such that the "projections" from $X + Y$ are jointly monic. These simple axioms, true for any abelian category, are adequate to develop the algebra of partially-defined binary sums. A natural generalization gives the *partially-additive categories* of [Arbib and Manes 1980, Theorem 5.3] which include **Pfn** and **Mfn**. – In such categories the set of morphisms between two objects has a sum operation $\sum$ which is defined on appropriately-defined summable families which may be infinite, the sum in **Pfn** being an illustration. Every partially-additive category has a canonical polymorphic iterate in terms of an infinite sum, the same formula given for **Mfn** above. The resulting power-series calculus is reasonably easy to work with and provides, as well, a sum-of-paths semantics (equivalent to least-fixed-point semantcs) for recursive specifications [Arbib and Manes 1982]. The sum operation satisfies the "partition-associative" property of **1.3** which asserts that introduction, deletion and rearrangement of parentheses does not affect summability or the value of the sum —a very strong property, much stronger than the properties of convergent real infinite series, for example. Additionally, complete commutativity holds, that is, the order in which terms are added does not change summability or sums. This gives an immediate proof that if $x \neq 0$ then no y exists with $x + y = 0$. For let $x + y = 0$. Then

$$
\begin{aligned}
0 &= (x+y) + (x+y) + (x+y) + \cdots \\
&= x + (y+x) + (y+x) + (y+x) + \cdots \\
&= x + 0 + 0 + 0 + \cdots \\
&= x \quad .
\end{aligned}
$$

Thus, partially-additive categories are never abelian.

We note in passing that it is sometimes possible to embed a partially-additive category in an abelian category in a useful way. See [Benson 1984] where the Perron-Frobenius theorem about the dominant eigenvalue of a nonnegative matrix is used to classify program divergence.

We came to see partially-additive categories as a successful model which, however, was not sufficiently general and with not quite enough structure. Given the inevitable evolution of programming languages, that is bound to be true about any semantic framework but, even so, one seeks reasonable plateaus. Boolean categories represent the first such plateau in our program and we now trace the path we followed from partially-additive categories to Boolean categories.

A major objective of a category-theoretic approach is to allow a broad (and unspecified) notion of state with as few syntax-driven assumptions as possible. It gradually became clear, however, that this virtue would not be compromised by seeking structure to incorporate the semantics of Hoare assertions $\{P\} \, \alpha \, \{Q\}$. Such an assertion should be equivalent to $P \subset [\alpha]Q$ and $[\alpha]Q$ has already been described in **Pfn** and **Mfn** in terms of pullbacks. Particularly compelling is the ease with which the Hoare assertion can be expressed in these categories (and, indeed, in just about any category), specifically

$$\{P\}\ \alpha\ \{Q\} \quad \Leftrightarrow \quad \exists\beta \qquad \begin{array}{ccc} P & \xrightarrow{\ \beta\ } & Q \\ {\scriptstyle i}\downarrow & & \downarrow{\scriptstyle j} \\ X & \xrightarrow[\ \alpha\ ]{} & Y \end{array}$$

(As j is mono, β is unique when it exists.) The technical problem at hand is, in essence, to decide what sort of monomorphisms should comprise the Boolean "predicates" $P \longrightarrow X$. Here an awareness of developments in topos theory (see [Johnstone 1977] for the tip of the iceberg) leads to a rapid resolution. A little background:

Work by algebraic geometers such as Grothendieck and Verdier focused attention on certain categories of sheaves. Analogous to the situation that culminated with abelian categories, a stage was reached where axiomatization could help. M. Tierney was thinking about this when he teamed up with F.W. Lawvere who was attempting to refine his earlier attempts to model set theory within the first-order theory of categories. The axioms of an elementary topos was the result [Tierney 1972] and this provided a foundation for *both* set theory and categories of sheaves. Many since have worked hard to develop the theory further and the impact on theoretical computer science has been considerable. Briefly, what is a topos?

First of all, a topos is *cartesian-closed* which means that it has cartesian products and function spaces, these expressed in a category using suitable universal mapping properties. These categories, more in the limelight because of topos theory but also developed earlier by [Lawvere 1964, 1966, 1969] are used to model the typed lambda calculus and it is common for categories of domains for Scott-Strachey denotational semantics to be cartesian-closed. Many have contributed to computer science applications of cartesian-closed categories. See [Lambek and Scott 1986] and [Spencer 1991].

A *topos* is a cartesian-closed category which has a subobject classifier Ω which provides a "two-element set" in that Ω–valued morphisms of X correspond (in a specific way involving pullbacks) to the subobjects of X generalizing "characteristic functions". The topos axioms imply that the poset $Sub(X)$ of subobjects of X forms a Brouwerian lattice so that every topos carries an intrinsic intuitionistic logic. A standard fact about Brouwerian lattices is that the subset of complemented elements is a Boolean algebra.

In a topos, $i : P \longrightarrow X$ is complemented in $Sub(X)$ if and only if there exists a coproduct $P \overset{i}{\longrightarrow} X \overset{j}{\longleftarrow} Q$. Hence, if in any category we define $Summ(X)$ (the *summands of* X) as the sub-poset of $Sub(X)$ of all subobjects represented by a coproduct injection, we have the result that $Summ(X)$ is a Boolean algebra in any topos.

Now back to our dilemma of finding a Boolean algebra of predicates in a category with finite coproducts. We have already seen above how to express the Hoare assertion $\{P\}\,\alpha\,\{Q\}$ when P, Q are subobjects. What happens in a topos suggests we might get the predicates to range over a Boolean algebra if we restrict these subobjects to being summands. The idea is especially intriguing since it further emphasizes the theory of coproducts. Further support comes from the observation that many semantic frameworks possess a subcategory containing all the objects which constitutes a topos whose coproducts coincide with those of the framework; for example, the "base morphisms" of an algebraic theory form a subcategory with all the objects which is equivalent to the topos of finite sets. Having a topos sit in the semantic framework in this way makes all topos constructions available to the objects. Thus products can be used to form record data types. The assignment of values to variables would employ the function-space construction in the context of imperative languages. "Domain equations" for data types could be formulated using the topos constructions but solved in the larger semantic framework. (While space does not permit a treatment of such applications, they will be pursued in future work.) This viewpoint strongly suggests that the desired Boolean algebra will be $Summ(X)$.

Of course we are not starting with a topos. We are starting with an arbitrary category with coproducts and must provide axioms which imply that $Summ(X)$, already a poset, is a Boolean algebra. In [Manes 1988] we offered "assertional categories" as a first-order stripped-down version of partially-additive categories for which $Summ(X)$ forms a Boolean algebra. The axioms were essentially as follows. There is a zero object and coproduct "projections" are jointly-monic leading to the (finite) partial sums discussed earlier; it is assumed that kernel-domain decompositions (**6.12**) and cokernel-range decompositions (**13.3**) exist; it is asumed that the relation $\alpha \leq \beta$ if $\beta = \alpha + \gamma$ for some γ is antisymmetric and hence a partial order; and, finally, it is assumed that if $(\alpha_1 + \cdots + \alpha_n) + \alpha_{n+1}$ exists then also $\alpha_1 + \cdots + \alpha_{n+1}$ exists. All of the theory to be developed for Boolean categories holds for assertional categories, and no wonder: every assertional category is Boolean. In effect, then, assertional categories are but a stepping stone. Their ultimate role is to provide a duality for certain Boolean categories as is discussed further below.

Assertional categories, partially-additive categories and indeed any category with iterate satisfying the original unrestricted polymorphic axiom **3.11** of [Arbib and Manes 1978] all suffer from a fundamental defect: zero morphisms. For some models this is fine, but in general one wants to distinguish between divergence and failing. Indeed the various forms of failing may have considerable structure (cf. [Goguen 1978].) What is meant by a "divergence" or "failing" in an abstract category? To this end, define an X-*sink* to be an object-indexed family of morphisms $\perp_Y : X \longrightarrow Y$ subject to the equations

$$X \xrightarrow{\;\perp_Y\;} Y \xrightarrow{\;\alpha\;} Z \;=\; X \xrightarrow{\;\perp_Z\;} Z$$

for all $\alpha : Y \longrightarrow Z$. Heuristically, $\perp_Y$ cannot be reset by future actions. An "abort" should be an example. The infinite loop of a polymorphic iterate, specifically

$$\perp_Y \;=\; (X \xrightarrow{\;in_X\;} X+Y)^\dagger$$

(see Section 3), is also an example. What is the relationship between sinks and zero morphisms? Since we assume even the empty case of finite coproducts, we always have an initial object 0. Let's prove a couple of elementary lemmas which we can use later.

LEMMA A *If a category with initial object 0 has zero morphisms then 0 is a zero object.*

Proof There is at least one morphism $X \longrightarrow 0$ namely the zero morphism. But if $t : X \longrightarrow 0$ is arbitrary then by the initiality of 0, the zero morphism $0 \longrightarrow 0$ and the identity morphism $0 \longrightarrow 0$ are both the unique morphism $0 \longrightarrow 0$ so $t = t\,id_0 = t\,0_{00} = 0_{X0}$. $\qquad\square$

Now suppose that 0 is initial. Say that $\alpha : X \longrightarrow Y$ is a *null morphism* if there exists β with

$$\alpha \;=\; X \xrightarrow{\;\;\beta\;\;} 0 \xrightarrow{\hspace{2cm}} Y \;.$$

By Lemma **A**, null morphisms coincide with zero morphisms if the latter exist. Null morphisms in a Boolean category will be studied in Section 6.

LEMMA B *Given* $\alpha : X \longrightarrow Y$, *there exists an X–sink $\perp$ with $\alpha = \perp_Y$ if and only if α is a null morphism.*

Proof Given an X–sink $\perp$,

$$\perp_Y \;=\; X \xrightarrow{\;\;\perp_0\;\;} 0 \xrightarrow{\hspace{2cm}} Y$$

is null. Conversely, given $\alpha \;=\; X \xrightarrow{\;\;\beta\;\;} 0 \xrightarrow{\hspace{2cm}} Y$, define

$$\perp_W \;=\; X \xrightarrow{\;\;\beta\;\;} 0 \xrightarrow{\hspace{2cm}} W \qquad\qquad\qquad \square$$

Since **Pfn** and **Mfn** have zero morphisms which correspond to the infinite loops induced by their natural iterates, Lemma **A** allows no separate notion of "abort". To add an abort a which differs from the infinite loop 0 one could, for instance, consider a category $\mathcal{C}$ whose objects are sets but whose morphisms $X \longrightarrow Y$ are partial functions $X \longrightarrow Y + \{a\}$ with composition $\alpha \circ \beta$ defined by

$$\begin{aligned} x(\alpha \circ \beta) \;&=\; (x\alpha)\beta \text{ if } x\alpha \text{ is defined and } x\alpha \neq a \\ &=\; a \text{ if } x\alpha = a \;. \end{aligned}$$

Notice that there are two morphisms $X \longrightarrow 0$ namely the empty function and the function constantly a. The former induces the X–sink for the infinite loop whereas the latter induces the X–sink for the abort. (Cf. **3.24** below for a similar example.) Our objective, of course, is to develop axioms sufficiently robust to remain true under modifications of the state such as "adding an abort".

How we arrived at the axioms for a Boolean category is now easy to explain.

Each of the four axioms of **4.7** is a well-known property of a topos. Zero morphisms play no role (a topos doesn't have them!) It was simply a matter of observing that these properties were enough to prove $Summ(X)$ is a Boolean algebra and to provide a calculus of Hoare assertions; though perhaps not surprising, it is pleasing that such simple axioms could have a great many consequences, but then again what happened with abelian categories and toposes was even more dramatic. We chalk it up to the surprising expressive power of the theory of categories!

The fundamental construct $I = if\ P\ then\ \alpha\ else\ \beta$ comes for free under this formalism. If $P \xrightarrow{\ i\ } X \xleftarrow{\ j\ } Q$ is a coproduct, the diagram

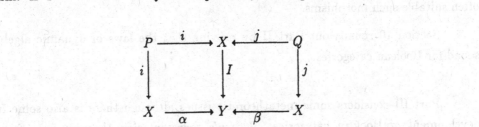

defines it.

Actually, our definition of Boolean category is a bit too general for the needs of semantics. For example **Set** (or any topos) is a Boolean category. Our approach has allowed for multiple divergences but has not guaranteed that any exist; yet any reasonable model of semantics possesses an iterate and hence its infinite loops. What is meant, precisely, by having a divergence? X–sinks here and there aren't enough; a coherent family of them is needed. This can be expressed in the form of a *projection system* which assigns a morphism of form $\rho_{XP} : X \longrightarrow P$ whenever $P \in Summ(X)$, subject to two axioms. For example, the projection system corresponding to an iterate $(-)^{\dagger}$ is given by $\rho_{XP} = \xi^{\dagger}$ for $\xi : X \longrightarrow X + P$, given the coproduct $P \xrightarrow{\ i\ } X \xleftarrow{\ j\ } Q$, by the equations $i\xi s = in_P$, $j\xi = jin_X$. It is seen in **6.11** that there is a bijective correspondence between projection systems and maximal Boolean subcategories with zero morphisms having all objects. The corresponding zero morphisms are the X–sinks induced by $\rho_{X0} : X \longrightarrow 0$ (noting that $0 \longrightarrow X$ is always the least element of $Summ(X)$.) The subcategory alluded to consists of all ρ–*nulling* morphisms, i.e. all $\alpha : X \longrightarrow Y$ with

$$X \xrightarrow{\ \alpha\ } Y \xrightarrow{\ \rho_{Y0}\ } 0 \ = \ X \xrightarrow{\ \rho_{X0}\ } 0 \ .$$

When ρ is induced by an iterate $(-)^\dagger$, the ρ–nulling morphisms are precisely the $\dagger$–pure morphisms mentioned earlier. A choice of projection system allows a calculus of *guards*, the guard morphism $\rho : X \longrightarrow X$ corresponding to $P \in Summ(X)$ being the intuitive one with ρ restricted to P being $P \longrightarrow X$ whereas ρ restricted to the complement P' being the ρ–null morphism $P' \longrightarrow X$. This passage from summands to guards is bijective with summand intersection corresponding to guard composition. The proof of the *while-do* rule is facilitated by the guard calculus; one needs morphisms to transform iterative specifications to apply the polymorphic axiom and guards are often suitable such morphisms.

Section 10 rounds out Part II by proving that the laws of dynamic algebra are sound for Boolean categories.

Part III considers some metatheoretic issues although there is also some further development of Boolean categories. Kozen's representation theorem for *-free PDL [Kozen 1980] appears in the form of Theorem **11.15** that "every Boolean category admits a representation by relations" and the same consequences are realized: the universally valid formulas for all Boolean categories coincide with the formulas satisfied by **Mfn**. We interpret this result as asserting "what can be expressed by predicate transformers is standard". "Formulas" as used here are constrained to be much weaker than arbitrary first-order sentences of Boolean categories. For example, the sentence

$$\forall P\ \forall Q\ \forall \alpha\ \forall \beta\ (\ \{P\}\ \alpha\ \{Q\}\ \Leftrightarrow\ \{P\}\ \beta\ \{Q\}\ )\ \Rightarrow\ \alpha = \beta$$

is true in **Pfn** and **Mfn** (indeed, this is a cornerstone of the philosophy of [Dijkstra 1976]) and yet fails in many Boolean categories with a more complex notion of "state". In Section 14, however, we isolate another standard fragment namely the equational theory of 3-valued *if-then-else* of [Manes 1992].

Section 12 applies the theory of predicate transformers to a further study of deterministic morphisms. We show in **12.17** that if $\xi : X \longrightarrow X + Y$ is deterministic then $\xi^\dagger$ can be expressed as a *while-do*. We also show that Dijkstra's "composition rule"

$$\forall \beta\quad wp(\alpha\beta, R)\ =\ wp(\alpha, wp(\beta, R))$$

is not universally valid in all Boolean categories but rather is equivalent to "α is deterministic". By imposing this rule in **Mfn** one effectively redefines composition so that $x\alpha\beta = \emptyset$ if any $y \in x\beta$ exists with $y\beta = \emptyset$. The resulting category is not Boolean. (This in itself does not invalidate the category but, as is pointed out in **4.12**, there are more objective reasons to consider the category pathological.) It is interesting to note that from a category-theoretic point of view composition is everything, whereas in the well-respected computer-science tradition of [Dijkstra 1976] based on an heuristic view of "state" underlying all the constructions, the definition of composition affects hardly anything else!

Unlike abelian categories, the dual of a Boolean category need not be Boolean. Section 13 adds further structure to Boolean categories so as to provide a duality theory. We have succeeded only for preadditive Boolean categories which, in particular, have zero morphisms. If these have not only the kernel-domain decompositions shared by all Boolean categories but also the dual cokernel-range decompositions, the resulting *preadditive ranged Boolean categories* admit a sum-ideal completion to a *semilattice-assertional category* which is a very nice sort of Boolean category whose dual again has the same form. As a result, the forward predicate transformers that can be defined on any ranged Boolean category are seen to be categorically dual to the inverse transformers.

In the final Part IV of the book we try to relate Boolean categories to work done with distributive categories. In Section 15 we show that the subcategory of atom-preserving morphisms of an *extensional Boolean category* form a distributive category which is a candidate for the semantics of data types. The last section, Section 16, considers *Kleisli categories* over an arbitrary base category, a well-known generalization of algebraic theories. Many Boolean categories are Kleisli over **Set**. For distributive categories with a suitable *atomic generator* there exists an extensional Boolean Kleisli category whose atom-preserving morphisms recapture the original distributive category.

It is a pleasure to thank the many colleagues and students who have patiently listened and made helpful suggestions, expecially David Benson who read the final manuscript. I especially want to thank Universitat de les Illes Balears in Mallorca and Universidade de Santiago in Galicia for invitations to give extensive lectures, the

National Science Foundation for support under grants CCR8701272 and CCR9903423 and the University of Massachusetts at Amherst for an excellent research environment despite fiduciary tribulations.

This book was prepared in EXP by Brooks/Cole, a lean, mean word processor which fit comfortably on the old XT laptop I carried everywhere in preparing this and earlier drafts.

Finally, I thank Chiggle —for everything.

PART I   FINITE COPRODUCTS

In this first part of the book we introduce a few categories as fundamental semantic frameworks and explore the formulation of general choice operators and iteration in arbitrary categories with finite coproducts.

1   FUNDAMENTAL FRAMEWORKS

This section presents a few basic examples of semantic frameworks along with some *ad hoc* definitions, e.g. assertions, predicate transformers, if-then-else and while-do. These concepts are among those formalized in the balance of the paper.

1 EXAMPLE The category **Mfn** of multivalued functions (= relations) has sets X, Y, Z as objects and a morphism $X \longrightarrow Y$ is a total function from X to the set of subsets of Y. If $\alpha : X \longrightarrow Y$ we may think of $x\alpha \subset Y$ as the set of "possible outcomes with input x". Composition is defined by

2   For $X \xrightarrow{\alpha} Y \xrightarrow{\beta} Z, \ x(\alpha\beta) = \{z \in Z : \exists \ y \in x\alpha, \ z \in y\beta\}$

with identity morphisms $X \longrightarrow X, \ x \mapsto \{x\}$.

In standard applications, the result of a computation is a partial function. We may comfortably regard a partial function as a relation α for which $x\alpha$ has at most one element. When the composition of **2** is restricted to partial functions the result is again a partial function and is indeed the usual composition of partial functions, that is, partial functions form a subcategory of **Mfn** and we call this category **Pfn**. The total functions form an important subcategory of **Pfn** and we call it simply **Set**.

One does not have to look towards concurrency or parallelism to justify the usefulness of **Mfn** in semantics. For example, the "Kleene iterate" $\alpha^* : X \longrightarrow X$ of $\alpha : X \longrightarrow X$ is multivalued even if α is a total function, $x\alpha^* = \bigcup x\alpha^n$. The interpretation is "$y \in x\alpha^*$ if α is allowed to iterate a random finite number n of times and $y \in x\alpha^n$". This operation is emphasized in dynamic algebra because it has pleasant algebraic properties and corresponds to e.g. while-do if "suitably guarded". For another example, let a subset of Y denote a pixel region on a monitor screen, whence it is not hard to think of menu scenarios for which **Mfn**-composition correctly captures program chaining.

3 DEFINITION   [Manes and Benson 1985.]   A *positive partial monoid* is $(M, \sum)$ with M a non-empty set and $\sum$ a partial operation (defined on not necessarily all families $(x_i : i \in I)$ in M, even if I is finite —we say (x_i) is *summable* if $\sum x_i$ is defined) subject to the axioms

3a   If I has one element i and $x_i = x$ then $\sum(x_i : i \in I)$ is defined and is x.

3b   (*Partition-associativity axiom.*) Given $(x_i : i \in I)$ and a partition $(I_j : j \in J)$ of I (we allow $I_j = \emptyset$ for any subset of j) then

$$\sum \left(\sum (x_i : i \in I_j) : j \in J \right) = \sum (x_i : i \in I)$$

in the strongest sense that if one side is defined than so is the other.

3c The relation $x \leq y$ defined by "$y = x + z$ for some z" is antisymmetric.

   The following properties are established in the paper just cited (and can easily be proved by the reader):

3d Isomorphic families have the same sum. In particular, reordering doesn't change sums.

3e Any subfamily of a subfamily is summable. Denote the empty sum as 0.

3f (*Additive positivity property*) If $\sum x_i = 0$ then each $x_i = 0$.

It is immediate that $\leq$ in **3c** is a partial order with 0 as least element. Further,

3g 0 is an additive zero, that is, $\sum (x_i : i \in I) = \sum (x_i : i \in J)$, if $J = \{i : x_i \neq 0\}$.

   A *positive partial semiring* is $(R, \sum, \cdot, 1)$ with $(R, \sum)$ a positive partial monoid and $(R, \cdot, 1)$ a monoid subject to the following positivity properties **3h, 3i**:

3h Given summable (x_i), for any y, $(z_i : i \in I)$, $(y x_i)$ and $(x_i z_i)$ are summable, $y(\sum x_i) = \sum y x_i$, and, if each $z_i = z$, $(\sum x_i)z = \sum x_i z$. In particular, $y0 = 0 = 0z$.

3i (*Multiplicative positivity property*) If $xy = 0$ then $x = 0$ or $y = 0$.

Note that the positive semirings of [Eilenberg 1974] are positive partial semirings in both the finite and complete cases. The significance of the positivity properties will be seen in Corollary 7.1 where they are used to prove $\mathbf{Mat}_R$ is a Boolean category.

4 EXAMPLE   If R is a positive partial semiring, we define the *matrix category* Mat_R of R as follows. The objects are sets. A morphism $\alpha : X \longrightarrow Y$ is an "array" $\alpha = (\alpha_{xy} : x \in X,\ y \in Y)$ satisfying the row-summability condition that $\sum_y \alpha_{xy}$ exists for every x. Composition is then defined by the usual matrix multiplication (use **3h**) and identities for the category are provided by the usual identity matrices.

If R is the two-element positive partial semiring $\{0,1\}$ for which multiplication is the usual numerical one whereas sum is given by maximum, then Mat_R may be identified with **Mfn** via incidence matrices. If we modify R so that $\sum x_i$ is undefined if x_i is 1 for more than one i then Mat_R may be identified with **Pfn** because the summability conditions in the definition of a matrix force each row in an incidence matrix to have at most one 1.

Another example of a positive partial semiring results if R is $\mathbf{N} \cup \{\infty\}$, with $\mathbf{N} = \{0,1,2,...\}$ the natural numbers, with the obvious numerical definitions for sum and product (e.g. $1+2+3 = 6$, $1+2+3+\cdots = \infty$.) Here morphisms represent "bag-valued functions" where a *bag* (or *multiset* or *suite*) is a "subset with repetitions" as occurs, e.g., in prime factorization of numbers. We shall denote the resulting category Mat_R as **Bag**. For a specific example, consider a chained-election scenario in which population P votes for electors in E who, in turn, cast their votes for selections in S. The vote of P is a morphism $\alpha : P \longrightarrow E$ in **Bag** as is the vote of E of form $\beta : E \longrightarrow S$. Even though α, β could be regarded as in **Mfn**, it is their **Bag**-composition $\alpha\beta : P \longrightarrow S$ which correctly tallies the net vote.

5 EXAMPLE   Let Ω be a *ranked alphabet* (or *signature*), that is, a disjoint sequence $\Omega_0, \Omega_1, \Omega_2, \ldots$ of (possibly empty) sets. For each set Y denote by $Y\Omega$ the set of all (possibly infinite-depth) finitely-branching rooted trees, each of whose n-way branch nodes is labeled by an element of Ω_n, and each of whose leaves is either an element of Y or a nullary label in Ω_0. [Note: More formally, if Y and Ω_0 are not disjoint, each leaf should belong to their disjoint union.]

The category Ω is defined to have sets as objects and to have total functions from X to $Y\Omega$ as morphisms from X to Y. The composition of $\alpha : X \longrightarrow Y$ and $\beta : Y \longrightarrow Z$ is defined as follows. For $x \in X$, consider the tree $x\alpha$; for each leaf in $x\alpha$

which is an element y of Y substitute the tree $y\beta$. The result of all such substitutions (possibly infinitely many) is the desired tree $x(\alpha\beta)$. The identity $X \longrightarrow X$ assigns to x the one-node tree with leaf x.

Possible uses of Ω as a semantic framework include program traces, the "output so far" in a parallel computation, and so forth. In [Moggi 1991], where a morphism is regarded as the semantics of a computation, Ω is called "interactive input".

We note that **Pfn** may be identified with Ω if $\Omega_0 = \{ \perp \}$ and all other Ω_n are empty. If all Ω_n are empty we get **Set**.

6 EXAMPLE A *causal monoid* is a monoid M with unit e satisfying the *causality axiom*

$$st = e \quad \Rightarrow \quad s = e = t.$$

(This axiom will be discussed further in Example 4.10.) We interpret M as a set of attributes about a computation. Let $\mathbf{Pfn}_M$ be the category whose objects are sets and for which a morphism from X to Y is a partial function from X to $Y \times M$. If $x\alpha$ is defined and takes the value (y,s) then we interpret this as "$x\alpha = y$ with attribute s". Composition is defined as follows: if $x\alpha = y$ with attribute s and if then $y\beta = z$ with attribute t, then $x(\alpha\beta) = z$ with attribute st. The identity morphism is $x \mapsto (x,e)$.

One possible further interpretation is that attributes measure computation time with addition as monoid operation so that the identity is a delayless skip. The causality axiom then amounts to "time's arrow". In another scenario, M can be a meet semilattice with greatest element whose elements measure the reliability of the computation —note that every such semilattice is a causal monoid. In [Moggi 1991], a closely-related example with M a free monoid is interpreted as "interactive output".

We recover **Pfn** if M is the trivial monoid.

So far, all frameworks have had sets as objects. This allows us to write down some natural definitions ad hoc with a view to later formalization.

We begin with the (Hoare) *partial correctness assertion* $\{P\}\ \alpha\ \{Q\}$ for $P \subset X$, $\alpha : X \longrightarrow Y$, $Q \subset Y$. The intended meaning is "with input $x \in X$, if $x \in P$ and α

is executed then all outputs entailed by $x\alpha$, if any, are in Q". There is a natural form of this definition in the examples so far as is recorded in Table 7.

Category	$\{P\} \; \alpha \; \{Q\} \; for \; \alpha : X \longrightarrow Y, \; P \subset X, \; Q \subset Y \; if \; \forall x \in P...$
Set	$x\alpha \in Q$
Pfn	if $x\alpha$ is defined, $x\alpha \in Q$
Mfn	$x\alpha \subset Q$
$\mathbf{Mat}_R$	$\alpha_{xy} \neq 0 \Rightarrow y \in Q$
Ω	each non-nullary leaf in $x\alpha$ is in Q
$\mathbf{Pfn}_M$	if $x\alpha$ (is defined and) is (y,s), $y \in Q$

TABLE 7: $\{P\} \; \alpha \; \{Q\}$ in basic examples.

Other operations of dynamic algebra and the weakest precondition operator are defined in terms of Hoare assertions. Thus, for $\alpha : X \longrightarrow Y$, $Q \subset Y$, we have

8
$$[\alpha]Q \; = \; \{x \in X : \{x\} \; \alpha \; \{Q\}\}$$
$$<\alpha> Q \; = \; ([\alpha]Q')'$$
$$Dom(\alpha) \; = \; <\alpha> Y$$
$$wp(\alpha,Q) \; = \; Dom(\alpha) \cap [\alpha]Q.$$

Here, $(-)'$ denotes set complement. The meaning of the formulas in 8 can be deduced from Table 7. For example, we give the meanings of $<\alpha> Q$ in Table 10 below.

9 DEFINITION   In the basic examples, for $P \subset X$, $\alpha : X \longrightarrow Y$, define
if P then α else β   to be the morphism $\gamma : X \longrightarrow Y$ as follows. In $\mathbf{Mat}_R$, $\gamma_{xy} = \alpha_{xy}$ if $x \in P$, else $= \beta_{xy}$. In all other examples, $x\gamma \; = \; x\alpha$ if $x \in P$, else $= x\beta$.

Category	*For $\alpha : X \longrightarrow Y$, $Q \subset Y$,* $x \in <\alpha>Q \Leftrightarrow \ldots$
Set	$x\alpha \in Q$
Pfn	$x\alpha$ is defined and $x\alpha \in Q$
Mfn	$x\alpha \cap Q \neq \emptyset$
Mat_R	$\exists\, y \in Q,\ \alpha_{xy} \neq 0$
Ω	$\exists\, y \in Q$ appearing as a leaf in $x\alpha$
Pfn_M	$x\alpha$ is defined and if $x\alpha = (y,s)$, $y \in Q$.

Table 10 : $<\alpha>Q$ in basic examples.

11 DEFINITION For $\alpha : X \longrightarrow X$, $P \subset X$, *while P do α* can be described by a repetitive algorithm in many of the frameworks we have so far considered.

Pfn: Given input $x \in X$, y is the output if and only if $y = x \notin P$ or there exists $n \geq 1$ such that $y = x\alpha^n$ is defined and $x, x\alpha, \ldots, x\alpha^{n-1} \in P$ but $y \notin P$. If neither case applies, the output is not defined.

Mfn: Given input $x \in X$, y is an output if and only if $y = x \notin P$ or there exist $x, x_1, \cdots, x_{n-1} \in P$ with $x_1 \in x\alpha$, $\ldots$, $x_{n-1} \in x_{n-2}\alpha$, $y \in x_{n-1}\alpha$ and $y \notin P$.

Mat_R: For $n \geq 0$ define a matrix $\beta^{(n)} : X \longrightarrow X$ in terms of P as follows. $\beta^{(0)}_{xy}$ is 1 if $x = y \notin P$ and is 0 otherwise. $\beta^{(1)}_{xy}$ is α_{xy} if $x \in P$, $y \notin P$ and is 0 otherwise. For $n \geq 1$, $\beta^{(n+1)}_{xy}$ is $\sum \alpha_{xx_1} \alpha_{x_1 x_2} \ldots \alpha_{x_{n-1}y}$, the sum taken over all $x_1, \cdots, x_{n-1} \in P$, if $x \in P$ and $y \notin P$ (this sum necessarily exists because α is a matrix) and is 0 otherwise. Then $(\text{while } P \text{ do } \alpha)_{xy} = \sum_n \beta^{(n)}_{xy}$. In general, this sum may not exist and so to ensure it does requires special assumptions on R. As already mentioned, **Pfn** and **Mfn** are both examples of Mat_R and the construction just given indeed captures the definitions already given there; in particular notice that it is not necessary that all countable sums exist. The needed sum also exists when R is $\mathbb{N} \cup \{\infty\}$ but ∞ is crucial for this.

Ω: If $\Omega_0 \neq \emptyset$ there is a canonical interpretation for *while-do* for each $\perp \in \Omega_0$.

First observe that the set $\Gamma = X \cup (\bigcup_n \Omega_n) \cup \{undefined\}$ is a poset under the ordering $undefined < \perp < \gamma$ ($\gamma \notin \{undefined, \perp\}$). In the usual way (see e.g. [Elgot, Bloom and Tindell 1978]), a tree in $X\Omega$ may be regarded as a partial function on the set $\mathbf{N}^*$ of strings of natural numbers (whose domain is the "shape" of the tree) so that $X\Omega$ is a subset of the set of total functions from $\mathbf{N}^*$ to Γ, one which is, in fact, closed under limits of ascending chains in the pointwise ordering. Given the input x, the output is the limit of the ascending chain of trees t_n defined as follows. First define $u_0 = x$ and then let u_{n+1} be obtained from u_n by replacing each leaf y of u_n with $y \in P$ by the tree $y\alpha$. Then t_n is obtained from u_n by replacing each leaf of u_n with $y \in P$ with $\perp$. It is easily checked that the same semantics of *while-do* in **Pfn** results when the only operation label is $\perp \in \Omega_0$.

Pfn$_M$: Given input x, if $x \notin P$ the output is (x, e). If there exists $n \geq 1$ with $x\alpha = (x_1, t_1)$, $\ldots$ $x_{n-2}\alpha = (x_{n-1}, t_{n-1})$, $x_{n-1}\alpha = (y, t)$ with $x, x_1, \cdots, x_{n-1} \in P$ but $y \notin P$ then the output is $(y, t_1 \cdots t_n)$. If neither case applies, the output is undefined.

The well-known "while rule" $\{P \cap Q\} \alpha \{Q\} \Rightarrow \{Q\}$ *while P do α* $\{Q \cap P'\}$ may be verified in all cases above. A much more efficient proof is given in Proposition **9.12** since this rule is valid in all Boolean categories.

2   NATURAL CHOICE OPERATORS

Both if-then-else and nondeterministic choice have the flavour of "choosing between" two actions subject to a "decision". Intuitively, we expect that the former decides on the basis of the current state whereas the latter has an aspect of unpredictability.

In this section we deal with choice operators axiomatically and present elementary consequences. Our emphasis is on the interaction with the semantic framework, which motivates the prominent role of coproducts in the approach overall. We shall show that commutative idempotent choice is inherently nondeterministic (Proposition 19) and that if-then-else has a functorial characterization (Proposition 29.)

1   DEFINITION Let $\mathcal{C}$ be a category and let X be an object of $\mathcal{C}$. A *choice operator on* X is a family $\star_Y$ of binary operations, one for each object Y of $\mathcal{C}$ of form

$$\mathcal{C}(X,Y) \times \mathcal{C}(X,Y) \xrightarrow{\quad \star_Y \quad} \mathcal{C}(X,Y)$$

(where $\mathcal{C}(X,Y)$ denotes the set of $\mathcal{C}$-morphisms from X to Y) such that the following right distributive law holds:

2   For $\alpha, \beta : X \longrightarrow Y$, $\gamma : Y \longrightarrow Z$, $(\alpha \star \beta)\gamma = (\alpha\gamma) \star (\beta\gamma)$.

Right distributivity reflects the interpretations that in a sequential composition $\alpha\beta$ α is finished before β begins, and that the choosing process for $\alpha \star \beta$ occurs first without interacting with either α or β.

We shall now prove that if binary copowers exist, that the intuition that "the choice is made first" can be formally established.

3 PROPOSITION *If the copower* $X \xrightarrow{in_1} X + X \xleftarrow{in_2} X$ *exists in* $\mathcal{C}$ *then there is a bijective correspondence between choice operators* $\star$ *on* X *and morphisms of form* $T : X \longrightarrow X + X$. *If* $\star$ *and* T *correspond,*

$$\alpha \star \beta \;=\; X \xrightarrow{\quad T \quad} X + X \xrightarrow{\quad <\alpha,\beta> \quad} X$$

where $<\alpha,\beta>$ *denotes the unique morphism* h *with* $in_1 h \;=\; \alpha$ *and* $in_2 h \;=\; \beta$, *whereas*

$$T \;=\; in_1 \star in_2.$$

Hence "the choice T is made first and the effects of α, β enter the process afterwards".

Proof   Given $T : X \longrightarrow X + X$,   define $\alpha \star \beta = T <\alpha,\beta>$.   Since $in_1(<\alpha,\beta>\gamma) \;=\; (in_1<\alpha,\beta>)\gamma \;=\; \alpha\gamma$ and, similarly, $in_2(<\alpha,\beta>\gamma) \;=\; \beta\gamma$, it follows that $<\alpha,\beta>\gamma \;=\; <\alpha\gamma,\beta\gamma>$. This establishes that $\star$ is right distributive: $(\alpha\star\beta)\gamma \;=\; T<\alpha,\beta>\gamma \;=\; T<\alpha\gamma,\beta\gamma> \;=\; (\alpha\gamma)\star(\beta\gamma)$.

$T \mapsto \star$ is injective because $<in_1, in_2> \;=\; id_{X+X}$ so that $T = T<in_1, in_2> = in_1 \star in_2$.

Finally, $T \mapsto \star$ is surjective because, given $\star$, define $T = in_1 \star in_2$ and observe that $T<\alpha,\beta> \;=\; (in_1<\alpha,\beta>)\star(in_2<\alpha,\beta>) \;=\; \alpha\star\beta$. $\square$

The preceding proposition makes it clear that the representation $T<\alpha,\beta>$ is independent of the choice of coproduct $X + X$.

We note that the right distributive law is equivalent to the assertion that $\star$ is a natural transformation

$$\mathcal{C}(X, -) \times \mathcal{C}(X, -) \xrightarrow{\quad \star \quad} \mathcal{C}(X, -).$$

If the coproduct $X + X$ exists, then the functor $\mathcal{C}(X,-) \times \mathcal{C}(X,-)$ is naturally equivalent to $\mathcal{C}(X + X, -)$. The well-known Yoneda lemma ([N. Yoneda, 1954], see [Mac Lane 1971, p, 61]) then gives Proposition **3**.

4 DEFINITION A *choice family* on $\mathcal{C}$ is an assignment of a choice operator on X to each object X of $\mathcal{C}$.

We say a choice family is *commutative, associative* or *idempotent* if the property holds for each choice operator of the family.

Two binary operations $*, \star$ *commute* if each is a homomorphism in the other, that is, if the "middle-four interchange"

$$(\alpha * \beta) \star (\gamma * \delta) = (\alpha \star \gamma) * (\beta \star \delta)$$

holds. Two choice families *commute* if their corresponding binary operations on $\mathcal{C}(X,Y)$ commute for each X, Y.

If $\mathcal{C}$ has binary copowers, a choice family is determined by a $\mathcal{C}$-object-indexed family of morphisms $F_X : X \longrightarrow X + X$. The choice family is *natural* if

5

$$
\begin{array}{ccc}
X & \xrightarrow{\;F_X\;} & X + X \\
{\scriptstyle \gamma}\Big\downarrow & & \Big\downarrow{\scriptstyle \gamma \oplus \gamma} \\
Y & \xrightarrow[\;F_Y\;]{} & Y + Y
\end{array}
$$

obtains for all $\gamma : X \longrightarrow Y$ —we use $\gamma \oplus \gamma$ for $< \gamma in_1, \gamma in_2 >$ rather than $\gamma + \gamma$ to prevent confusion with a different meaning for "sum of morphisms" in **11** and in Section 7. Thus a natural choice family is simply a natural transformation $id \longrightarrow id + id$ for id the identity functor of $\mathcal{C}$.

We do not regard **5** as a universal law for a choice (although a better case could be made for **2**.) For example, in the context of [Kasangian, Labella and Pettorossi 1990], the two paths of **5** would be related but not equal if choices can be promoted.

6 PROPOSITION *Let* (F_X) *be a choice family in a category with binary copowers and let* $\alpha \star \beta = F_X < \alpha, \beta >$ *be the corresponding choice operators of* **3**. *Then* (F_X) *is natural if and only if* $\star$ *is left distributive, that is,*

$$\gamma(\alpha \star \beta) \;=\; (\gamma\alpha)\star(\gamma\beta)$$

for all $\gamma : X \longrightarrow Y, \quad \alpha, \beta : Y \longrightarrow Z.$

Proof For any $\gamma : X \longrightarrow Y, \quad \alpha, \beta : Y \longrightarrow Z, \quad (\gamma \oplus \gamma)<\alpha, \beta > \;=\; <\gamma\alpha, \gamma\beta >.$ Thus if **5** commutes, $F_X < \gamma\alpha, \gamma\beta > \;=\; \gamma F_Y < \alpha, \beta >.$ Conversely, $F_Y = in_1 \star in_2$ for $in_i : Y \longrightarrow Y + Y$ by **3**, so if left distributivity holds, $F_X(\gamma \oplus \gamma) = F_X < \gamma in_1, \gamma in_2 > \;=\; \gamma in_1 \star \gamma in_2 \;=\; \gamma(in_1 \star in_2) \;=\; \gamma F_Y.$ □

7 EXAMPLE It is clear that $in_1 : id \longrightarrow id + id$ is natural so $x \star y = x$ is a natural choice family. Similarly for $x * y = y$. These operations are associative and idempotent but not commutative.

The theory of **8-11** below is part of the folklore of abelian categories. [See Freyd 1964, Mitchell 1965, Section 18.]

8 PROPOSITION *On a category with binary copowers, any natural choice family commutes with every choice family.*

Proof Let $\star$ be a natural choice family and let $*$ be a choice family. The proof requires only that $\star$ is left-distributive and that $*$ is right-distributive as follows.

$$
\begin{aligned}
(\alpha * \beta)\star(\gamma * \delta) &= (in_1 < \alpha, \beta > *in_2 < \alpha, \beta >)\star(in_1 < \gamma, \delta > * < in_2 < \gamma, \delta >) \\
&= (in_1 * in_2) < \alpha, \beta > \star(in_1 * in_2) < \gamma, \delta > \\
&= (in_1 * in_2)(< \alpha, \beta > \star < \gamma, \delta >) \\
&= (in_1 < \alpha, \beta > \star in_1 < \gamma, \delta >) * (in_2 < \alpha, \beta > \star < in_2 < \gamma, \delta >) \\
&= (\alpha \star \gamma) * (\beta \star \delta).
\end{aligned}
$$
  □

Certain categories of interest in program semantics, e.g. of domains, may fail to have coproducts and yet still have weak coproducts (meaning the uniqueness condition of induced maps is dropped.) It is worth commenting, then, that only weak binary copowers were used in the above proof.

9 DEFINITION A category *has zero morphisms* if there exists a family of morphisms $0_{XY} : X \longrightarrow Y$ indexed by pairs of objects such that for all $\alpha : W \longrightarrow X$, $\beta : Y \longrightarrow Z$, $\alpha 0_{XY} \beta = 0_{WZ}$.

Such 0_{XY} are clearly unique if they exist so we abbreviate 0_{XY} to $0 : X \longrightarrow Y$.

10 DEFINITION A *semiadditive category* is a category with zero morphisms and binary copowers for which there exists a natural transformation $\Delta : id \longrightarrow id + id$ such that the diagram shown below commutes for all objects X.

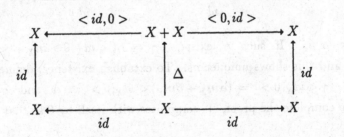

See **20** and Sections 7 and 13 for examples of semiadditive categories. Indeed Proposition **13.13** is an important special case of the duality assertion in the next result.

11 PROPOSITION *For a semiadditive category, the following two statements hold:*

1. $X \xleftarrow{\ <id,0>\ } X + X \xrightarrow{\ <0,id>\ } X$ *is a product. (In particular, Δ_X is unique.)*

2.   *The corresponding choice operator* $\alpha + \beta = \Delta_X < \alpha, \beta >$ *is associative and commutative and has zero morphism as unit, that is, each* $\mathbb{C}(X, Y)$ *is an abelian monoid.*

Additionally, the dual of a semiadditive category is again semiadditive.

Proof The diagram in **10** implies that $\alpha + 0 = \alpha = 0 + \alpha$.   Now consider any binary coproduct that happens to exist, $X + Y$. We observe

12            $< id_X, 0 > in_X + < 0, id_Y > in_Y = id_{X+Y}.$

To check this, observe that the left hand side preceded by in_X is $id_X in_X + 0 = in_X$ and similarly for in_Y. This established, consider the diagram

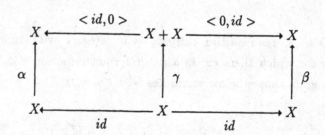

for arbitrary α, β.   If such γ exists, $\gamma = \gamma(< id_X, 0 > in_X + < 0, id_Y > in_Y) = \alpha in_X + \beta in_Y$ and this shows uniqueness. To extablish existence, define γ this way. We then have $\gamma < id_X, 0 > = (\alpha in_X + \beta in_Y) < id_X, 0 > = \alpha$ and $\gamma < 0, id_Y > = \beta$ similarly. To complete the proof, $+$ commutes with itself by **8** so that

$$(\alpha + \beta) + (\gamma + \delta) = (\alpha + \gamma) + (\beta + \delta) .$$

The commutativity and associativity of $+$ then follow from judicious substitution of zeroes. The duality assertion amounts mainly to the fact already shown that $X + X$ is a product as well as a coproduct; for the remaining details, observe that $in_X = [id_X, 0]$: $X \longrightarrow X + X$ and that $< id_X, id_X > \gamma = (\gamma \oplus \gamma) < id_Y, id_Y >$: $X + X \longrightarrow Y.$

□

Semiadditive categories will be developed a little further in the next section in connection with iteration.

We now turn toward formally establishing that a commutative, idempotent choice operator is inherently nondeterministic, Proposition 19 below. The definition of "deterministic" of the next definition is essentially that of [Dijkstra 1976] as will be discussed further in Section 12.

13 DEFINITION A morphism $\alpha : X \longrightarrow Y$ is *deterministic* if for every coproduct of form $Q \xrightarrow{\ j\ } Y \xleftarrow{\ j'\ } Q'$ there exists a coproduct of form $P \xrightarrow{\ i\ } X \xleftarrow{\ i'\ } P'$ and a commutative diagram

14

$$
\begin{array}{ccccc}
P & \xrightarrow{\ i\ } & X & \xleftarrow{\ i'\ } & P' \\
\downarrow{t} & & \downarrow{\alpha} & & \downarrow{u} \\
Q & \xrightarrow[\ j\ ]{} & Y & \xleftarrow[\ j'\ ]{} & Q'
\end{array}
$$

The intuition behind this definition is as follows. A coproduct in **Set** is a disjoint union decomposition, that is, $P \xrightarrow{\ i\ } X \xleftarrow{\ i'\ } P'$ is a coproduct if and only if i, i' are injective and their images partition X. While it is true that coproducts can be very different in other categories, it is this disjoint-union model that we wish to emulate. Beginning with Section 4, the axioms we impose on the semantic framework will be designed to support this interpretation of coproducts. Thus the intuitive meaning of the definition of a deterministic morphism is "subject to available tests, it is impossible to witness 2-valued behaviour". In somewhat more detail, the various coproduct decompositions Q, Q' represent the ability of the semantic framework to divide Y into two disjoint alternatives. To witness 2-valued behaviour some element of X must be mapped by α in such a way as to be neither wholly inside Q nor wholly inside Q'. We interpret the left hand square in **14** as asserting that each element of P is mapped by α wholly inside Q and similarly the right hand square for P' and Q'. But our viewpoint on coproducts is that every element of X is in exactly one of P, P'.

Table 15 presents examples of deterministic morphisms. (Formal proofs are more easily given using the theory to be developed later.)

Category	Deterministic $X \xrightarrow{\alpha} Y$
Set, Pfn, Pfn$_M$	all
Mfn	the partial functions
Mat$_R$	$\forall x \, \exists$ at most one $y \in Y, \alpha_{xy} \neq 0$
Ω	$\forall x \in X \, \exists$ at most one $y \in Y$ appearing as a leaf in $x\alpha$

Table 15:   Examples of deterministic morphisms

Our interpretation of coproducts supports the following term:

16   DEFINITION An object X of $\mathbb{C}$ is *trivial* if there exists a morphism $t :$ $X \longrightarrow Y$ such that $X \xrightarrow{t} Y \xleftarrow{t} X$ is a coproduct.

The examples of Section 1 all have exactly one trivial object, the empty set. It is obvious from the coproduct property that a trivial object never admits two distinct morphisms to any object. It follows that $\alpha \star \beta = \alpha = \beta$ is the only choice operator on such an object, so trivial objects have only trivial choice operators.

17   LEMMA *Let* $X \xrightarrow{in_1} X + X \xleftarrow{in_2} X$ *be a coproduct and let* $s :$ $X + X \longrightarrow X + X$ *be the "switch map" defined by* $in_1 s = in_2$, $in_2 s = in_1$. *Let* T $: X \longrightarrow X + X$ *and define* $T' = Ts$.   *Assume that* T *is deterministic and idempotent. Then*

$$X \xrightarrow{T} X + X \xleftarrow{T'} X$$

is a coproduct.

Proof   As T is deterministic and idempotent there exists a commutative diagram

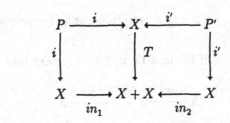

18

in which the top row is a coproduct. (Idempotency $\Leftrightarrow T < id_X, id_X > \; = id_X$ and this is used to see that both the horizontal and vertical i are equal, i' similarly.) Composing with s gives rise to

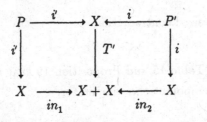

To complete the proof, given arbitrary $\alpha, \beta : X \longrightarrow Y$ we must find unique $h : X + X \longrightarrow Y$ such that $Th = \alpha$, $T'h = \beta$. For such h the following equations must hold:

$$
\begin{aligned}
i\, in_1 h &= iTh &= i\alpha \\
i'\, in_1 h &= i'T'h &= i'\beta \\
i\, in_2 h &= iT'h &= i\beta \\
i'\, in_2 h &= i'Th &= i'\alpha .
\end{aligned}
$$

As $P \xrightarrow{\ i\ } X \xleftarrow{\ i'\ } P'$ is a coproduct there exists unique $in_1 h$ satisfying the first two equations and unique $in_2 h$ satisfying the second two. But then as $X \xrightarrow{\ in_1\ } X + X \xleftarrow{\ in_2\ } X$ is a coproduct, the desired h exists uniquely. $\qquad\square$

We have paved the way for

19 PROPOSITION *Commutative idempotent choice is inherently nondeterministic. More precisely, given* $T : X \longrightarrow X + X$ *with* X *non-trivial and whose choice* operator $\alpha \bigstar \beta = T <\alpha, \beta>$ is commutative and idempotent, T is not deterministic.

Proof   In the notation of Lemma 17, if T were deterministic then

$$X \xrightarrow{\ T\ } X + X \xleftarrow{\ T'\ } X$$

is a coproduct with $T' = Ts$, $s : X + X \longrightarrow X + X$ the switch map. For any α, β we have $T' <\alpha, \beta> = Ts <\alpha, \beta> = T <\beta, \alpha> = \beta \bigstar \alpha = \alpha \bigstar \beta = T <\alpha, \beta>$. Setting $\alpha = in_1$, $\beta = in_2$, we see that $T = T'$. Using the coproduct above, any two morphisms $\alpha, \beta : X \longrightarrow Y$ are equal so that $X \xrightarrow{\ id\ } X \xleftarrow{\ id\ } X$ is a coproduct and X is trivial, the desired contradiction. $\square$

It follows from Table 15 and Proposition 19 that no object in **Set**, **Pfn**, or **Pfn**$_M$ has a commutative, idempotent choice operator.

20 EXAMPLE In **Mfn**, $if\ P \to \alpha \ \square\ Q \to \beta\ fi$ is a choice operator. More precisely, for P, Q subsets of X, define the choice operator $\bigstar$ on X by

$$x(\alpha \bigstar \beta) = (x \in P) \cdot x\alpha \ \bigcup\ (x \in Q) \cdot x\beta$$

where $true \cdot S = S$, $false \cdot S = \emptyset$. The resulting $T : X \longrightarrow X + X$ is $xT = P_1 \bigcup Q_2$ where S_i is the image of S under $in_i : X \longrightarrow X + X$. Such $\bigstar$ is idempotent if and only if $P \bigcup Q = X$ and is commutative if and only if $P = Q$. When $P = Q = X$, the resulting commutative, idempotent choice is $\alpha \bigstar \beta = \alpha \bigcup \beta$ with T the "nondeterministic fork map" sending x to two copies of x. Such T is better written Δ since it provides **Mfn** with its unique semiadditive structure.

We devote the balance of the section to a discussion of *if–then–else* in an arbitrary category with an initial object 0.

21 DEFINITION Let $X \xrightarrow{\ in_1\ } X + X \xleftarrow{\ in_2\ } X$ be a coproduct. For each coproduct decomposition $P \xrightarrow{\ i\ } X \xleftarrow{\ i'\ } P'$ of X, define the *fanout* $F : X \longrightarrow X + X$ of X by

22

$$
\begin{array}{ccccc}
P & \xrightarrow{\ i\ } & X & \xleftarrow{\ i'\ } & P' \\
\scriptstyle i \downarrow & & \scriptstyle F \downarrow & & \downarrow \scriptstyle i' \\
X & \xrightarrow[in_1]{} & X + X & \xleftarrow[in_2]{} & X
\end{array}
$$

It is clear that an isomorphic coproduct decomposition of X gives rise to the same fanout. The resulting *if–then–else operator* is the choice operator on X given by $if_{PP'}(\alpha,\beta) = F < \alpha,\beta >$. Thus

23

$$
\begin{array}{ccccc}
P & \xrightarrow{\ i\ } & X & \xleftarrow{\ i'\ } & P' \\
\scriptstyle i \downarrow & & \scriptstyle if_{PP'}(\alpha,\beta) \downarrow & & \downarrow \scriptstyle i' \\
X & \xrightarrow[\alpha]{} & Y & \xleftarrow[\beta]{} & X
\end{array}
$$

characterizes $if_{PP'}(\alpha,\beta)$. This is a choice operator whether or not $X + X$ exists.

24 PROPOSITION *Each if–then–else operator $\star$ in a category with finite coproducts is idempotent and associative and satisfies*

$$\alpha \star \beta \star \gamma = \alpha \star \gamma.$$

Proof Use the notation of **23**. As $< i\alpha, i'\alpha > = \alpha$, $\alpha \star \alpha = \alpha$. Further, $\alpha \star (\beta \star \gamma) = < i\alpha, i'(\beta \star \gamma) > = < i\alpha, i' < i\beta, i'\gamma > > = < i\alpha, i'\gamma > = \alpha \star \gamma = < i < i\alpha, i'\beta >, i'\gamma > = (\alpha \star \beta) \star \gamma$.
The proof is complete. $\qquad\qquad\square$

It was observed in **18** that any deterministic, idempotent choice is an if–then–else operator. The converse fails in the category of real vector spaces. For consider the choice operator on $\mathbb{R}$ given by $\alpha \star \beta = \alpha$. This is the if–then–else operator corresponding to the coproduct $\mathbb{R} \xrightarrow{id} \mathbb{R} \longleftarrow 0$, but it is not deterministic. (Proof: The corresponding fanout is $F : \mathbb{R} \longrightarrow \mathbb{R} \oplus \mathbb{R}$, $x \mapsto (x, 0)$. If L, M are two lines through the origin distinct from the x–axis, $L \longrightarrow \mathbb{R} \oplus \mathbb{R} \longleftarrow M$ is a coproduct but F maps no nonzero element to either L or M.) We will see later in Proposition **5.13** that fanouts are deterministic in a Boolean category.

The next definition is needed to set up a polymorphic characterization of if–then–else.

25 DEFINITION Let $\mathbb{C}$ be a category. Let $\mathbb{C}^{\bullet}$ denote the category whose objects are all $(P, i, P', i', X, \alpha, \beta, Y)$ where

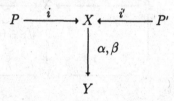

is such that the top row is a coproduct. A *morphism* from $(P, i, P', i', X, \alpha, \beta, Y)$ to $(Q, j, Q', j', X_1, \alpha_1, \beta_1, Y_1)$ is (t, u, h, k) such that

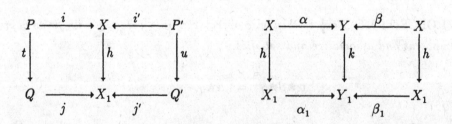

$\mathbb{C}^{\bullet}$ is a category with identity morphism $(id_P, id_{P'}, id_X, id_Y)$ and with the same composition as $\mathbb{C}$.

Define $\mathbb{C}^{\rightarrow}$ to be the morphism category of $\mathbb{C}$ with objects all $v : X \longrightarrow Y$ and with a morphism $v \longrightarrow v_1$ being (h, k) such that $hv_1 = vk$. $\mathbb{C}^{\rightarrow}$ is a category with identity morphisms (id_X, id_Y) and with composition as in $\mathbb{C}$.

Notice that the definition of $if_{PP'}(\alpha, \beta)$ in **23** has the form of mapping an object of $\mathbb{C}^\bullet$ to an object of $\mathbb{C}^\rightarrow$.

26 PROPOSITION *For any category $\mathbb{C}$, if–then–else satisfies the following "polymorphic property": For any morphism (t, u, h, k) in $\mathbb{C}^\bullet$ (so that 27 holds with both*

27

$$
\begin{array}{ccccc}
P & \xrightarrow{\ i\ } & X & \xleftarrow{\ i'\ } & P' \\
\downarrow{t} & & \downarrow{h} & & \downarrow{u} \\
Q & \xrightarrow{\ j\ } & X_1 & \xleftarrow{\ j'\ } & Q'
\end{array}
\qquad
\begin{array}{ccccc}
X & \xrightarrow{\ \alpha\ } & Y & \xleftarrow{\ \beta\ } & X \\
\downarrow{h} & & \downarrow{k} & & \downarrow{h} \\
X_1 & \xrightarrow{\ \alpha_1\ } & Y_1 & \xleftarrow{\ \beta_1\ } & X_1
\end{array}
$$

rows of the left rectangle being coproducts), then $(h, k) : if_{PP'}(\alpha, \beta) \longrightarrow if_{QQ'}(\alpha_1, \beta_1)$ is a morphism in $\mathbb{C}^\rightarrow$, that is, diagram 28 holds:

28

$$
\begin{array}{ccc}
X & \xrightarrow{\ if_{PP'}(\alpha, \beta)\ } & Y \\
\downarrow{h} & & \downarrow{k} \\
X_1 & \xrightarrow{\ if_{QQ'}(\alpha_1, \beta_1)\ } & Y_1
\end{array}
$$

Proof Because of the equations in **27** and **23**, the two paths $X \longrightarrow Y_1$ in **28** agree preceded by either of the coproduct injections i, i' and so are equal. □

Thus $if_{PP'}(\alpha, \beta)$ has the right form to be a functor $\mathbb{C}^\bullet \longrightarrow \mathbb{C}^\rightarrow$. It is routine to verify that it in fact is.

When $\mathbb{C}$ has an initial object 0, $X \xrightarrow{\ id\ } X \longleftarrow 0$ is a coproduct for any X. It is clear that $if_{X0}(\alpha, \beta) = \alpha$, $if_{0X}(\alpha, \beta) = \beta$. We then have the following converse to Proposition **26**:

29 PROPOSITION *For any category* $\mathbb{C}$ *with initial object* 0, *there is exactly one function* I *assigning an object* $I_{PP'}(\alpha,\beta) : X \longrightarrow Y$ *of* $\mathbb{C}^{\rightarrow}$ *to each object* $(P, i, P', i', X, \alpha, \beta, Y)$ *of* $\mathbb{C}^{\bullet}$ *subject to the laws*

30
$$I_{X0}(\alpha,\beta) = \alpha$$
$$I_{0X}(\alpha,\beta) = \beta$$

and the polymorphic property 27 $\Rightarrow$ 28, *namely* $(P, i, P', i', X, \alpha, \beta, Y) \mapsto if_{PP'}(\alpha,\beta)$ *as in 23.*

Proof   If $P \xrightarrow{\;i\;} X \xleftarrow{\;i'\;} P'$ is a coproduct and $\alpha, \beta : X \longrightarrow Y$ then

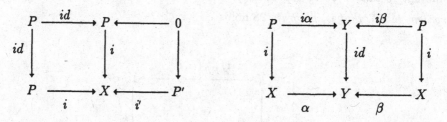

is an instance of 27 so that $i\alpha = I_{P0}(i\alpha, i\beta)\, id_Y = i\, I_{PP'}(\alpha,\beta)$. Similarly, $i'\, I_{PP'}(\alpha,\beta) = i'\beta$. Thus $I_{PP'}(\alpha,\beta) = \,<i\alpha, i'\beta> \,= if_{PP'}(\alpha,\beta)$. $\square$

Traditionally, the choice operators $if_{PP'}(-,-)$ for $P \longrightarrow X \longleftarrow P'$ a coproduct with X fixed, range over Boolean algebra. There is no problem in describing the desired Boolean operations:

31
$$(if_{not\ PP'})(\alpha,\beta) = if_{PP'}(\beta,\alpha)$$
$$(if_{PP' \vee QQ'})(\alpha,\beta) = if_{PP'}(\alpha, if_{QQ'}(\alpha,\beta))$$
$$(if_{PP' \wedge QQ'})(\alpha,\beta) = if_{PP'}(if_{QQ'}(\alpha,\beta),\, \beta).$$

Here, $if_{not\ PP'}(-,-) = if_{P'P}(-,-)$. As de Morgan's laws hold, either of $\vee$, $\wedge$ will suffice to get both. While $if_{PP' \vee QQ'}$ is always a choice operator it is not an if–then–else operator in general. We state the following result which is easily adapted from [Bloom and Ésik, 1988]:

32 PROPOSITION *Let Γ be a set of choice operators on X in any category $\mathbb{C}$. Assume*

1. *Each operator in Γ satisfies the three equations of proposition 24, namely*
   $$\alpha \star \alpha = \alpha, \ \alpha \star (\beta \star \gamma) = \alpha \star \gamma = (\alpha \star \beta) \star \gamma.$$

2. *The trivial operation $\alpha \star \beta = \alpha$ is in Γ.*

3. *Γ is closed under the operations not and $\vee$ of 31.*

4. *Any two operations in Γ commute* (in the sense of Proposition 8.)

Then $(\Gamma, not, \vee)$ is a Boolean algebra with $\alpha \star \beta = \alpha$ as greatest element. $\qquad\square$

Bloom and Ésik use this approach to build Boolean structure into their categories. As will be seen in Section 5, we shall employ different axiomatics to develop Boolean structure in categories.

3   POLYMORPHIC ITERATES

Motivated by the polymorphic characterization of *if–then–else in* Proposition **2.29**, we offer a related concept of "polymorphic iterate" in any category with binary coproducts. In the category of partial functions, the only polymorphic iterate is the usual one. In semiadditive categories, polymorphic iterates correspond to "Kleene stars", and a lax version of the polymorphic axioms leads to the familiar idea that the Kleene star is the reflexive–transitive closure in suitable ordered categories. The ideas of this section stem from the work of many hands over the past two decades including M.A. Arbib, S.L. Bloom, V.E. Căsănescu, C.C. Elgot, Z. Ésik, J.A. Goguen, S. Ginali, J.D. Rutledge, J.W. Thatcher, Gh. Ştefănescu, E.G. Wagner, J.B. Wright and others. More detailed historical remarks were given in the introduction.

Examples of   *while P do α* : $X \longrightarrow X$ for $P \subset X$, $\alpha : X \longrightarrow X$ were given in **1.12**. In these cases there is a coproduct $P \overset{i}{\longrightarrow} X \overset{i'}{\longleftarrow} P'$ with P' the set-theoretic complement of P and i, i' inclusion functions interpreted as morphisms in **Pfn**, **Mfn**, **Mat**$_R$, ... in the natural way, with fanout $F : X \longrightarrow X + X$ as in **2.22**. Define

1 $\qquad\qquad \xi \;=\; X \overset{F}{\longrightarrow} X + X \overset{\alpha \oplus id_X}{\longrightarrow} X + X \quad .$

(See **2.5** for the definition of $\alpha \oplus id_X$.) Then *while P do α* on input x is obtained by iterating ξ so long as the result is in the first component X of $X + X$ to get the trace sequence $x, x\xi, x\xi^2, \ldots, x\xi^{n-1}$ until (if ever) $x\xi^n$ is achieved in the second component X in which case such $x\xi^n$ is the output value. A mild generalization is the construction (*while P do α*) ; k for $k : X \longrightarrow Y$ in which case the appropriate ξ is

2 $\qquad\qquad \xi \;=\; X \overset{F}{\longrightarrow} X + X \overset{\alpha \oplus k}{\longrightarrow} X + Y$

and the description simplifies to "iterate ξ as long as possible". Following [Elgot 1975] we then allow ξ to be any morphism $\xi : X \longrightarrow X + Y$ and attempt to axiomatize "repeat ξ" as a construction of form $\xi : X \longrightarrow X + Y \mapsto \xi^{\dagger} : X \longrightarrow Y$ in a category with coproducts. [Note: It is formally proved for "preadditive Boolean categories" in Proposition **12.17** below that if ξ is deterministic then, for suitable P, α and k, $\xi^{\dagger}$ is indeed $(while\ P\ do\ \alpha)\,;\,k$. This need not hold for nondeterministic ξ, however.] This leads to the next definition.

3 DEFINITION Let C be a category with finite coproducts. An *iterative specification in* C is (X, Y, C, i, j, ξ) with $X \overset{i}{\longrightarrow} C \overset{j}{\longleftarrow} Y$ a coproduct and $\xi : X \longrightarrow C$. A *pre-iterate on* C is an assignment $(-)^{\dagger}$ of a morphism $X \longrightarrow Y$ to each iterative specification (X, Y, C, i, j, ξ).

To maximize expressiveness it is conventional to use more concise notation and to denote an iterative specification by $\xi : X \longrightarrow X + Y$ and its assigned value as $\xi^{\dagger}$. This is not dangerous so long as it is understood that such ξ is not just a morphism but includes how $X + Y$ is a coproduct. The following example explicates this point.

4 EXAMPLE Consider $C = \mathbf{Pfn}$ with $(-)^{\dagger}$ as discussed above. Let $\mathbb{N} = \{0, 1, 2, \ldots\}$ with even numbers $\mathbb{E} = \{0, 2, 4, \ldots\}$ and odd numbers $\mathbb{O} = \{1, 3, 5, \ldots\}$. The morphism $\xi : \mathbb{E} \longrightarrow \mathbb{N}$ given by $x \mapsto 2x$ is part of an iterative specification in various ways. For the specification given by $(\mathbb{E}, \mathbb{O}, \mathbb{N}, i, j, \xi)$ (with i, j the inclusions), $\xi^{\dagger}$ is the empty partial function because iterating ξ never produces an odd number. On the other hand, $(\mathbb{E}, \mathbb{N}, \mathbb{N}, t, u, \xi)$ is an iterative specification if $xt = x + 1$ and $xu = 2x$, in which case $x\xi$ is not iterated for any x so that $\xi^{\dagger} = \xi$.

We seek axioms on a pre-iterate which will generate a useful first-order theory. The least-fixed-point-semantics of iteration is well established, so we shall review some of that theory here and use it as a springboard to motivate a more general formulation.

5 DEFINITION An ω–*complete poset* is a poset with a least element in which every ascending sequence has a least upper bound. A function between ω–complete posets is *continuous* if it preserves suprema of ascending sequences. A function between posets with a least element is *strict* if it preserves these least elements.

Notice that while ω–complete posets always have least elements, continuous maps are not required to preserve them.

6 KLEENE FIXED POINT THEOREM *A continuous endomorphism ψ of an ω-complete poset has a least fixed point x_0. Further, x_0 is the least x with $x\psi \leq x$.*

Proof Comments Let $(X, \leq)$ be ω–complete with least element $\bot$ and consider continuous $\psi : (X, \leq) \longrightarrow (X, \leq)$. As ψ is monotone there is an ascending sequence (called the *Kleene sequence*) $\bot \leq \bot\psi \leq \bot\psi^2 \leq \ldots$ with limit $x_0 = Sup(\bot x\psi^n)$ having the desired properties because ψ is continuous.   □

It was observed by [Elgot 1975] that the familiar fixed point property for iteration was easily expressed for categories with pre-iterate.

7 DEFINITION Let $\xi : X \longrightarrow X + Y$ be an iterative specification. The *Elgot fixed point equation* for ξ is the equation in the variable α given by

$$\alpha \;=\; X \xrightarrow{\quad \xi \quad} X + Y \xrightarrow{\quad <\alpha, id_Y> \quad} Y$$

For ξ as in 1 in the context of *while P do α* in **Pfn**, this equation with $\alpha = $ *while P do β* asserts that

$$(while \; P \; do \; \beta)(x) \;=\; if \; P(x) \; then \; (while \; P \; do \; \beta)(\beta(x)) \; else \; x \;.$$

The Elgot fixed point equation 7 is $\alpha\psi = \alpha$ for $\psi : \mathbb{C}(X,Y) \longrightarrow \mathbb{C}(X,Y)$ defined by $\alpha\psi = \xi <\alpha, id_Y>$. For a given $\bot : X \longrightarrow Y$, the resulting Kleene sequence is given by

$$8 \qquad \perp \psi^n \;=\; X \xrightarrow{\;in_X\;} X+Y \xrightarrow{\;<\xi,id_Y>^{\,n}\;} X+Y \xrightarrow{\;<\perp,id_Y>\;} Y \;.$$

To prove both sides are the same, let ξ_n denote the right hand side of 8. Clearly $\xi_0 = \perp$. Noting that $in_Y < \xi, id_Y >^{\,n} \;=\; id_Y$, we then calculate

$$
\begin{aligned}
\xi_{n+1} \;&=\; in_X <\xi,id_Y> <\xi,id_Y>^{\,n} <\perp,id_Y> \\
&=\; \xi <\xi,id_Y>^{\,n} <\perp,id_Y> \\
&=\; \xi < in_X <\xi,id_Y>^{\,n} <\perp,id_Y> ,\; in_Y <\xi,id_Y>^{\,n} <\perp,id_Y> > \\
&=\; \xi <\xi_n,id_Y> \;=\; \xi_n \psi \;.
\end{aligned}
$$

This represents the n–fold application of ψ as an n–fold composition in $\mathbb{C}$ and one whose interpretation in, say, **Pfn** is clear: $<\xi,id_Y>^{\,n}$ maps y to y and x to $x\xi^n$ if $m \leq n$, or to $x\xi^n$ else; the prefix in_X limits inputs to those in X and the suffix $<\perp,id_Y>$ is undefined on X so keeps only outputs truly in Y.

Given all this it is very natural to axiomatize a class of categories with pre-iterate for which ψ in 8 is continuous. This is easily done and there are lots of examples.

9 DEFINITION

An ω-*complete category* is a category with chosen binary coproducts in which each set $\mathbb{C}(X,Y)$ is provided with an ω–complete poset structure possessing a least element $\perp$ in such a way that

$$\mathbb{C}(X,Y) \xrightarrow{\;\alpha \circ -\;} \mathbb{C}(W,Y)$$

$$\mathbb{C}(X,Y) \xrightarrow{\;- \circ \beta\;} \mathbb{C}(X,Z)$$

are continuous and strict, and

$$\mathbb{C}(X,Y) \xrightarrow{\qquad} \mathbb{C}(X+Y,Y), \quad \gamma \mapsto <\gamma,id_Y>$$

are continuous. Here X,Y,Z, $\alpha : W \xrightarrow{\quad} X$, $\beta : Y \xrightarrow{\quad} Z$ are arbitrary.

Pfn is ω–complete via the extension ordering. Mfn is ω–complete under the inclusion ordering.

The definition of an ω–complete category and **8** makes the next result immediate.

10 PROPOSITION *Let* $\mathcal{C}$ *be an* ω*–complete category, and let* $\bot : X \longrightarrow Y$ *denote the least element of* $\mathcal{C}(X,Y)$. *Given an iterative specification* $\xi : X \longrightarrow X+Y$ *define*

10a $\qquad \xi_n = X \xrightarrow{in_X} X+Y \xrightarrow{<\xi,id_Y>^n} X+Y \xrightarrow{<\bot,id_Y>} Y$.

Then $\psi : \mathcal{C}(X,Y) \longrightarrow \mathcal{C}(X,Y)$, $\alpha\psi = \xi<\alpha,id_Y>$ *is continuous with Kleene sequence* ξ_n *so that*

10b $\qquad\qquad \xi^\dagger = Sup\ \xi_n$

is a pre-iterate on $\mathcal{C}$ *satisfyng the Elgot fixed point equation* **7**. $\qquad\qquad\square$

We now begin to explore axioms satisfied by the canonical iterate **10b**. We begin with a polymorphic property in the style of that of **2.29**. The term "unrestricted" in the following definition owes to **26** below, our ultimate definition in which h,k are subject to restrictions.

11 DEFINITION A pre-iterate $(-)^\dagger$ satisfies the *unrestricted polymorphic axiom* if given iterative specifications $\xi : X \longrightarrow X+Y$, $\overline{\xi} : \overline{X} \longrightarrow \overline{X}+\overline{Y}$ and $h : X \longrightarrow \overline{X}$, $k : Y \longrightarrow \overline{Y}$

$$\begin{array}{ccc} X \xrightarrow{\xi} X+Y & & X \xrightarrow{\xi^\dagger} Y \\ h\downarrow \quad \downarrow h\oplus k & \Rightarrow & h\downarrow \quad \downarrow k \\ \overline{X} \xrightarrow{\overline{\xi}} \overline{X}+\overline{Y} & & \overline{X} \xrightarrow{\overline{\xi}^\dagger} \overline{Y} \end{array}$$

12 PROPOSITION *The canonical iterate* **10b** *on an ω-complete category satisfies the unrestricted polymorphic axiom.*

Proof Let $\xi(h \oplus k) = h\bar{\xi}$ as in **11**. Then $in_X(h \oplus k) = h\, in_{\overline{X}}$ (definition of $h \oplus k$), $<\xi, in_Y>(h \oplus k) = (h \oplus k)<\bar{\xi}, in_{\overline{Y}}>$ and $<\perp, id_Y>k = (h \oplus k)<\perp, id_{\overline{Y}}>$ (because $h \circ -$ is strict) so that $\xi_n k = h\bar{\xi}_n$. Thus $h\xi^{\dagger} = \bar{\xi}^{\dagger}k$ since $h \circ -$ and $- \circ k$ are continuous. $\square$

Notice that $\xi^{\dagger} = 0$ satisfies the unrestricted polymorphic axiom, though not the Elgot equation. In the basic example of **Pfn** we have

13 PROPOSITION [Arbib and Manes 1978.] *In the ω-complete category* **Pfn**, *the canonical pre-iterate is the only one satisfying the Elgot fixed point equation* 7 *and the unrestricted polymorphic axiom* 11.

Proof Let $(-)^{\dagger}$ be the canonical pre-iterate and let $(-)^{\ddagger}$ be a pre-iterate satisfying the Elgot equation and the unrestricted polymorphic axiom. Let $\xi : X \longrightarrow X + Y$ be an iterative specification. As $\xi^{\dagger}$ is the least fixed point, $\xi^{\dagger} \leq \xi^{\ddagger}$ in the extension ordering so it suffices to show that if $K = \{x \in X : x\xi^{\dagger}$ is not defined$\}$ then $x \in K \Rightarrow x\xi^{\ddagger}$ is not defined. For $x \in K$, there is an infinite trace sequence $x, x\xi, \ldots$ of elements of X obtained by iterating ξ and $x\xi$ has the same trace with x truncated, so $x\xi \in K$ and there exists a commutative diagram

$$
\begin{array}{ccc}
K & \xrightarrow{\ \theta\ } & K + \emptyset \\
\scriptstyle i \downarrow & & \downarrow \scriptstyle i \oplus 0 \\
X & \xrightarrow[\ \xi\ ]{} & X + Y
\end{array}
$$

where $i : K \longrightarrow X$ is inclusion and $0 : \emptyset \longrightarrow Y$ is the empty function. By the unrestricted polymorphic axiom we have the diagram

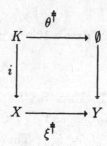

so that $i\xi^{\dagger}$ is empty as desired.   □

As is well-known, the behaviour of a general iterative network is the simultaneous solution of a system of fixed point equations. Such a system in the notation of pre-iterates takes the form $\xi_1, \ldots, \xi_n$ with $\xi_i : X_i \longrightarrow X_1 + \cdots + X_n + Y$ or, in vector form, $\langle \xi_1, \ldots, \xi_n \rangle : X_1 + \cdots + X_n \longrightarrow X_1 + \cdots + X_n + Y$. There is little evidence that the Elgot equation and unrestricted polymorphism can, alone, generate a reasonable theory of vector iteration and Ésik has shown us an example in which these hold but the pairing axiom of **16** below does not.

In the vector case with $n = 2$, we have $\langle \xi, \theta \rangle : X + Y \longrightarrow Z$ and the Elgot equation for $\langle \xi, \theta \rangle$ resolves into the system

14
$$\begin{aligned}
\alpha &= \xi \langle \alpha, \beta, id_Y \rangle \\
\beta &= \theta \langle \alpha, \beta, id_Y \rangle \ .
\end{aligned}$$

For the ω-complete case, we can rely on the following well-known technique for ω-complete posets. Before stating it we recall that if P, Q, R are ω-complete posets, a function $\psi : P \times Q \longrightarrow R$ is jointly continuous (with respect to the coordinatewise order on the product which *is* ω-complete) if and only if it is continuous in each variable separately.

15 PROPOSITION Let P, Q be ω-complete posets and let $\varphi : P \times Q \longrightarrow P$, $\psi : P \times Q \longrightarrow Q$ be continuous. For each $\beta \in Q$ set

15a $$\alpha_\beta = \text{least } \alpha \text{ with } \alpha = (\alpha, \beta)\varphi .$$

Then $\beta \mapsto \alpha_\beta$ is continuous $Q \longrightarrow P$, and if

15b $$\beta_0 = \text{least } \beta \text{ with } \beta = (\alpha_\beta, \beta)\psi$$
$$\alpha_0 = \alpha_{\beta_0}$$

then (α_0, β_0) is the least (α, β) with $(\alpha, \beta) = ((\alpha, \beta)\varphi, (\alpha, \beta)\psi)$ that is, is the least-fixed-point solution of the system

15c $$\alpha = (\alpha, \beta)\varphi$$
$$\beta = (\alpha, \beta)\psi .$$

Proof Outline That $\alpha_0 = (\alpha_0, \beta_0)\varphi$, $\beta_0 = (\alpha_0, \beta_0)\psi$ is trivial. If $\beta \le \beta_1$, $(\alpha_{\beta_1}, \beta)\varphi \le (\alpha_{\beta_1}, \beta_1)\varphi = \beta_1$ whereas α_β is the least α with $(\alpha, \beta)\varphi \le \alpha$ so $\alpha_\beta \le \alpha_{\beta_1}$. Let β_n be an ascending chain with limit β and let $\alpha = Sup\, \alpha_{\beta_n}$. As $(\alpha_{\beta_n}, \beta_n)\psi = \alpha_{\beta_n} \le \alpha$, $(\alpha, \beta)\psi \le \alpha$ whereas α_β is the least γ with $(\gamma, \beta)\psi \le \gamma$, $\alpha_\beta \le \alpha$. This shows that $\beta \mapsto \alpha_\beta$ is continuous.

Now let (α, β) solve **15c**. As $\alpha_\beta \le \beta$, $(\alpha_\beta, \beta)\psi \le (\alpha, \beta)\psi = \beta$ whereas β_0 is the least γ with $(\alpha_\gamma, \gamma)\psi \le \gamma$ so $\beta_0 \le \beta$. Thus $\alpha_0 = \alpha_{\beta_0} \le \alpha_\beta \le \alpha$. $\qquad\square$

As **14** is a special case of **15c**, Proposition 15 can be unravelled into an axiom about pre-iterates which is true, at least, for the canonical pre-iterate in any ω–complete category. Here

$$P = \mathfrak{C}(X, Z), \quad Q = \mathfrak{C}(Y, Z)$$

$$\varphi : P \times Q \longrightarrow P, \quad (\alpha, \beta) \mapsto X \xrightarrow{\;\xi\;} X + Y + Z \xrightarrow{\;<\alpha, \beta, id_Z>\;} Z$$

$$\psi : P \times Q \longrightarrow Q, \quad (\alpha, \beta) \mapsto Y \xrightarrow{\;\theta\;} X + Y + Z \xrightarrow{\;<\alpha, \beta, id_Z>\;} Z .$$

But observe that φ can be factored as

$$(\alpha, \beta) \mapsto X \xrightarrow{\xi} X+Y+Z \xrightarrow{<in_X, \beta in_Z, in_Z>} X+Z \xrightarrow{<\alpha, id_Z>} Z$$

so that for fixed β, $\alpha = (\alpha, \beta)\varphi$ is the Elgot equation for $\xi <in_X, \beta in_Z, in_Z>$, that is,

$$X \xrightarrow{\alpha_\beta} Z = (X \xrightarrow{\xi} X+Y+Z \xrightarrow{<in_X, \beta in_Z, in_Z>} X+Z)^\dagger .$$

But by reassociating the coproduct, $<in_X, \beta in_Z, in_Z> = id_X \oplus <\beta, id_Z>$. It thus follows from the unrestricted polymorphic axiom, true in all ω-complete categories by Proposition 14, that

$$\alpha_\beta = \xi^\dagger <\beta, id_Z>$$

for all β. This gives

$$(\alpha_\beta, \beta)\psi = Y \xrightarrow{\theta} X+Y+Z \xrightarrow{<\xi^\dagger, in_Y, in_Z>} Y+Z \xrightarrow{<\beta, id_Z>} Z$$

making $\beta = (\alpha_\beta, \beta)\psi$ the Elgot equation for the specification $\gamma = \theta <\xi^\dagger, in_Y, in_Z>$. This yields the equations

$$\beta_0 = \gamma^\dagger, \ \gamma = \theta <\xi^\dagger, in_Y, in_Z>$$

$$\alpha_0 = \alpha_{\beta_0} = \xi^\dagger <\gamma^\dagger, id_Z> .$$

We have then motivated the following *pairing axiom* of [Bloom, Ginali and Rutledge 1977].

16 DEFINITION A pre-iterate $(-)^\dagger$ satisfies the *pairing axiom* if given two iterative specifications $\xi : X \longrightarrow X+Y+Z$, $\theta : Y \longrightarrow X+Y+Z$,

$$(X+Y \xrightarrow{<\xi, \theta>} X+Y+Z)^\dagger = <\xi^\dagger <\gamma^\dagger, id_Z>, \gamma^\dagger>$$

for

$$\gamma \;=\; Y\xrightarrow{\;\;\theta\;\;}X+Y+Z\xrightarrow{\;<\xi^{\dagger},in_Y,in_Z>\;}Y+Z\;.$$

Here $X+Y+Z$ refers to any choice of coproduct (with specific given injections in_X, in_Y, in_Z) of X,Y,Z; similarly for $Y+Z$. Observe that the canonical isomorphism $X+Y+Z \cong X+(Y+Z)$ is used to define $\xi^{\dagger}$.

We also present two additional axioms.

17 DEFINITION [Elgot 1975, p. 220.] A pre-iterate satisfies the *parameter axiom* if for every iterative specification $\xi : X\longrightarrow X+Y$ and every $k : Y\longrightarrow Z$,

$$(\xi(id_X \oplus k))^{\dagger} \;=\; \xi^{\dagger}k\;.$$

18 DEFINITION A pre-iterate satisfies the *left-zero axiom* if for every $\alpha : X\longrightarrow Y$ and coproduct $X+Y$, $(\alpha\, in_Y)^{\dagger} = \alpha$.

It is easy to see that the parameter axiom follows from unrestricted polymorphism: use $\xi(id_X \oplus k) = id_X(\xi(id_X \oplus k))$. On the other hand, the Elgot fixed point equation implies the left-zero axiom since $(\alpha\, in_Y)^{\dagger} = \alpha\, in_Y < (\alpha\, in_Y)^{\dagger}, id_Y > =$ $\alpha\, id_Y = \alpha$. Thus the canonical pre-iterate of an ω-complete category satisfies all of axioms **16-18**, and so is a "pre-polymorphic iterate" in the sense of the next definition.

19 DEFINITION A pre-iterate $(-)^{\dagger}$ on a category $\mathfrak{C}$ is a *pre-polymorphic iterate* if it satisfies the pairing axiom **16**, the parameter axiom **17** and the left-zero axiom **18**. The *polymorph of* $(-)^{\dagger}$ is the class $\mathfrak{H}_{\dagger}$ of all morphisms $h : X\longrightarrow \overline{X}$ satisfying

$$
\begin{array}{ccc}
X \xrightarrow{\;\;\xi\;\;} X+Y & & X \xrightarrow{\;\;\xi^{\dagger}\;\;} Y \\
\Big\downarrow h \quad\quad \Big\downarrow h\oplus id_Y & \Rightarrow & \Big\downarrow h \quad\quad \Big\downarrow id_Y \\
\overline{X} \xrightarrow[\;\;\overline{\xi}\;\;]{} \overline{X}+Y & & \overline{X} \xrightarrow[\;\;\overline{\xi}^{\dagger}\;\;]{} Y
\end{array}
$$

for all iterative specifications $\xi : X \longrightarrow X + Y$, $\overline{\xi} : \overline{X} \longrightarrow \overline{X} + Y$.

Notice that the commutative square

$$
\begin{array}{ccc}
X & \xrightarrow{\ \xi\ } & X + Y \\
h \downarrow & & \downarrow h \oplus k \\
\overline{X} & \xrightarrow[\ \overline{\xi}\ ]{} & \overline{X} + \overline{Y}
\end{array}
$$

may be presented equivalently as

$$
\begin{array}{ccccc}
X & \xrightarrow{\ \xi\ } & X + Y & \xrightarrow{\ id_X \oplus k\ } & X + \overline{Y} \\
h \downarrow & & & & \downarrow h \oplus id_{\overline{Y}} \\
\overline{X} & & \xrightarrow[\quad\quad\quad\overline{\xi}\quad\quad\quad]{} & & \overline{X} + \overline{Y}
\end{array}
$$

This justifies the use of id_Y instead of the $k : Y \longrightarrow \overline{Y}$ that appeared in **11**, since the parameter axiom allows us to recover the more general form. Specifically, given the diagrams above with $h \in \mathcal{H}_\dagger$ we have $h\overline{\xi}^\dagger = (\xi(id_X \oplus k))^\dagger = \xi^\dagger k$ as desired. In particular, the unrestricted polymorphic axiom takes the form of the assertion $\mathcal{H}_\dagger = \mathcal{C}$.

20 PROPOSITION *If* $(-)^\dagger$ *is a pre-polymorphic iterate, every coproduct injection belongs to its polymorph* $\mathcal{H}_\dagger$.

Proof Let $P \xrightarrow{\ i\ } X \xleftarrow{\ j\ } Q$ be a coproduct. We must show

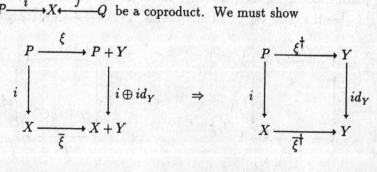

Now $\bar{\xi} = <\alpha, \beta>$ with $\alpha = i\bar{\xi} : P \longrightarrow P + Q + Y$, $\beta = j\bar{\xi} : Q \longrightarrow P + Q + Y$. By the pairing axiom,

$$i\bar{\xi}^{\dagger} \;=\; P \xrightarrow{\quad \alpha^{\dagger} \quad} Q + Y \xrightarrow{\quad <\gamma^{\dagger}, id_Y> \quad} Y$$

for

$$\gamma \;=\; Q \xrightarrow{\quad \beta \quad} P + Q + Y \xrightarrow{\quad <\alpha^{\dagger}, in_Q, in_Y> \quad} Y \;.$$

But by hypothesis, $\alpha = i\bar{\xi} = \xi(i \oplus id_Y)$ and $i \oplus id_Y : P + Y \longrightarrow X + Y$ may be reassociated as $id_P \oplus in_Y$ so, by the parameter axiom,

$$\alpha^{\dagger} \;=\; P \xrightarrow{\quad \xi^{\dagger} \quad} Y \xrightarrow{\quad in_Y \quad} Q + Y$$

whence $i\bar{\xi}^{\dagger} = \xi^{\dagger} in_Y <\gamma^{\dagger}, id_Y> = \xi^{\dagger} id_Y = \xi^{\dagger}.$ □

We now explain why some limitation on $\mathcal{H}_{\dagger}$ is to be expected. Associated with any pre-polymorphic iterate $(-)^{\dagger}$ is an "infinite loop" morphism $\perp_{XY} : X \longrightarrow Y$ for arbitrary X, Y defined by

21 $$X \xrightarrow{\quad \perp_{XY} \quad} Y \;=\; (X \xrightarrow{\quad in_X \quad} X + Y)^{\dagger} \;.$$

For any $k : Y \longrightarrow \overline{Y}$ the parameter axiom gives

$$(X \xrightarrow{\quad in_X \quad} X + Y \xrightarrow{\quad id_X \oplus k \quad} X + \overline{Y})^{\dagger} \;=\; X \xrightarrow{\quad in_X^{\dagger} \quad} Y \xrightarrow{\quad k \quad} \overline{Y}$$

that is,

22 $$X \xrightarrow{\quad \perp_{XY} \quad} Y \xrightarrow{\quad k \quad} \overline{Y} \;=\; X \xrightarrow{\quad \perp_{X\overline{Y}} \quad} \overline{Y} \;.$$

This shows that $\perp_{XY}$ is independent of the choice of coproduct $X + Y$ in the iterative specification $in_X : X \longrightarrow X + Y$ and also shows that for fixed X the family of $\perp_{XY}$ is an X–sink as defined in the introduction. The interpretation of 22 is that chaining a program to an infinite loop only changes the formal codomain of that loop.

In general, the $\perp_{XY}$ will not constitute a family of zero morphisms as in Definition 2.9. This is because other sinks may exist. If $h : X \longrightarrow Y$ on input x causes an abort, $h \perp_{YZ} : X \longrightarrow Y$ should also be an abort rather than $\perp_{XZ}$. This leads us to

23 DEFINITION Given a pre-polymorphic iterate $(-)^{\dagger}$, $h : X \longrightarrow X$ is $\dagger$-*pure* if for all Z, $h \perp_{\overline{X}Z} = \perp_{XZ}$.

This is an abstract way of saying that h does not fail to terminate normally in any sense except possibly that of an infinite loop.

24 EXAMPLE We introduce a category studied by [Main and Black 1990] to be further explored in 8.20. The category $\mathbf{Mfn}_{\perp}$ of *strict multivalued functions* has sets as objects and morphism $\mathbf{Mfn}_{\perp}(X, Y) = \mathbf{Mfn}(X, Y + \{\perp\})$. Given two morphisms $\alpha : X \longrightarrow Y$, $\beta : Y \longrightarrow Z$ in $\mathbf{Mfn}_{\perp}$ their composite $\alpha\beta$ is defined to be the $\mathbf{Mfn}$–composite $\alpha\hat{\beta}$ where $\hat{\beta} : X + \{\perp\} \longrightarrow Y + \{\perp\}$ extends β by $\perp\hat{\beta} = \perp$. The interpretation is that the computation of $x\alpha$ results in many computation paths, some of which terminate. The terminating paths yield an output subset of Y. The nonterminating paths contribute value $\perp$ to the output.

Each object X admits two sinks, the constantly empty multivalued function $\emptyset_{XY} : X \longrightarrow Y$ and the infinite loop $\perp_{XY} : X \longrightarrow Y$. Since every ω–complete category has zero morphisms and hence only one sink for each object, we see that $\mathbf{Mfn}_{\perp}$ is not ω–complete. Even so, there is a natural pre-iterate $(-)^{\dagger}$ on this category. First of all, observe that "avoiding $\perp$" describes a subcategory $\mathbf{Mfn} \longrightarrow \mathbf{Mfn}_{\perp}$ and that the $\mathbf{Mfn}$–coproducts provide coproducts in $\mathbf{Mfn}_{\perp}$ as well. Thus given an iterative specification $\xi : X \longrightarrow X + Y$ in $\mathbf{Mfn}_{\perp}$ define $\xi^{\dagger} : X \longrightarrow Y$ as follows. First define a ξ–*trace* of $x \in X$ in the usual way as either a finite sequence of form $x, x_1, x_2, \ldots, x_n, y$ with $x_1 \in x\xi$, $x_2 \in x_1\xi$, $\ldots$, $x_n \in x_{n-1}\xi$, $y \in x_n\xi$, $y \in Y$ or as an infinite sequence $x, x_1, x_2, \ldots$ with $x_1 \in x\xi$, $x_2 \in x_1\xi$, $\ldots$. Define $\tau : X \longrightarrow Y$ by

$$x\tau \quad = \quad \{\perp\} \text{ if some infinite } \xi\text{–trace of } x \text{ exists}$$

$$= \emptyset \quad \text{otherwise}$$

and then

$$x\xi^\dagger \;=\; \{y : \text{there exists a finite } \xi\text{--trace of } x \text{ ending in } y\} \;\bigcup\; x\tau \;.$$

The construction of **22** indeed produces the constantly-$\perp$ morphisms since $in_X : X \longrightarrow X + X$ has only the infinite trace $x, x, x, \dots$. We leave it as an exercise for the reader to check that $(-)^\dagger$ is a pre-polymorphic iterate with pure maps those α with $x\alpha \neq \emptyset$ for all x.

We see, then, that the following proposition prevents unrestricted polymorphism.

25 PROPOSITION *Let* $(-)^\dagger$ *be a pre-iterate. Then if* $h : X \longrightarrow \overline{X} \in \mathcal{H}_\dagger$, h *is* $\dagger$– *pure.*

Proof The diagram

$$
\begin{array}{ccc}
X & \xrightarrow{\;in_X\;} & X + Y \\[2pt]
{\scriptstyle h}\Big\downarrow & & \Big\downarrow{\scriptstyle h \oplus id_Y} \\[2pt]
\overline{X} & \xrightarrow[\;in_{\overline{X}}\;]{} & \overline{X} + Y
\end{array}
$$

always commutes. $\square$

We have motivated the central definition of this section.

26 DEFINITION A *polymorphic iterate* is a pre-polymorphic iterate $(-)^\dagger$ for which every $\dagger$–pure morphism belongs to the polymorph $\mathcal{H}_\dagger$ of $\dagger$.

In detail, $(-)^\dagger$ satisfies the pairing, parameter and left-zero axioms of **16-18** and

$$
\begin{array}{ccc}
X \xrightarrow{\ \xi\ } X+Y & & X \xrightarrow{\ \xi^\dagger\ } Y \\
\Big\downarrow h \qquad\quad \Big\downarrow h \oplus id_Y & \Rightarrow & \Big\downarrow h \qquad\quad \Big\downarrow id_Y \\
\overline{X} \xrightarrow[\ \overline{\xi}\ ]{} \overline{X}+Y & & \overline{X} \xrightarrow[\ \overline{\xi}^\dagger\ ]{} Y
\end{array}
$$

whenever h is $\dagger$–pure, that is, whenever h is such that $\ \bot_{XZ} = h\,\bot_{\overline{X}Z}\ $ for all Z where $\bot_{AB}$ is $(A \xrightarrow{\ in_A\ } A+B)^\dagger$. Notice that h is $\dagger$–pure $\Leftrightarrow h \in \mathcal{K}_\dagger$ by **25**.

An *unrestricted polymorphic iterate* is a polymorphic iterate with all morphisms pure. It is clear from the discussion above that a polymorphic iterate is unrestricted if and only if it lives in a category with zero morphisms.

27 OBSERVATION *A pre-iterate* $(-)^\dagger$ *is an unrestricted polymorphic iterate if and only if it satisfies the pairing axiom* **16**, *the unrestricted polymorphic axiom* **11** *and satisfies the law* $(Y \xrightarrow{\ in_2\ } Y+Y)^\dagger = id_Y$. We have already commented following Definition **23** that unrestricted polymorphism implies the parameter axiom. For the left-zero axiom observe that

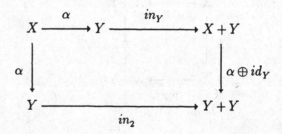

implies that $(\alpha\, in_Y)^\dagger = \alpha\, in_2^\dagger$.   □

28 PROPOSITION *For a polymorphic iterate, the following two statements hold.*

    1.   [Ésik 1983, Statement 1.] *The Elgot fixed point equation* **7** *is true for all* ξ.

2.   *The double-dagger identity holds: for* $\xi : X \longrightarrow X + X + Y$,

$$\xi^{\dagger\dagger} \;\; = \;\; (X \xrightarrow{\ \xi\ } X + X + Y \xrightarrow{\ <id_X, id_X> \;\oplus\; id_Y\ } X + Y)^{\dagger} \; .$$

Proof Let $\delta : X \longrightarrow X + X + Y$. We will prove independently in **8.21** below that $\sigma \;=\; <id_X, id_X> \;:\; X + X \longrightarrow X + X$ is †-pure. Thus, by hypothesis, $\sigma \in \mathcal{K}_{\dagger}$ and we have

$$
\begin{array}{ccc}
X + X \xrightarrow{\ <\delta, \delta>\ } X + X + Y & \qquad & X + X \xrightarrow{\ <\delta, \delta>^{\dagger}\ } Y \\
\sigma \downarrow \qquad\qquad \downarrow \sigma \oplus id_Y & \Rightarrow & \sigma \downarrow \qquad\qquad\qquad \downarrow id_Y \\
X + X \xrightarrow[\ \delta(\sigma \oplus id_Y)\ ]{} X + X + Y & & X + X \xrightarrow[\ (\delta(\sigma \oplus id_Y))^{\dagger}\ ]{} Y
\end{array} .
$$

(The left square commutes because restricted to either injection, both paths are $\delta(\sigma \oplus id_Y)$.) Resolving the right square into its components yields

$$<\delta, \delta>^{\dagger} \;\; = \;\; <(\delta(\sigma \oplus id_Y))^{\dagger}, \; (\delta(\sigma \oplus id_Y))^{\dagger}> \; .$$

On the other hand, we may evaluate $<\delta, \delta>^{\dagger}$ using the pairing identity. Thus for

$$\gamma_{\delta} \;\; = \;\; X \xrightarrow{\ \delta\ } X + X + Y \xrightarrow{\ <\delta^{\dagger}, in_X, in_Y>\ } X + Y$$

we get the fundamental equations

29 $\qquad \delta^{\dagger} <\gamma_{\delta}^{\dagger}, id_X> \;\; = \;\; (\delta(\sigma \oplus id_Y))^{\dagger} \;\; = \;\; \gamma_{\delta}^{\dagger} \; .$

To apply this to the Elgot equation, let $\xi : X \longrightarrow X + Y$ be an iterative specification and set

$$\delta \;\; = \;\; X \xrightarrow{\ \xi\ } X + Y \xrightarrow{\ <in_2, in_Y>\ } X + X + Y \; .$$

As $<in_2, in_Y>$ is just the second coproduct injection under the association $X + (X + Y)$, it follows from the left-zero axiom that $\delta^{\dagger} = \xi$. We further compute

that $\delta(\sigma \oplus id_Y) = \xi < in_2, in_Y > < id_X, id_X, id_Y > = \xi < id_X, id_Y > = \xi$ and also
$\gamma_\delta = \xi < in_2, in_Y > <\xi, in_X, in_Y > = \xi < in_X, in_Y > = \xi$. Thus the first equation in
29 is $\xi < \xi^\dagger, id_Z > = \xi$ which is the Elgot equation.

For the double-dagger identity let $\delta = \xi$. Then $\gamma_\xi = \xi < \xi^\dagger, in_X, in_Y > = \xi < \xi^\dagger, id_{X+Y} >$ which, by the Elgot equation already established, is $\xi^\dagger$. Thus the
second equation in **29** is the desired result.   □

In **1.12**, examples of *while-do* were given in fundamental frameworks. All of
these arise as special cases of polymorphic iterates. **Pfn** , **Mfn** , **Bag**, **Pfn**$_M$ are ω–
complete and we have seen that the canonical iterate is a polymorphic one in such
cases. Ω is ω-complete when $\Omega_0 = \{ \perp \}$ has one element; in general, by a similar
construction (as indicated in **1.12**) there is a polymorphic iterate for each element of Ω_0
(cf. [Bloom, Elgot and Wright 1980].) Here if $\perp \in \Omega_0$ induces iterate $(-)^\dagger$, the $\dagger$–pure
morphisms are those such that for each x, $x\alpha$ has no nullary leaf except possibly $\perp$.

The categories **Mat**$_R$ that work in **1.12** are all partially-additive. Such categories
have a canonical unrestricted polymorphic iterate and the axioms may be established by
manipulating formal power series. See [Arbib and Manes 1985] for this power-series
calculus.

In general, the axioms for a polymorphic iterate are not easy to establish and it
is useful to have classes of categories such as "ω–complete" and "partially-additive" for
which a canonical polymorphic iterate is available. In the balance of this section we
will study polymorphic iterates on the semiadditive categories of **2.10**. Here we will
introduce the notion of *lax Kleene-$*$* whose axioms are usually easy to verify but which
imply a polymorphic iterate. Such categories have zero morphisms by definition, so
this yet another example of a broad class of categories with unrestricted polymorphic
iterate. Note that the theory of Section 8 below makes some headway in reducing the
general case to the unrestricted one.

For the balance of the section we will work in a semiadditive category (**2.10**.)
We recall that

$$X \xleftarrow{\ \rho_X\ } X + Y \xrightarrow{\ \rho_Y\ } Y$$

is a product where $\rho_X = [id_X, 0]$, $\rho_Y = [0, id_Y]$ so that every $\xi : X \longrightarrow X + Y$ has the form $[\alpha, \beta] : X \longrightarrow X + Y$ for $\alpha : X \longrightarrow X$, $\beta : X \longrightarrow Y$. In particular, $[\alpha, id_X] : X \longrightarrow X + X$ exists leading to the concept of the "Kleene-$*$-operation" $\alpha \mapsto \alpha^* = [\alpha, id_X]^\dagger$ of a polymorphic iterate. To motivate the axioms on such a Kleene-$*$, we make use of a well-known matrix calculus associated with a semiadditive category (see e.g. [Freyd 1964, Mitchell 1965]) which we review briefly here.

By iterating the binary case, a coproduct $in_i : Y_i \longrightarrow Y_1 + \cdots + Y_n$ is also a product $\rho_i : Y_1 + \cdots + Y_n \longrightarrow Y_i$ where ρ_i is defined by $in_i \rho_j = \delta_{ij}$, where δ_{ij} is the "Kronecker delta" with 1 denoting the identity morphism. Each morphism of form $\alpha : X \longrightarrow Y_1 + \cdots + Y_n$ has unique representation $[a_1, \cdots, a_n]$ with $a_i = \alpha \rho_i$ and, of course, each map $\beta : Y_1 + \cdots + Y_n \longrightarrow Y$ has unique form $< b_1, \cdots, b_n >$ with $b_i = in_i \beta$. (Note that some authors in the category-theory literature reverse our use of $<>$ and $[\ ]$ but the version here is most consistent with the iterative-theories literature.) We will also write $[a_1, \cdots, a_n]$ as a row vector $[a_1 \cdots a_n]$ and similarly write $< b_1, \cdots, b_n >$ as a column vector. To understand this convention, observe that a composition of form

$$X \xrightarrow{\;[a_1 \cdots a_n]\;} Y_1 + \cdots + Y_n \xrightarrow{\;\begin{bmatrix} b_1 \\ \vdots \\ b_m \end{bmatrix}\;} Y$$

evaluates by matrix multiplication. To prove it, **2.12** generalizes from 2 to n so that

$$[a_1 \cdots a_n] < b_1 \cdots b_n > \; = \; [a_1 \cdots a_n] \left(id_{Y_1 + \cdots + Y_n} \right) < b_1 \cdots b_n >$$

$$= \; [a_1 \cdots a_n] \left(\sum \rho_i \, in_i \right) < b_1 \cdots b_n > \; = \; \sum_i \left([a_1 \cdots a_n] \rho_i \right) \left(in_i < b_1 \cdots b_n > \right)$$

$$= \; \sum a_i b_i.$$

More generally, each morphism $\alpha : X_1 + \cdots + X_m \longrightarrow Y_1 + \cdots + Y_n$ corresponds to a unique $m \times n$ matrix $[a_{ij}]$ with $a_{ij} = in_i \, \alpha \, \rho_j$ (define either rows or columns first, it doesn't matter) and the composition of two such morphisms is given by the matrix product.

Our objective is to use the matrix calculus to simplify the form of an iterate. To begin, observe that an iterative specification takes the form of a matrix

$$[\alpha, \beta] : X \longrightarrow X + Y$$

with $\alpha : X \longrightarrow X$, $\beta : X \longrightarrow Y$.

30 OBSERVATION *A polymorphic iterate* $(-)^\dagger$ *on a semiadditive category is determined by the operation* $\alpha : X \longrightarrow X \mapsto \alpha^* : X \longrightarrow X$ *with* α^* *defined by*

30a $$X \xrightarrow{\ \alpha^*\ } X \quad = \quad (X \xrightarrow{\ [\alpha, id_X]\ } X + X)^\dagger$$

and $(-)^\dagger$ *defined by*

30b $$[\alpha, \beta]^\dagger \ = \ \alpha^* \beta \ .$$

This follows from the matrix identity

$$\begin{bmatrix} \alpha & \beta \end{bmatrix} \ = \ \begin{bmatrix} \alpha & id_X \end{bmatrix} \begin{bmatrix} id_X & 0 \\ 0 & \beta \end{bmatrix}$$

whereas

$$\begin{bmatrix} id_X & 0 \\ 0 & \beta \end{bmatrix} \ = \ id_X \oplus \beta$$

(check!) so **30b** is just the parameter axiom **17**.   □

The following simplifies the polymorphic hypothesis:

31   LEMMA   *In a semiadditive category,*

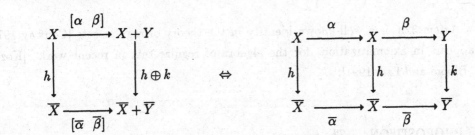

Proof By the matrix calculus, $h\,[\overline{\alpha}\ \overline{\beta}] = [h\overline{\alpha}\ h\overline{\beta}]$ whereas $h \oplus k$ is the diagonal matrix with diagonal entries h, k so that $[\alpha\ \beta](h \oplus k) = [\alpha h\ \beta k]$. Equating the matrices gives the commutative squares comprising the diagram on the right. □

The next definition and proposition characterize polymorphic iterates on semiadditive categories.

32   **DEFINITION**   A *Kleene-* on a semiadditive category $\mathcal{C}$ is an assignment

$$\mathcal{C}(X, X) \longrightarrow \mathcal{C}(X, X), \qquad \alpha \mapsto \alpha^*$$

for each object X, subject to three axioms as follows:

32a
$$(X \xrightarrow{\ 0\ } X)^* = id_X$$

32b $X + X \xrightarrow{\begin{bmatrix} a & b \\ c & d \end{bmatrix}^*} X + X = \begin{bmatrix} a^*b(ca^*b + d)^*ca^* + a^* & a^*b(ca^*b + d)^* \\ (ca^*b + d)^*ca^* & (ca^*b + d)^* \end{bmatrix}$

32c

$$
\begin{array}{ccc}
X & \xrightarrow{\ \alpha\ } & X \\
{\scriptstyle h}\downarrow & & \downarrow{\scriptstyle h} \\
\overline{X} & \xrightarrow{\ \overline{\alpha}\ } & \overline{X}
\end{array}
\qquad \Rightarrow \qquad
\begin{array}{ccc}
X & \xrightarrow{\ \alpha^*\ } & X \\
{\scriptstyle h}\downarrow & & \downarrow{\scriptstyle h} \\
\overline{X} & \xrightarrow{\ \overline{\alpha}^*\ } & \overline{X}
\end{array}
$$

Axiom **32b** is a well-known identity in the theory of regular sets [Conway 1971] and appears in axiomatizations for the algebra of regular sets in recent work [Kozen 1990, Bloom and Ésik 1991].

33   PROPOSITION   *The passages*

$$\alpha^* = [\alpha, id_X]^\dagger$$

$$[\alpha, \beta]^\dagger = \alpha^* \beta$$

$(\alpha : X \longrightarrow X, \ \beta : X \longrightarrow Y)$ *establish a bijection between Kleene-$*$'s and polymorphic iterates on any semiadditive category.*

Proof That the correspondence is bijective is clear from **30** noting that $\alpha^* id_X = \alpha^*$. We must show that the axioms of **28** translate to those of **32**. As $in_2 : X \longrightarrow X + X$ has matrix form $[0 \ id_X]$, $in_2^\dagger = id_X \Leftrightarrow 0^* = id_X$. Given the polymorphic hypothesis in the form of the right hand diagram in **31** we must show $h [\alpha, \beta]^\dagger = [\overline{\alpha}, \overline{\beta}]^\dagger k \Leftrightarrow \alpha^* h = h\alpha^*$. For $\Rightarrow$, set $\beta = id_X$, $\overline{\beta} = id_{\overline{X}}$; conversely, $h\alpha^* = \overline{\alpha}^* h\beta = \overline{\alpha}^* \overline{\beta} k$. Finally we show that the pairing axiom **16** is expressed by **32b**. Let

$$\xi = X \xrightarrow{\quad [a \ b \ t] \quad} X + Y + Z$$

$$\theta = Y \xrightarrow{\quad [c \ d \ u] \quad} X + Y + Z \ .$$

Thus $\xi^\dagger = a^* [b \ t] = [a^* b \ a^* t]$. As in **16** define

$$\gamma = Y \xrightarrow{\quad \theta \quad} X + Y + Z \xrightarrow{\quad <\xi^\dagger, in_Y, in_Z> \quad} Y + Z$$

$$= [c \quad d \quad u] \begin{bmatrix} a^* b & a^* t \\ id_Y & 0 \\ 0 & id_Z \end{bmatrix}$$

$$= [ca^* b + d \quad ca^* t + u]$$

so that

$$\gamma^{\dagger} \;=\; (ca^*b + d)^* (ca^*t + u)$$

and

$$\xi^{\dagger} <\gamma^{\dagger}, id_Z> \;=\; [\; a^*b \quad a^*t \;] \begin{bmatrix} (ca^*b + d)^* (ca^*t + u) \\[2mm] id_Z \end{bmatrix}$$

It is now routine to check that the right hand side $<\xi^{\dagger} <\gamma^{\dagger}, id_Z>, \gamma^{\dagger}>$ of **16** is the matrix product of the 2×2 matrix on the right side of **32b** followed by the column vector $<t, u>$. On the other hand

$$<\xi, \theta> \;=\; \begin{bmatrix} a & b & t \\ c & d & u \end{bmatrix}$$

so the left hand side of **16** is

$$<\xi, \theta>^{\dagger} \;=\; \begin{bmatrix} a & b \\ c & d \end{bmatrix}^* \begin{bmatrix} t \\ u \end{bmatrix}.$$

Since Z, t, u are arbitrary and can be set $t = id_X$, $u = 0$ or $t = 0$, $u = id_Y$, **16** is equivalent to **32b**.   ☐

34   PROPOSITION   *For any Kleene-$*$, the following hold:*

1.   *The Elgot fixed point equation for* $[\alpha, \beta]^{\dagger} : X \longrightarrow Y$ *takes the form* $t = \alpha t + \beta$.

2. $\alpha \alpha^* = \alpha^* \alpha$

3. $(\alpha \beta)^* \alpha = \alpha (\beta \alpha)^*$

4. $(\alpha \beta)^* = id_X + \alpha (\beta \alpha)^* \beta$.

Proof   The first statement follows from matrix algebra:

$$[\ a \quad b \ ] \begin{bmatrix} \gamma \\ id_Y \end{bmatrix} \ = \ a\gamma + b \ .$$

The second statement is immediate from **32c** since $\alpha\alpha \ = \ \alpha\alpha$. For (3), $(\alpha\beta)\alpha \ = \ \alpha(\beta\alpha)$ $\Rightarrow \ \alpha(\beta\alpha)^* \ = \ (\alpha\beta)^*\alpha$ and this yields (4): $(\alpha\beta)^* \ = \ id_X \ + \ \alpha\beta(\alpha\beta)^* \ =$ $id_X \ + \ (\alpha\beta)^*\alpha\beta \ = \ id_X \ + \ \alpha(\beta\alpha)^*\beta.$ $\square$

In treatments of regular algebra it is common to assume $id_X^* \ = \ id_X$. This axiom collapses the addition operation on morphisms in a semiadditive category as follows:

35   PROPOSITION   *If a semiadditive category* $\mathcal{C}$ *admits a Kleene-$*$ satisfying* id_X^* $= \ id_X$ *for all objects* X *then* $\alpha + \alpha \ = \ \alpha$ *for all* $\alpha : X \longrightarrow Y$; *that is, the abelian monoid* $\mathcal{C}(X,Y)$ *is a join-semilattice with least element* 0. *Further, given* $\alpha, \alpha_1 : X \longrightarrow Y$, $\beta, \beta_1 : Y \longrightarrow Z$, *then* $\alpha \le \alpha_1$, *and* $\beta \le \beta_1 \ \Rightarrow \ \alpha\beta \le \alpha_1\beta_1$.

Proof $id_Y \ = \ id_Y^* \ = \ id_Y id_Y^* \ + \ id_Y \ = \ id_Y \ + \ id_Y$. For the second statement, $\alpha_1 + \beta_1 \ = \ (\alpha + \alpha_1)(\beta + \beta_1)$ expands to the form $\alpha\beta + t$. $\square$

As promised, we now define a strengthened form of the Kleene-$*$ whose axioms, nonetheless, are often easy to verify.

36   DEFINITION   A *lax Kleene-$*$* on a semiadditive category $\mathcal{C}$ is an assignment

$$\mathcal{C}(X,X) \longrightarrow \mathcal{C}(X,X), \qquad \alpha \mapsto \alpha^*$$

subject to the axioms

36a   (*Fixed point axiom.*)   For all $\alpha : X \longrightarrow X$, $\alpha^* \ = \ \alpha\alpha^* \ + \ id_X.$

36b $id_X^* \ = \ id_X$ for all X.

36c   (*Lax polymorphic axiom.*) With respect to the partial order $\le$ defined above in Proposition **35**, given $X \xrightarrow{\alpha} X \xrightarrow{h} \overline{X} \xrightarrow{\overline{\alpha}} \overline{X}$ then $h\overline{\alpha} \leq \alpha h \Rightarrow$ $h\overline{\alpha}^* \leq \alpha^* h$ and $h\overline{\alpha} \geq \alpha h \Rightarrow h\overline{\alpha}^* \geq \alpha^* h$.

We show in **38** below that a lax Kleene-$*$ is a Kleene-$*$.

With regard to the next result, say that $\beta : X \longrightarrow X$ is *reflexive* if $id_X \leq \beta$ and that such β is *transitive* if $\beta\beta \leq \beta$.

37   THEOREM   *A lax Kleene-$*$ satisfies the following properties for any   two endomorphisms* $\alpha, \beta : X \longrightarrow X$:

1. α^* is the least γ with $id_X \leq \gamma$, $\alpha\gamma \leq \gamma$. (In particular, α^* is the least solution of the fixed point equation $\gamma = id_X + \alpha\gamma$.)

2. If $\alpha \leq \beta$, $\alpha^* \leq \beta^*$.

3. $\alpha^*\alpha^* = \alpha^*$.

4. $\alpha^{**} = \alpha^*$.

5. α^* is the least reflexive, transitive γ with $\alpha \leq \gamma$.

6. $(\alpha + \beta)^* = (\alpha^*\beta)^*\alpha^*$.

Proof   (1)   As $\alpha^* = id_X + \alpha\alpha^*$, $id_X \leq \alpha^*$ and $\alpha\alpha^* \leq \alpha^*$. Now let $id_X \leq \beta$, $\alpha\beta$ $\leq \beta$. As $\alpha\beta \leq \beta id_X$, $\alpha^*\beta \leq \beta \, id_X^* = \beta$, so $\alpha^* = \alpha^* id \leq \alpha^*\beta \leq \beta$.

(2)   As $\alpha \, id \leq id \, \beta$, $\alpha^* \, id \leq id \, \beta^*$.

(3)   As $id \leq \alpha^*$, $id = id \, id \leq \alpha^*\alpha^*$. Additionally, $\alpha\alpha^* \leq \alpha^* \Rightarrow \alpha\alpha^*\alpha^* \leq$ $\alpha^*\alpha^*$. It follows from (1) that $\alpha^* \leq \alpha^*\alpha^*$. Conversely, $\alpha\alpha^* \leq \alpha^* \, id \Rightarrow \alpha^*\alpha^* \leq \alpha^* id^*$ $= \alpha^*$.

(4) $\alpha \leq \alpha^*$ because $\alpha \, id \leq \alpha\alpha^* \leq \alpha^*$, so $\alpha^* \leq \alpha^{**}$ by (2). Conversely, as $id_X \leq \alpha^*$ and $\alpha^*\alpha^* \leq \alpha^*$, it follows from (1) that $\alpha^{**} \leq \alpha^*$.

(5)   We have already shown that α^* is reflexive and transitive and that $\alpha \leq \alpha^*$. Now suppose that $\alpha \leq \beta$, $id_X \leq \beta$ and $\beta\beta \leq \beta$. Then $\beta\beta \leq \beta \, id_X \Rightarrow \beta^*\beta \leq \beta \, id_X^*$ $= \beta$ so $\beta\beta^* \leq \beta$ (**16(2)**) and $\beta^* = id_X + \beta\beta^* \leq \beta$. But by (2), $\alpha^* \leq \beta^*$ so $\alpha^* \leq$ β.

(6)   This follows from (1,...,5) by a standard argument in regular algebra.   See

[Conway 1971].   □

38 THEOREM *A lax Kleene-* is a Kleene-* in the sense of Definition* **32**.

Proof For **32a**, $0^* = 00^* + id_X = id_X$. **32c** is clearly a consequence of the lax polymorphic axiom and antisymmetry . It remains to establish **32b**. But the argument is standard regular algebra using **37**.   □

PART II STRUCTURE OF A BOOLEAN CATEGORY

Part II introduces Boolean categories and establishes their basic structure. A Boolean category is intended to be a minimal framework for the semantics of loop-free control structures including a high-level specification language based on propositional dynamic logic. Coproducts are given a fundamental role in this approach. The axioms on a Boolean category are designed to justify the intuition that a binary coproduct decomposes an object into two disjoint alternatives.

4   THE AXIOMS

Before stating the axioms for a Boolean category we must first provide some basic definitions necessary for their formulation.

1 DEFINITION   A morphism $i : P \longrightarrow X$ in a category $\mathcal{C}$ is a *summand* of X if there exists a coproduct of form $P \overset{i}{\longrightarrow} X \overset{i'}{\longleftarrow} P'$. Say that two summands $i : P \longrightarrow X$, $j : Q \longrightarrow X$ are *isomorphic* if there exists an isomorphism $\psi : P \longrightarrow Q$ in $\mathcal{C}$ with $\psi j = i$. The class of all isomorphism classes of summands of X will be denoted   *Summ(X)*.

The term "summand" owes to the fact that coproducts are often called "direct sums" in algebra.

By a standard abuse of language in category theory, we shall use the term "summand" both for an element of $Summ(X)$ (i.e., an equivalence class) and a single summand (i.e., a representative of that equivalence class.) This leads to no difficulty in practice because the needed constructions are independent of choice of representative. The overall objective is to keep terminology to a minimum. Thus if we say "$Q \in Summ(X)$" an unmentioned $Q \longrightarrow X$ is understood to be a summand representative and the same symbol Q is both an object and an equivalence class of such representatives.

Given $Q \in Summ(Y)$, $\alpha : X \longrightarrow Y$, how are we to define $[\alpha]Q \in Summ(X)$ to capture the spirit of 1.7-8? The ad hoc definitions there seem quite consistent with "$[\alpha]Q$ is the inverse image of Q under α" and it is well-understood in the category-theoretic folklore [Mitchell 1965, §11] that inverse images in a category are constructed with pullbacks. This is the definition we shall choose.

2 DEFINITION A morphism $\alpha : X \longrightarrow Y$ *pulls back summands* if for every $Q \in Summ(Y)$ there exists $P \in Summ(X)$ and a pullback square

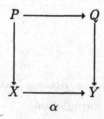

In this case we write $[\alpha]Q$ for P. It is trivial to check that as a summand of X, $[\alpha]Q$ is independent of all choices made.

It is possible to strengthen Definition 2 as follows.

3 DEFINITION A morphism $\alpha : X \longrightarrow Y$ is *crisp* if for every coproduct $Q \xrightarrow{j} Y \xleftarrow{j'} Q'$ there exists a coproduct $P \xrightarrow{i} X \xleftarrow{i'} P'$ and a commutative

diagram

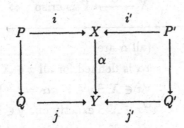

in which the squares are pullbacks.

Thus every crisp morphism is deterministic (see Definition **2.13.**)

4 EXAMPLE In the fundamental examples **Set, Pfn, Mfn, Bag,** Ω of Section 1 it is easily checked that isomorphisms are just the bijective total functions, that the inclusion functor of **Set** is coproduct-preserving and that every summand of X is represented by the inclusion function of a subset of X. (In the case of Ω, the value of a function is represented as a 1-node tree.) The functor from **Set** in the case of other categories is obvious. In each of these categories, given $\alpha : X \longrightarrow Y$ and a subset Q of Y there exists a subset $[\alpha]Q$ of X and a pullback diagram

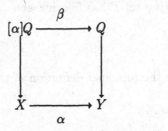

where $[\alpha]Q \longrightarrow X$, $Q \longrightarrow Y$ are inclusions. The constructions are those of 1.7-8 with β "the same as α but with codomain Q". Table 5 supports the view that crisp morphisms are total and deterministic, a result which will be proved later in **12.3.**

Though the pullbacks which construct $[\alpha]Q$ will play a major role in this book, general pullbacks may fail to exist as is shown by the next example.

Category	$X \xrightarrow{\alpha} Y$ is crisp $\Leftrightarrow$
Set	(all α are)
Pfn	$x\alpha$ is defined for all $x \in X$
Mfn	$\forall x \in X \; \exists \, y \in Y \; x\alpha \, = \, \{y\}$
Bag	$\forall x \in X \; \exists$ exactly one $y \in Y \; \alpha_{xy} \neq 0$
Ω	$\forall x \in X. \; \exists$ exactly one $y \in Y$ as a leaf in $x\alpha$

Table 5: Examples of crisp morphisms

6 EXAMPLE **Mfn** does not have pullbacks. For if $Y \longleftarrow P \longrightarrow X$ were a pullback of $X \xrightarrow{\alpha} Z \xleftarrow{\beta} Y$ there would be a bijective correspondence between the set of subsets of P (= **Mfn**-morphisms from a 1-element set!) and pairs (A, B), $A \subset X$, $B \subset Y$ with $\bigcup_A a\alpha = \bigcup_B b\beta$. Now consider the specific case $X = \{a\}$, $Y = \{b, c, d\}$, $Z = \{e, f, g\}$ with $a\alpha = Z$, $b\beta = \{e, f\}$, $c\beta = \{e, g\}$, $d\beta = \{f, g\}$. Then there are exactly five such pairs (A, B), namely $(\emptyset, \emptyset)$ and (X, B) with B having at least two elements. But no set P has five subsets.

We can now give the principal definition of this book.

7 DEFINITION A *Boolean category* is a category $\mathfrak{B}$ satisfying the following four axioms.

1. $\mathfrak{B}$ has binary coproducts and an initial object 0.

2. Every morphism in $\mathfrak{B}$ pulls back summands, that is, $[\alpha]Q$ exists for all $\alpha : X \longrightarrow Y$ and $Q \in Summ(Y)$.

3. Every summand is crisp.

4. Every trivial object (Definition 2.16) is initial.

The initial object will be seen to play two roles in a Boolean category. First of all, it is obvious that $0 \longrightarrow X \xleftarrow{\;id\;} X$ is a coproduct, so $0 \in Summ(X)$. In 5.11 below it will be shown that $Summ(X)$ is a Boolean algebra with 0 as least element, so 0 represents "false". Additionally, while there is exactly one morphism $0 \longrightarrow X$ there may be any number of morphisms $X \longrightarrow 0$ (consider Ω where a morphism $X \longrightarrow 0$ is a total function mapping each x to a tree all of whose leaves are in Ω_0) which can be thought of as "divergences/failings". These "null morphisms" will be studied in Sections 6 and 8.

The following example shows that the axiom that 0 is the only trivial object is necessary if the promised theorem that $Summ(X)$ is a Boolean algebra is to hold.

8   EXAMPLE   Let $\mathfrak{B}$ be the poset qua category with objects $0, 1, 2$ and with morphisms $\mathfrak{B}(m, n) = \emptyset$ or $\{\alpha_{m,n}\}$ accordingly as $m > n$, $m \le n$. In this category, any diagram of form $k \longrightarrow n \longleftarrow m$ is a coproduct and every square commutes and is a pullback. 0 is the initial object. Every morphism is a summand and is crisp. Thus the only axiom which fails is the one that asserts that 0 is the only trivial object since, in fact, all objects are trivial. Yet $Summ(2)$ is not a Boolean algebra since it has three elements.

9   EXAMPLE   With $0 = \emptyset$, **Set**, **Pfn**, **Mfn**, **Bag**, Ω are all Boolean categories with the constructions detailed in Example 4.

10   EXAMPLE   If M is a causal monoid then the category **Pfn**$_M$ of 1.6 is Boolean. To understand the role of the causality condition consider morphisms $\alpha : X \longrightarrow Y$, $\beta : Y \longrightarrow X$ in **Pfn**$_M$. Then α is tantamount to a pair $[f, t]$ for $f : X \longrightarrow Y$, $t : X \longrightarrow M$ partial functions with the same domain, and $\beta = [g, u]$ similarly. If α is an isomorphism with inverse β then f, g are mutually-inverse bijective (total) functions whereas, for each x, $x\alpha$ and $x\beta$ are mutually inverse in the monoid M. The causality condition forces $x\alpha = e = x\beta$, e the monoid unit. But the canonical embedding of **Set** in $\mathbf{Pfn}_M$ maps f to $[f,t]$ with t constantly e, that is, the isomorphisms of $\mathbf{Pfn}_M$ coincide with those of **Set**. It follows that if $P\xrightarrow{\ i\ }X\xleftarrow{\ i'\ }P'$ is a coproduct in $\mathbf{Pfn}_M$ and if $P\xrightarrow{\ j\ }Y\xleftarrow{\ j'\ }Y'$ is the standard disjoint-union coproduct in **Set** (hence also a coproduct in $\mathbf{Pfn}_M$) then the unique isomorphism transforming one to the other is in **Set**. This shows that i is just an injective function, that is, that the summands are just the subsets. The remaining details that $\mathbf{Pfn}_M$ is Boolean are routine, using $[\alpha]Q$ as in 1.7-8.

To better appreciate the role of causality in the argument just given consider the two-element group M (which is not causal.) For this monoid, $\mathbf{Pfn}_M$ is not Boolean because a 1-element set has three non-isomorphic summands so is not a Boolean algebra which contradicts **5.11** below.

11   EXAMPLE   If R is a positive partial semiring, then the category $\mathbf{Mat}_R$ of Example 1.4 is a Boolean category. This is proved in detail in Corollary **7.13** below.

12   EXAMPLE   [Dijkstra 1976] (implicitly) models nondeterminism by working in the category $\mathcal{C}$ whose objects, morphisms and identities are exactly as for **Mfn**, but whose composition $\alpha*\beta$ is defined by letting $x(\alpha*\beta)$ be the usual value in **Mfn** when $y\beta \neq \emptyset$ for all $y \in x\alpha$, but $x(\alpha*\beta) = \emptyset$ otherwise. Thus "the whole program diverges if any of its possible computation paths does". This category is not Boolean, even though coproducts, isomorphisms and summands (= subsets) are exactly as in **Mfn**. The axiom that fails is 7(2). To see this, let $X = Y$ have at least two elements and let $x_0 \in X$, $y_0 \in Y$. Define $\alpha : X\longrightarrow Y$ by $x_0\alpha = Y$, $x\alpha = \emptyset$ $(x \neq x_0)$. Let 1 denote a 1-element set. Define $\beta : 1\longrightarrow X$ to map the unique element of 1 to all of X. Then the following diagram commutes:

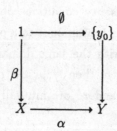

This guarantees that if $[\alpha]\{y_0\}$ exists, it is all of X. But then α factors through $\{y_0\}$ which is the desired contradiction.

A more fundamental objection to this category in program semantics is its incompatibility with Scott-Strachey semantics [Stoy 1977]. For let $\delta, \epsilon : 1 \longrightarrow Y$ be defined by $\delta = \{y_0\}$, $\epsilon = Y$ and let $\eta : Y \longrightarrow Y$ map y_0 to $\{y_0\}$ and other y to $\emptyset$. Then $\delta \subset \epsilon$, $\delta\eta \neq \emptyset$, $\epsilon\eta = \emptyset$ which violates monotonicity of composition.

Cartesian products of categories, diagram categories and functor categories are well-known [Mac Lane, 1971]. "Noninteracting processes" are captured by the cartesian product. The following is trivial from the definitions and elementary category theory:

13 PROPOSITION Any cartesian product of Boolean categories is Boolean. (The empty case is included —the 1-morphism category is Boolean.) If $\mathfrak{B}$ is a Boolean category and if Δ is a small diagram scheme [Mac Lane, 1971], then the diagram category $\mathfrak{B}^\Delta$ is a Boolean category and, as well, for $\mathfrak{S}$ a small category the functor category $\mathfrak{B}^\mathfrak{S}$ is a Boolean category. $\square$

We remark that the algebraic theory models favoured by Bloom and Ésik and others do not satisfy Proposition **13**; there is a cartesian product of theories but it is not the desired cartesian product of categories.

"Boolean functors" between Boolean categories preserve the Boolean structure. Such functors are defined as follows.

14 DEFINITION Let $\mathfrak{B}, \mathfrak{C}$ be Boolean categories. A functor $F : \mathfrak{B} \longrightarrow \mathfrak{C}$ is *Boolean* if F preserves initial objects and binary coproducts and if F preserves $[\alpha]Q$, that is, given the pullback diagram associated with $[\alpha]Q$, the commutative square obtained by applying F is again a pullback (and hence necessarily a model for $[\alpha F](QF)$ —"$([\alpha]Q)F = [\alpha F](QF)$" .) We say a Boolean functor F is *strict* if XF initial $\Rightarrow X$

initial. A subcategory $\mathfrak{B}$ of the Boolean category $\mathfrak{C}$ is a *Boolean subcategory* if it is a Boolean category and its inclusion functor is (necessarily strict) Boolean. $\mathfrak{B} \subset \mathfrak{C}$ is a *(Boolean) extension* and $\mathfrak{B}$ is a *wide Boolean subcategory* of $\mathfrak{C}$ if $\mathfrak{B}$ is a Boolean subcategory of $\mathfrak{C}$ such that all $\mathfrak{C}$–isomorphisms belong to $\mathfrak{B}$ (so, in particular, $\mathfrak{B}$, $\mathfrak{C}$ share the same objects.)

·Strict Boolean functors play a major role in the metatheory to be developed in Part III.

The usual way to establish that $\mathfrak{B} \subset \mathfrak{C}$ is an extension is as follows. Verify that $0 \longrightarrow X$ is in $\mathfrak{B}$. Verify that each two objects of $\mathfrak{B}$ admit a coproduct in $\mathfrak{C}$ which is a $\mathfrak{B}$–coproduct. Since every $\mathfrak{C}$–isomorphism is in $\mathfrak{B}$, $Summ(X)$ is the same in both $\mathfrak{B}$ and $\mathfrak{C}$. Finally, verify that given $\alpha : X \longrightarrow Y$ in $\mathfrak{B}$ and $Q \in Summ(Y)$ there exists a pullback square for $[\alpha]Q$ in $\mathfrak{C}$ which is a pullback in $\mathfrak{B}$.

15 EXAMPLE   Set is a wide Boolean subcategory of any of **Pfn**, **Mfn**, **Bag**, Ω and **Pfn**$_M$. Similarly, **Pfn** is a wide Boolean subcategory of **Mfn** and **Bag**.

16 EXAMPLE $F : \Omega \longrightarrow$ **Mfn** defined by $XF = X$ and, for $\alpha : X \longrightarrow Y$, $x(\alpha F)y \Leftrightarrow y$ is a leaf of $x\alpha$ is a strict Boolean functor.

17 EXAMPLE   A projection from a product of two or more Boolean categories to one of its factors is a Boolean functor which is not strict.

18 EXAMPLE   Let M be the causal monoid $\{1,2,3,...\}$ under numerical multiplication, with unit 1. Define $F :$ **Pfn**$_M \longrightarrow$ **Bag** by $XF = X$ on objects and, for $\alpha \in$ **Pfn**$_M(X,Y)$, let $(\alpha F)_{xy}$ be defined to be m if $x\alpha$ is defined and $x\alpha = (y,m)$, but otherwise defined to be 0. Then F is a strict Boolean functor.

19 EXAMPLE   For any category $\mathfrak{C}$ and object Z of $\mathfrak{C}$, the *category $\mathfrak{C}/Z$ of objects* over Z has as objects all pairs (C, α) with $\alpha : C \longrightarrow Z$ in $\mathcal{C}$ and has as morphisms ψ : $(C, \alpha) \longrightarrow (D, \beta)$ all $\mathcal{C}$-morphisms $\psi : C \longrightarrow D$ with $\psi\beta = \alpha$. Composition and identities are defined at the level $\mathcal{C}$. There is a forgetful functor $F : \mathcal{C}/Z \longrightarrow \mathcal{C}$. If $\mathcal{C}$ is Boolean, each $\mathcal{C}/Z$ is Boolean in such a way that the corresponding F is strict Boolean. We leave the obvious (but slightly tedious) details to the reader.

20 EXAMPLE Let $\psi : R \longrightarrow S$ be a morphism of positive partial semirings, that is, if $\sum r_i$ exists then so too does $\sum(r_i\psi)$ and then $(\sum r_i)\psi = \sum(r_i\psi)$; also, $1\psi = 1$ and $(rs)\psi = (r\psi)(s\psi)$. We prove in **7.13** below that $\mathbf{Mat}_R$, $\mathbf{Mat}_S$ are Boolean categories. Such ψ induces a strict Boolean functor $F_\psi : \mathbf{Mat}_R \longrightarrow \mathbf{Mat}_S$ by $XF_\psi = X$, $[\alpha_{xy}]\psi = [\alpha_{xy}\psi]$. To prove that F_ψ preserves $[\alpha]Q$ observe that ψ preserves 0.

5 THE BOOLEAN ALGEBRA OF SUMMANDS

In this section, $\mathfrak{B}$ is a Boolean category. We will establish that every Boolean category has considerable Boolean structure.

1 LEMMA *The following statements are valid.*

    1.   *If* $X\xrightarrow{\;id\;}X\xleftarrow{\;\;i\;\;}P$ *is a coproduct then* $P = 0$.

    2.   *If* $P\xrightarrow{\;\;i\;\;}X\xleftarrow{\quad}0$ *is a coproduct, i is an isomorphism.*

Proof For the first statement, by axiom **4.7(4)** it suffices to prove i is an isomorphism. As i is crisp, there exists a diagram

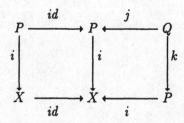

with both rows coproducts and both squares pullbacks (note that the leftmost square is necessarily a pullback for any morphism i and so we may choose it.) Using the pullback property of the rightmost square there exists unique $g : P\longrightarrow Q$ such that $gj = id_P = gk$. By the coproduct property of the top row there exists a unique morphism h : $P\longrightarrow Q$ with $id_P h = g$, $jh = id_Q$. As $h = g$, we have $jg = id_Q$, so that g, j

are mutually-inverse isomorphisms as desired.

The second statement is true in any category. By the coproduct property there exists unique $g: X \longrightarrow P$ with $ig = id_P$. As $i(gi) = (ig)i = i = i\, id_X$, it follows from the uniqueness of coproduct-induced maps that $gi = id_X$.   □

2 LEMMA (Disjointness of coproducts.) If $P \overset{i}{\longrightarrow} X \overset{i'}{\longleftarrow} P'$ is a coproduct then i, i' are monomorphisms and in the commutative diagram

$$
\begin{array}{ccccc}
P & \xrightarrow{\ id\ } & P & \longleftarrow & 0 \\
{\scriptstyle id}\downarrow & (A) & {\scriptstyle i}\downarrow & (B) & \downarrow \\
P & \xrightarrow{\ i\ } & X & \overset{i'}{\longleftarrow} & P'
\end{array}
$$

both squares are pullbacks.

Proof There exists a commutative diagram as shown below in which the rows are

$$
\begin{array}{ccccc}
R & \xrightarrow{\ j\ } & P & \overset{j}{\longleftarrow} & R' \\
{\scriptstyle t}\downarrow & & {\scriptstyle i}\downarrow & & \downarrow{\scriptstyle u} \\
P & \xrightarrow{\ i\ } & X & \overset{i'}{\longleftarrow} & P'
\end{array}
$$

coproducts and the squares are pullbacks. Now consider the diagram

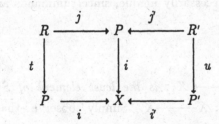

in which f, g are arbitrary morphisms. As $R \overset{j}{\longrightarrow} P \overset{j'}{\longleftarrow} R'$ is a coproduct there exists unique h with $jh = jf$, $j'h = g$. Now consider the unique $v: P \longrightarrow R$ with

$vt = id_P = vj$. We have $h = (vj)h = v(jh) = v(jf) = (vj)f = f$. This proves that $P \xrightarrow{\quad id \quad} P \xleftarrow{\quad j' \quad} R'$ is a coproduct so that $R' = 0$ by Lemma 1, and (B) is a pullback. Again by Lemma 1, j is an isomorphism so that i is a monomorphism (i.e. there exists u with $uj = id_P = ut$ so $u = j^{-1}$ and $t = j$; thus if $xi = yi$ the pullback property gives $x = y$.) This shows that (A) is a pullback. As now any summand is a monomorphism, i, i' are in particular.   □

By Lemma 2, $Summ(X)$ is a subset of the poset of all subobjects of X. Because of the importance of this idea in what follows we review the definition:

3 OBSERVATION   *For any object* X, $(Summ(X), \subset)$ *is a poset whose partial order* $P \subset Q$ *is defined by the assertion that there exists* $t : P \xrightarrow{\quad} Q$ *with*

$$P \xrightarrow{\quad\quad} X \quad = \quad P \xrightarrow{\quad t \quad} Q \xrightarrow{\quad\quad} X .$$

The morphism t which witnesses $P \subset Q$ will sometimes be called the *inclusion morphism* of P *in* Q; it is necessarily unique, since summands are monomorphisms by Lemma 2.   □

4 OBSERVATION $0 \xrightarrow{\quad\quad} X$ *is the least element of* $Summ(X)$ *whereas the greatest element is* $id : X \xrightarrow{\quad\quad} X$. Simply observe that, in any category, $0 \xrightarrow{\quad\quad} X \xleftarrow{\quad id \quad} X$ is a coproduct.   □

5   LEMMA   *For* $R \in Summ(X)$, $Summ(R)$ *is order-isomorphic to* $\{S \in Summ(X) : S \subset R\}$. *If* $k : R \xrightarrow{\quad\quad} X$ *is a summand, the order-isomorphism is the function* Δ *which maps* $i : P \xrightarrow{\quad\quad} R$ *to* $ik : P \xrightarrow{\quad\quad} X$.

Proof   Consider arbitrary $P \in Summ(R)$, $R \in Summ(X)$ so that there exist coproducts $P \xrightarrow{\ i\ } R \xleftarrow{\ i' \ } P'$ and $R \xrightarrow{\ k\ } X \xleftarrow{\ k' \ } R'$. To show that Δ is well-defined we must exhibit a coproduct $P \xrightarrow{\ ik\ } X \xleftarrow{\quad\quad} Q$. Intuitively, "$Q$ is the union of P' and R'" and this can be implemented as follows. A Boolean category has binary coproducts, so let $P' \xrightarrow{\ t\ } Q \xleftarrow{\ u\ } R'$ be a coproduct. We shall show that the top row of the diagram

$$
\begin{array}{ccccc}
 & \xrightarrow{ik} & & \xleftarrow{<i'k,k'>} & \\
P & \longrightarrow & X & \longleftarrow & Q \\
f \downarrow & & \psi \downarrow & & \downarrow\, \varphi \,=\, <g,h> \\
Y & \longrightarrow & Y & \longleftarrow & Y \\
 & id & & id &
\end{array}
$$

6

is a coproduct. To this end, let f, φ be arbitrary morphisms as shown and write $\varphi = <g,h>$ for unique $g : P' \longrightarrow Y$, $h : R' \longrightarrow Y$. Thus there exist unique Γ, ψ constructed by the requirements that $i\Gamma = f$, $i'\Gamma = g$; $k\psi = \Gamma$, $k'\psi = h$. Then $ik\psi = i\Gamma = f$, $i'k\psi = i'\Gamma = g$, $k'\psi = h$ so **6** commutes. Conversely, given any ψ such that diagram **6** commutes, $k'\psi = h$ and $(ik\psi = f, i'k\psi = g) \Rightarrow k\psi = \Gamma$ so ψ is unique.

So far Δ is a well-defined function $Summ(R) \longrightarrow Summ(X)$. Next apply Lemma 2: since k is a monomorphism, for two given summands $i : P \longrightarrow R$ and $i_1 : P_1 \longrightarrow R$, i factors through i_1 if and only if ik factors through $i_1 k$, and this shows that Δ is an order-isomorphism onto its image. It is obvious that we have the inclusion $ik : P \longrightarrow R \subset R$. The proof is then complete once we establish

7 OBSERVATION *Given* $P \xrightarrow{\ i\ } R \xrightarrow{\ k\ } X$ *with both* $k : R \longrightarrow X$ *and* $ik : P \longrightarrow X$ *summands then* $i : P \longrightarrow R$ *is also a summand*. This follows from the fact that k is a monomorphism because then

$$
\begin{array}{ccc}
 & \xrightarrow{\ i\ } & \\
P & \longrightarrow & R \\
id \downarrow & & \downarrow\, k \\
P & \longrightarrow & X \\
 & ik &
\end{array}
$$

is a pullback. Hence $i : P \longrightarrow R = [ik](R \xrightarrow{\ k\ } X) \in Summ(R)$. $\square$

8   LEMMA   *Summ(X) is a meet semilattice.* $P \bigcap Q$ *is given by the common path* ti
$= uj : R \longrightarrow X$ *in the pullback*

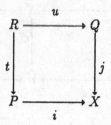

Proof   Lemma **6** is needed to know that $R \longrightarrow X \in Summ(X)$; this is so because
$u : R \longrightarrow Q = [j]P \in Summ(Q)$. That $(S \subset P \ \wedge \ S \subset Q) \Leftrightarrow S \subset R$ for all
$S \in Summ(X)$ is then immediate from the pullback property. $\square$

9   LEMMA   *Coproduct complements are unique.*

Proof   Let $P \overset{i}{\longrightarrow} X \overset{j}{\longleftarrow} Q$, $P \overset{i}{\longrightarrow} X \overset{k}{\longleftarrow} R$ be coproducts. We must
prove $Q = R$ in $Summ(X)$. It suffices to show $Q \subset R$. By Lemma **8** and axiom **4.7**(3)
applied to j , the inclusions $P \bigcap Q \longrightarrow Q \longleftarrow R \bigcap Q$ consitute a coproduct. By
Lemma **2**, $P \bigcap Q = 0$ so $R \bigcap Q = Q$ by Lemma **1**. $\square$

10   NOTATION   For $P \in Summ(X)$, the unique coproduct complement of P will be
denoted P' .

Observe that $P'' = P$.

We have finally set up the main result of this section.

11   THEOREM   *In a Boolean category, for each object X the poset $(Summ(X), \subset)$*
is a Boolean algebra with operations as follows:

   Least element : 0

$$Greatest\ element\ :\ X$$

$$Intersection\ :\ via\ pullback\ as\ in\ 8$$

$$Complement\ :\ The\ coproduct\ complement\ P'$$

Further, if $Q, R \in Summ(X)$ with $Q \bigcap R = 0$, the poset inclusions $Q \longrightarrow Q \bigcup R \longleftarrow R$ constitute a coproduct.

Proof We freely use the previous results of this section. Begin by observing that $P \mapsto P'$ is an anti-involution, that is, $P \subset Q \Leftrightarrow Q' \subset P'$. For if $P \subset Q$, $P \bigcap Q' \subset Q \bigcap Q' = 0$ then $P \bigcap Q' = 0$ and, reasoning as in 9, $P' \bigcap Q' \longrightarrow Q'$ is an isomorphism. It has already been seen that $0' = X$ so $Summ(X)$ is a lattice with join $P \bigcup Q = (P' \bigcap Q')'$. $P \bigcup P' = X$ because $P \bigcap P' = 0$. Hence $Summ(X)$ will be a Boolean algebra if for $P, Q, R \in Summ(X)$ we can establish the distributive law $P \bigcap (Q \bigcup R) = (P \bigcap Q) \bigcup (P \bigcap R)$. For this we may assume without loss of generality that $Q \bigcap R = 0$. [Proof: Using only that case we have $Q = Q \bigcap (R \bigcup R') = (Q \bigcap R) \bigcup (Q \bigcap R')$. As $Q \bigcap R \subset R$, $Q \bigcup R = R \bigcup (Q \bigcap R')$. As $R \bigcap (Q \bigcap R') = 0$, $P \bigcap (Q \bigcup R) = P \bigcap (R \bigcup (Q \bigcap R')) = (P \bigcap R) \bigcup (P \bigcap Q \bigcap R') \subset (P \bigcap Q) \bigcup (P \bigcap R)$. The reverse inequality is trivial.]

By Lemma 5, $Q, R \in Summ(Q \bigcup R)$ and so have coproduct complements Q', R' $\in Summ(Q \bigcup R)$. Pulling back the coproduct $Q \longrightarrow Q \bigcup R \longleftarrow Q'$ under $R \longrightarrow Q \bigcup R$ produces a coproduct $Q \bigcap R \longrightarrow R \longleftarrow Q' \bigcap R$. As $Q \bigcap R = 0$ in $Summ(X)$, $Q \bigcap R = 0$ in $Summ(Q \bigcup X)$ (Lemma 5) so $Q' \bigcap R \longrightarrow R$ is an isomorphism and $Q' \subset R$. But, in $Summ(Q \bigcup R)$, $Q \bigcup R = (Q' \bigcap R')'$ so $0 = (Q \bigcup R)' = Q' \bigcap R'$ whence, by the same reasoning, $R \subset Q'$. Thus $Q' = R$ and $Q \longrightarrow Q \bigcup R \longleftarrow R$ is a coproduct. This establishes that last part of the statement of this theorem.

Continuing, $P \bigcap (Q \bigcup R)$ is a summand of X contained in $Q \bigcup R$ so may be regarded in $Summ(Q \bigcup R)$. We then have the following commutative diagram in which both rows are coproducts and both squares are pullbacks:

$$
\begin{array}{ccccc}
S & \longrightarrow & P \bigcap (Q \bigcup R) & \longleftarrow & T \\
\downarrow & & \downarrow & & \downarrow \\
Q & \longrightarrow & Q \bigcup R & \longleftarrow & R
\end{array}
$$

But $S = Q\bigcap P\bigcap(Q\bigcup R) = P\bigcap Q$ (as $Q\bigcap(Q\bigcup R) = Q$) and $T = P\bigcap R$ similarly. As established above, there is a coproduct

$$S\longrightarrow(P\bigcap Q)\bigcup(P\bigcap R)\longleftarrow T .$$

The uniqueness of coproducts produces the needed distributive law. $\square$

12 EXAMPLE In the Boolean categories **Set, Pfn, Mfn, Bag** and Ω, $Summ(X)$ is the usual Boolean algebra of subsets of X.

We turn next to characterizing *if-then-else* operators in a Boolean category. Recall the definitions (2.21-2.23): if $P \in Summ(X)$, its fanout $F: X\longrightarrow X + X$ depends only on P because P' is unique and so the corresponding choice operator may be written

$$if_P(\alpha,\beta) = F < \alpha,\beta > .$$

We then have

13 PROPOSITION *In a Boolean category, "if-then-else is characterized as deterministic idempotent choice". More precisely, the passage from $P \in Summ(X)$ to its fanout in 2.22 establishes a bijection of $Summ(X)$ onto the deterministic morphisms $F: X\longrightarrow X + X$ whose choice operator $F < \alpha,\beta > = if_P(\alpha,\beta)$ is idempotent.*

Proof Given a fanout $F: X\longrightarrow X + X$ as in 2.22, we have $iF < \alpha,\alpha > = i\,in_1 < \alpha,\alpha > = i\alpha$, and $i'F < \alpha,\alpha > = i'\alpha$ similarly, so $F < \alpha,\alpha > = \alpha$. In 12.12 below we will independently prove that if $P\overset{i}{\longrightarrow}X\overset{i'}{\longleftarrow}P'$ is a coproduct in a Boolean category and if $\alpha: X\longrightarrow Y$ is such that $i\alpha$ and $i'\alpha$ are deterministic then α itself is deterministic. In particular, every fanout is deterministic since in the diagram of 2.22 the restrictions of the fanout to the coproduct injections i, i' are summands of $X + X$ (Lemma 5) and so are crisp by the definition of a Boolean category, deterministic in particular. (Recall the example following 2.24 which showed that in a non-Boolean category, fanouts need not be deterministic.)

So far, the map $P \mapsto F$ is well-defined. Lemma 2.17 established that a deterministic idempotent choice is a fanout, that is, that $P \mapsto F$ is surjective. To show that $P \mapsto F$ is injective, we rely on Theorem 11 and a closer look at the proof of 2.17. Suppose $Q \mapsto T$. As 2.17 in fact proved that $T \in Summ(X + X)$, T is even crisp and so we may choose P in 2.18 so that the squares are pullbacks. Thus $P \mapsto T$ as well and it suffices to prove $P = Q$ since P is canonically dependent upon T. It is immediate from the pullback property that $Q \subset P$. Symmetrically, $Q' \subset P'$, so also $P \subset Q$.   □

We isolate the following fact just proved:

14 OBSERVATION   *In a Boolean category, the squares in the diagram 2.22 defining a fanout are always pullbacks.*   □

We showed that summands are monomorphisms in 2. This can be strengthened as follows.

15 PROPOSITION   *Summands are equalizers. More precisely, if* $i : P \longrightarrow X$ *is a summand with corresponding fanout* $F : X \longrightarrow X + X$ *as in 13 then* $i = eq(in_1, F)$.

Proof   Immediate from 14.   □

The Boolean structure of $Summ(X)$ leads to the definition of Hoare assertions, the modal operators of dynamic algebra [Kozen 1980], [Pratt 1980] and the weakest precondition operator {Dijkstra 1976] as follows.

16 DEFINITION   Given $\alpha : X \longrightarrow Q$, $Q \in Summ(Y)$ we have already defined the "box operator" $[\alpha](-)$, $Q \mapsto [\alpha]Q \in Summ(X)$ in 4.2. Also define the *diamond operator* $< \alpha > (-)$ of α, the *domain of definition* $Dom(\alpha)$ of α, the *weakest precondition operator* $wp(\alpha, -)$ of α and the *kernel* $Ker(\alpha)$ of α by

$$< \alpha > Q \ = \ ([\alpha]Q')' \ \in \ Summ(X)$$
$$Dom(\alpha) \ = \ < \alpha > Y \ \in \ Summ(X)$$
$$wp(\alpha, Q) \ = \ Dom(\alpha) \bigcap [\alpha]Q \ \in \ Summ(X)$$
$$Ker(\alpha) \ = \ (Dom(\alpha))' \ = \ [\alpha]0$$

(That the two versions of $Ker(\alpha)$ coincide is obvious.)

Because of the logical origins of these operators (in dynamic logic as opposed to dynamic algebra) they are often called "predicate transformers", the "predicates" being properties of the state, here being the summands. While α is a morphism from X to Y, $[\alpha](-)$, $< \alpha > (-)$, $wp(\alpha, -)$ map in the opposite direction from $Summ(Y)$ to $Summ(X)$; for this reason, they are called *inverse predicate transformers*. Direct operators mapping from $Summ(X)$ to $Summ(Y)$ will appear in Section 13.

17 PROPOSITION   *For any* $\alpha : X \longrightarrow Y$, *the three operators* $[\alpha](-)$, $< \alpha > (-)$, $wp(\alpha, -)$ *are mutually interexpressible.*

Proof To see that $[\alpha](-)$ and $< \alpha > (-)$ can be expressed in terms of each other, observe that $[\alpha]Q = (< \alpha > Q')'$.   Since $wp(\alpha, Q) = ([\alpha]0)' \bigcap [\alpha]Q$, $wp(\alpha, -)$ is expressible in terms of $[\alpha](-)$. It then suffices to prove

18              $Dom(\alpha) \ = \ wp(\alpha, Y)$

19                    $[\alpha]Q \ = \ Ker(\alpha) \bigcup wp(\alpha, Q)$

since then $[\alpha]Q = (wp(\alpha, Y))' \bigcup wp(\alpha, Q)$. For 18, the square $\alpha \, id_Y = id_X \alpha$ is a pullback, so $[\alpha]Y = X$. Pursuant to 19, we state a standard result which is frequently useful (and whose proof is safely left to the reader):

20 PROPOSITION (Pullback-pasting.)   *In any category, given a commutative diagram*

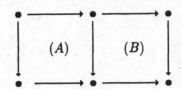

if (A), (B) *are pullbacks then so is the outer rectangle* (AB); *and, if* (B),(AB) *are pullbacks, so too is* (A). □

It follows immediately from **20** that $[\alpha](-)$ is monotone, that is, that $Q \subset R \Rightarrow [\alpha]Q \subset [\alpha]R$ (a result which will be improved in Lemma **6.8.**) In particular, $Ker(\alpha) = [\alpha]0 \subset [\alpha]Q$. Thus **19** (and hence the proof of **17**) is established by the following calculation:

$$
\begin{aligned}
Ker(\alpha) \bigcup wp(\alpha, Q) &= Ker(\alpha) \bigcup (Dom(\alpha) \bigcap [\alpha]Q) \\
&= X \bigcap (Ker(\alpha) \bigcup [\alpha]Q) \\
&= [\alpha]Q.
\end{aligned}
$$
□

21 DEFINITION Two morphisms α, β are *indiscernible* if $[\alpha]Q = [\beta]Q$ (equivalently, $<\alpha>Q = <\beta>Q$, $wp(\alpha, Q) = wp(\beta, Q)$) for all $Q \in Summ(Y)$. The Boolean category $\mathfrak{B}$ is *faithful* if any two indiscernible morphisms are equal. (Later, in **11.18** we shall observe that $\mathfrak{B}$ is faithful if and only if a canonical functor representing $\mathfrak{B}$ is faithful, and this explains the terminology.)

22 EXAMPLE For Set, Pfn, Mfn, Bag and Ω, $<\alpha>Q$ is as in Table **1.9**. Set, Pfn and Mfn are faithful whereas Bag and Ω are not.

6   NULL AND TOTAL MORPHISMS

In **Mfn**, the empty relation is a "null map" whereas a total morphism α satisfies $x\alpha \neq \emptyset$ for all x.   These definitions generalize to arbitrary Boolean categories.   In this section we study the simplest properties of null and total morphisms.   Examples are given in Table 18.

1 DEFINITION   In any category with an initial object 0, say that $\alpha : X \longrightarrow Y$ is *null* if it factors through 0, i.e. there exists $\beta : X \longrightarrow 0$ with

$$\alpha \ = \ X \xrightarrow{\ \beta\ } 0 \longrightarrow Y$$

where the unnamed morphism $0 \longrightarrow Y$ is, of course, the unique one.   Say that α is *total* if for all $\gamma : W \longrightarrow X$, if $\gamma\alpha$ is null then γ is null.

We think of null morphisms as divergences or failings but have chosen a neutral term so as not to prejudice future applications.   Speaking heuristically, a total map α never diverges or fails in that so long as its input γ is non-null, so too is its output $\gamma\alpha$.

In the category **Set** of sets and total functions, all morphisms are total and the only null maps have form $\emptyset \longrightarrow Y$.   In **Pfn**, there is exactly one null map $X \longrightarrow Y$ for each X, Y namely the one with empty domain of definition, and total has its usual meaning.   Unique null maps (= zero morphisms, see Observation 4 below) as enjoyed by **Pfn** and **Mfn** lead to nice algebraic properties but it is somewhat limiting in that there is no way to distinguish between divergence and failing, so we insist that a general theory should allow more arbitrary null maps. As already mentioned following Definition 4.7, there may be many null maps $X \longrightarrow Y$ in the Boolean category Ω. Here $\alpha : X \longrightarrow Y$ is total if and only if for every x there exists some y appearing as a leaf in $x\alpha$. The canonical divergence $\perp_{XY} : X \longrightarrow Y$ of a polymorhic iterate as defined in **3.22** is always a null morphism; this follows from **2.23** setting $Y = 0$.

2 OBSERVATION *The following statements are valid.*

1. *For* $W \xrightarrow{\alpha} X \xrightarrow{\beta} Y \xrightarrow{\gamma} Z$, β *null* $\Rightarrow \alpha\beta\gamma$ *null.*

2. *If* $\alpha : X \longrightarrow Y$ *is null and* $\beta : W \longrightarrow Y$ *is arbitrary then there exists null* $\gamma : X \longrightarrow W$ *with* $\alpha = \gamma\beta$.

3. *For any object* X, id_X *is null* $\Leftrightarrow X = 0$.

4. *In a Boolean category, if* $\alpha : X \longrightarrow Y$ *is null and* $Q \in Summ(Y)$, $[\alpha]Q \longrightarrow Q$ *is null.*

5. *If* $P \xrightarrow{i} X \xleftarrow{i'} P'$ *is a coproduct and if* $\alpha : P \longrightarrow Y$, $\alpha' : P' \longrightarrow Y'$, *then* $< \alpha, \alpha' > : X \longrightarrow Y$ *is null* $\Leftrightarrow \alpha, \alpha'$ *are null.*

The proof is routine. For (3), if $\beta : X \longrightarrow 0$ with $id_X = X \xrightarrow{\beta} 0 \xrightarrow{u} X$ then $u\beta = id_0$ so β is an isomorphism. For (4), use the pullback pasting proposition **5.20** and observe that $[0 \rightarrow Y]Q = Q \cap 0 = 0$. $\qquad\square$

The next observation is left to the reader.

3 OBSERVATION *The following statements are valid.*

1. *Every monomorphism is total.*

2. *Given* $X \xrightarrow{\alpha} Y \xrightarrow{\beta} Z$, α, β *total* $\Rightarrow \alpha\beta$ *total; and,* $\alpha\beta$ *total* $\Rightarrow \alpha$ *total.* $\qquad\square$

4 OBSERVATION *If a category with initial object admits a family of zero morphisms (Definition 2.9), such zeroes are the only null maps.* To see that this is so, given $\alpha : X \longrightarrow 0$, $X \xrightarrow{\ \alpha\ } 0 \longrightarrow X \xrightarrow{\ 0\ } 0$ is both $\alpha \, id_0 = \alpha$ and 0 so $\alpha = 0$.

$\square$

For the balance of this section, we work in a Boolean category $\mathfrak{B}$.

In the theory of modules over a ring, the kernel of a homomorphism is the submodule on which it vanishes. The universal property of the kernel is exploited in homological algebra [Freyd 1964, Mitchell 1965]. Essentially the same universal property exists in a Boolean category:

5   PROPOSITION   (Universal property of $Ker(\alpha)$.) *For $\alpha : X \longrightarrow Y$, $Ker(\alpha)$ is the (necessarily unique) summand $i : P \longrightarrow X$ of X satisfying the following two properties:*

1. $i\alpha$ *is null.*

2.   *If $\beta : W \longrightarrow X$ and $\beta\alpha$ is null then β factors uniquely through i.*

Proof By definition 5.16, $i : Ker(\alpha) \longrightarrow X = [\alpha]0$. It is obvious from the diagram below that $i\alpha$ is null. Now let $\beta\alpha$ be null so that there exists δ with $\beta\alpha = A \xrightarrow{\ \delta\ } 0 \longrightarrow Y$. By the pullback property there exists unique ψ with $\psi i = \beta$,

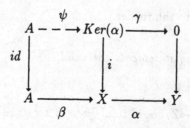

$\psi\gamma = \delta$. As i is a monomorphism, ψ is in fact unique with $\psi i = \beta$. $\square$

6 COROLLARY   *Given* $\alpha : X \longrightarrow Y$, α *is null* $\Leftrightarrow$ $Ker(\alpha) = X$ $\Leftrightarrow$ $Dom(\alpha)$
$= 0$.

$\square$

Before stating the next proposition, we need

7 LEMMA   *For any* $\alpha : X \longrightarrow Y$, $n \geq 2$, $Q_1, \ldots, Q_n \in Summ(Y)$,

$$[\alpha](Q_1 \bigcap \cdots \bigcap Q_n) = [\alpha]Q_1 \bigcap \cdots \bigcap [\alpha]Q_n.$$

Proof   Given $i : P \longrightarrow X \in Summ(X)$, by the pullback property of $[\alpha]Q$ and the
fact that intersections in $Summ(Y)$ are constructed as pullbacks as stated in Theorem
5.11, we have

$$P \subset \bigcap [\alpha]Q_j \Leftrightarrow P \subset [\alpha]Q_j \text{ for all } j$$
$$\Leftrightarrow i\alpha \text{ factors through } Q_j \text{ for all } j$$
$$\Leftrightarrow i\alpha \text{ factors through } \bigcap Q_j$$
$$\Leftrightarrow P \subset [\alpha](\bigcap Q_j). \qquad \square$$

8 LEMMA   *For any* $\alpha : X \longrightarrow Y$ *and any* $Q \in Summ(Y)$, $Ker(\alpha) = [\alpha]Q \bigcap$
$[\alpha]Q'$.

Proof   Immediate from 7. $\square$

We then easily deduce the following equivalent characterizations of total. The
fourth condition is very intuitive: only the empty summand can belong to both Q and
its complement so no input x produces empty $x\alpha$.

9 PROPOSITION   *For* $\alpha : X \longrightarrow Y$, *the following four statements are equivalent.*

1. α *is total, that is, if $\beta\alpha$ is null then β is null.*

2. $Ker(\alpha) = 0.$

3. $Dom(\alpha) = X.$

4. *For all $Q \in Summ(Y)$, $[\alpha]Q \bigcap [\alpha]Q' = 0.$*

Proof Use **6** for $(1) \Rightarrow (2)$: if $i : P \longrightarrow X = Ker(\alpha)$, $i\alpha$ null $\Rightarrow i$ null, that is, $P \subset 0$ in $Summ(X)$, so $P = 0$. For $(2) \Rightarrow (1)$, let $\beta\alpha$ be null. By **6** again, β factors through $Ker(\alpha)$ so β is null if $Ker(\alpha) = 0.$ $\Box$

10 COROLLARY   *Every crisp morphism is total.*

Proof   Use **9**(4) and **5.2** since, if α is crisp, $[\alpha]Q \longrightarrow X \longleftarrow [\alpha]Q'$ is a coproduct. $\Box$

The next proposition establishes an intuitive property of $Dom(\alpha)$ which, though weaker than the universal property analogous to that of $Ker(\alpha)$, nonetheless characterizes it.

11 PROPOSITION   *For any $\alpha : X \longrightarrow Y$, $i : Dom(\alpha) \longrightarrow X$ is the largest summand restricted to which α is total.*

Proof We must show that $i\alpha$ is total and that if $j : P \longrightarrow X \in Summ(X)$ with $j\alpha$ total then $P \subset Dom(\alpha)$. For $k : S \longrightarrow X$ a summand, construct the pullbacks for $Ker(\alpha)$ and for $S \bigcap Ker(\alpha)$:

$$
\begin{array}{ccccc}
S \bigcap Ker(\alpha) & \longrightarrow & Ker(\alpha) & \overset{\beta}{\longrightarrow} & 0 \\
{\scriptstyle t}\big\downarrow & & \big\downarrow & & \big\downarrow \\
S & \underset{k}{\longrightarrow} & X & \underset{\alpha}{\longrightarrow} & Y
\end{array}
$$

By pullback pasting (5.20), $Ker(k\alpha) = S \bigcap Ker(\alpha)$ qua summand of S, that is, $Ker(k\alpha) = t$ as shown. Setting $S = Dom(\alpha) = (Ker(\alpha))'$, $k = i$ and $Ker(i\alpha) = 0$ so $i\alpha$ is total by 9. Setting $S = j : P\longrightarrow X$ with $j\alpha$ total, $Ker(j\alpha) = 0$ so $S \bigcap Ker(\alpha) = 0$ whence $S \subset (Ker(\alpha))' = Dom(\alpha)$. $\quad\quad\square$

12 DEFINITION For $\alpha : X\overset{}{\longrightarrow}Y$, a *kernel-domain decomposition of* α is a coproduct decomposition $K\overset{i}{\longrightarrow}X\overset{j}{\longleftarrow}D$ such that $i\alpha$ is null and $j\alpha$ is total.

13 PROPOSITION $K = Ker(\alpha)$, $D = Dom(\alpha)$ *is the unique kernel-domain decomposition of* $\alpha : X\longrightarrow Y$.

Proof We already have shown in Propositions 5, 11 that $Ker(\alpha)$, $Dom(\alpha)$ provide a kernel-domain decomposition. Now let $K\overset{i}{\longrightarrow}X\overset{j}{\longleftarrow}D$ be an arbitrary one. As $i\alpha = 0$ it follows from 5 that $K \subset Ker(\alpha)$. As $j\alpha$ is total, Proposition 11 gives $D \subset Dom(\alpha)$. Thus $Ker(\alpha) = (Dom(\alpha))' \subset D' = K$ so $K = Ker(\alpha)$ and $D = Dom(\alpha)$ in $Summ(X)$. $\quad\quad\square$

14 DEFINITION Let $\mathcal{B}$ be any Boolean category. The *category* $\mathcal{B}_{part}$ *of partial morphisms of* $\mathcal{B}$ has the same objects as $\mathcal{B}$ but a morphism $X\longrightarrow Y$ is an equivalence class $[P,t]$ of (P,t) with $P \in Summ(X)$, $t : P\longrightarrow X$ total (with respect to the obvious equivalence relation $(P,t) \sim (P_1,t_1)$) if there exists a summand isomorphism transforming t to t_1. Composition is by pullback and the identity morphism of X is represented by $X\overset{id}{\longrightarrow}X\overset{id}{\longleftarrow}X$. This is the standard way to define "categories of partial morphisms" in the literature.

Proposition **13** establishes a function $\mathcal{B}(X,Y)\longrightarrow\mathcal{B}_{part}(X,Y)$. In spite of that, $\mathcal{B}\longrightarrow\mathcal{B}_{part}$ is *not* a functor in general. In **12.8** below we will see that functoriality is a statement of determinism.

15 PROPOSITION *A pullback of a total map is total, that is, given a pullback square* $a\beta = b\alpha$, *if* α *is total then so is* a.

Proof Let $a\beta = b\alpha$ be a pullback square and paste on the pullback square for $Ker(a)$.

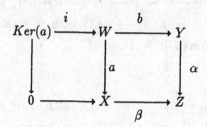

By pullback pasting **5.20**, $i\,b : Ker(a) \longrightarrow Y = Ker(\alpha) = 0$ so $Ker(a) = 0$ and a is total.   □

16 PROPOSITION   Let $P \overset{i}{\longrightarrow} X \overset{j}{\longleftarrow} Q$ be a coproduct and let $\alpha : X \longrightarrow Y$. If $i\alpha$, $j\alpha$ are total then α is total.

Proof Consider the following diagram with $K = Ker(\alpha)$:

$$
\begin{array}{ccccc}
P \cap K & \longrightarrow & K & \longleftarrow & Q \cap K \\
{\scriptstyle a}\downarrow & & {\scriptstyle k}\downarrow & & \downarrow{\scriptstyle b} \\
P & \underset{i}{\longrightarrow} & X & \underset{j}{\longleftarrow} & Q
\end{array}
$$

Then the squares are pullbacks. As $ai\alpha$ factors through $k\alpha$, $ai\alpha$ is null so, as $i\alpha$ is total, a is null and then ai is. Similarly, bj is null. But the top row is a coproduct, so k is null by **2(5)**. Now let $t\alpha$ be null. Then t factors through k so t is null.   □

17 PROPOSITION   The category $\mathcal{B}_{tot}$ of $\mathcal{B}$–objects and total $\mathcal{B}$–morphisms forms a Boolean subcategory of $\mathcal{B}$, and $\mathcal{B}_{tot}$ is a wide Boolean subcategory of $\mathcal{B}$.

Proof That $0 \longrightarrow X$ is total is obvious, so 0 acts as an initial object in $\mathcal{B}_{tot}$. It follows from **3, 14, 15** that the $\mathcal{B}$–coproduct acts as a coproduct in $\mathcal{B}_{tot}$ and that $[\alpha]Q$ is a pullback in $\mathcal{B}_{tot}$. Isomorphisms are total.   □

Table 18 gives examples of null and total maps in examples of Boolean categories. (Mat_R is a Boolean category by Corollary 7.13 below.)

Category	$X \xrightarrow{\alpha} Y$ is null $\Leftrightarrow$	α is total $\Leftrightarrow$
Set	$X = \emptyset$	(all α are total)
Pfn	α is always undefined	$\forall x \; x\alpha$ is defined
Mfn	$\forall x \; x\alpha = \emptyset$	$\forall x \; x\alpha \neq \emptyset$
Mat_R	$\alpha_{xy} = 0 \; \forall x, y$	$\forall x \; \exists y \; \alpha_{xy} \neq 0$
Ω	$\forall x \; x\alpha$ has only nullary leaves	$\forall x \; \exists$ non-nullary leaf in $x\alpha$

Table 18: Examples of null and total maps.

7   PREADDITIVE CATEGORIES

Semiadditive categories were introduced and briefly studied in **2.10 ff**. In such categories, there is a sum operation $\alpha + \beta$ on morphisms $X \longrightarrow Y$. Yet in **1.3-4** we introduced the matrix category $\mathbf{Mat}_R$ of a partial semiring R in which $\alpha + \beta$ is only sometimes defined, and pointed out that even the fundamental example of $\mathbf{Pfn}$ has this feature. The preadditive categories of this section (really "presemiadditive", but that is too cumbersome; more accurately "pre-partially-additive" [cf. Arbib and Manes 1980]) allow a rudimentary theory of partially-defined sums. We shall give sufficient conditions for a preadditive category to be Boolean and use them to find conditions on R so that $\mathbf{Mat}_R$ is Boolean.

Prior to stating the first definition, we recall that a *zero object* in a category is an object which is both initial and terminal. We proved in Lemma **A** of the introduction that the initial object is a zero object if and only if there are zero morphisms. These zero morphisms are constructed as $X \longrightarrow 0 \longrightarrow Y$ when 0 is a zero object.

1   DEFINITION   A category is *preadditive* if it has a zero object, has binary coproducts, and is such that whenever $P \xrightarrow{i} X \xleftarrow{i'} P'$ is a coproduct, the *projections* $\rho : X \longrightarrow P$, $\rho' : X \longrightarrow P'$ defined by the equations

2

$$i\rho = id_P$$
$$i\rho' = 0$$

$$i'\rho = 0$$
$$i'\rho' = id_{P'}$$

are

jointly monic (that is, recall, for all $\alpha, \beta : W \longrightarrow X$, if $\alpha\rho = \beta\rho$ and $\alpha\rho' = \beta\rho'$ then $\alpha = \beta$.)

In such a category, say that $\alpha, \beta : X \longrightarrow Y$ are *summable* if there exists a coproduct $Y \xrightarrow{in_1} Y + Y \xleftarrow{in_2} Y$ (with projections $\rho_i : Y + Y \longrightarrow Y$) and a morphism $F : X \longrightarrow Y + Y$ such that $F\rho_1 = f$, $F\rho_2 = g$. In that case F is unique because ρ_1, ρ_2 are jointly monic, so we may define the *sum* of α, β written $\alpha + \beta$ by

3
$$\alpha + \beta = X \xrightarrow{F} Y + Y \xrightarrow{\sigma} Y$$

where σ is defined by

4
$$in_i\sigma = id_Y.$$

It is routine to check that $\alpha + \beta$ is independent of the choice of copower $Y + Y$. In particular, $\alpha + \beta = \beta + \alpha$.

5 EXAMPLE Pfn is preadditive since $\rho : X \longrightarrow P$ maps $x \mapsto x$ if $x \in P$, and is undefined otherwise. Thus α, β are summable if and only if $Dom(\alpha) \bigcap Dom(\beta) = \emptyset$ in which case $\alpha + \beta = \alpha \bigcup \beta$.

6 EXAMPLE Any semiadditive category is preadditive by Proposition 2.11. Conversely, a preadditive category in which all $\alpha, \beta : X \longrightarrow Y$ are summable is semiadditive since there exists unique $F_X : X \longrightarrow X + X$ with $F_X\rho_i = id_X$ and F is natural by the joint monicity of the ρ_i.

7 EXAMPLE   The category of semigroups has $\emptyset$ as initial object and coproducts $M + N$ as follows. As a set, $M + N$ consists of all nonempty strings in which no two adjacent elements are both from M or from N (M, N should be viewed as disjoint.) The semigroup operation is obtained by concatenating and reducing, if necessary, by multiplying the last symbol of the first string with the first symbol of the second string if they are in the same semigroup. With the obvious injections this does form a coproduct.   But this category is not preadditive because the projections $\rho_i :$ $M + M \longrightarrow M$ are not jointly monic.   To see this,   let $S = \{1, 2, \dots\}$ with numerical addition as semigroup operation, so that S is the free semigroup on one generator. Let u, v be, respectively, 1 in the first, second copy of S in $S + S$. Then F $: S \longrightarrow S + S$, $n \mapsto (uv)^n$ and $G : S \longrightarrow S + S$, $n \mapsto (vu)^n$ are distinct semigroup homomorphisms but $F\rho_i = id_S = G\rho_i$ for $i = 1, 2$.

For the balance of this section, we work in a preadditive category $\mathcal{P}$.

8 PROPOSITION   *The following statements hold.*

1. *For $\alpha : X \longrightarrow Y$, $\alpha + 0$ exists and is α.*

2. *For $\alpha : W \longrightarrow X$, $\beta_1, \beta_2 : X \longrightarrow Y$, $\gamma_1, \gamma_2 : Y \longrightarrow Z$,*
    if $\beta_1 + \beta_2$ exists then $\alpha\beta_1\gamma_1 + \alpha\beta_2\gamma_2$ exists and, when $\gamma_1 = \gamma$
    $= \gamma_2$, coincides with $\alpha(\beta_1 + \beta_2)\gamma$.

Proof For the first statement, if $F = \alpha\, in_1 : X \longrightarrow Y + Y$, then $F\rho_1 = \alpha$, $F\rho_2$ $= 0$ and $F\sigma = \alpha$. For the second, let $F : X \longrightarrow Y + Y$ satisfy $\rho_i F = \beta_i$, and define $G : X \longrightarrow Z + Z$ by

$$ G = W \xrightarrow{\quad\alpha\quad} X \xrightarrow{\quad F\quad} Y + Y \xrightarrow{\quad\gamma_1 \oplus \gamma_2\quad} Z + Z $$

(where the notation $\gamma_1 \oplus \gamma_2$ was explained in **2.5**.) The diagrams

9

$$
\begin{array}{ccc}
Y + Y & \xrightarrow{\gamma_1 \oplus \gamma_2} & Z + Z \\
{\scriptstyle \rho_i}\downarrow & & \downarrow{\scriptstyle \rho_i} \\
Y & \xrightarrow[\gamma]{} & Z
\end{array}
\qquad\qquad
\begin{array}{ccc}
Y + Y & \xrightarrow{\gamma \oplus \gamma} & Z + Z \\
{\scriptstyle \sigma}\downarrow & & \downarrow{\scriptstyle \sigma} \\
Y & \xrightarrow[\gamma]{} & Z
\end{array}
$$

commute since they do so preceded by $in_i : Y \longrightarrow Y + Y$. It follows easily that $G\rho_i$ $= \alpha\beta_i\gamma_i$ and $G\sigma = \alpha(\beta_1 + \beta_2)\gamma$. $\qquad\qquad\qquad\qquad\qquad\qquad\qquad\qquad\square$

The next result is analogous to a well-known theorem about semiadditive categories [Mitchell 1965].

10 PROPOSITION *Let* $P \overset{i}{\longrightarrow} X \overset{i'}{\longleftarrow} P'$, $P \overset{\rho}{\longleftarrow} X \overset{\rho'}{\longrightarrow} P'$ *in a preadditive category. Then the following two statements are equivalent.*

1. $P \overset{i}{\longrightarrow} X \overset{i'}{\longleftarrow} P'$ *is a coproduct with projections* ρ, ρ'.

2. $i\rho = id_P$, $i'\rho = 0$, $i\rho' = 0$, $i'\rho' = id_{P'}$ *and* $\rho i + \rho' i'$ *exists and is* id_X.

We say that $(X, P, i, \rho, P', i', \rho')$ is a *coproduct system*.

Proof For $1 \Rightarrow 2$, let $F : X \longrightarrow X + X$ be the fanout of P, P' (2.21.) It is routine to check that $F\rho_1 = i\rho$, $F\rho_2 = i'\rho'$ and $F\sigma = id_X$. For $2 \Rightarrow 1$, consider morphisms $\alpha : P \longrightarrow Y$, $\beta : P' \longrightarrow Y$. If $\gamma : X \longrightarrow Y$ exists with $i\gamma = \alpha$, $i'\gamma = \beta$ then $\gamma = id_X\gamma = (\rho i + \rho' i')\gamma = \rho i\gamma + \rho' i'\gamma = \rho\alpha + \rho'\beta$ which establishes uniqueness. For existence, apply 8(2) with $\alpha = id_X$, $\beta_1 = \rho i$, $\beta_2 = \rho' i'$, $\gamma_1 = \rho\alpha$, $\gamma_2 = \rho'\beta$ to see that $(\rho i)(\rho\alpha) + (\rho' i')(\rho'\beta) = \rho\alpha + \rho'\beta$ exists. Define $\gamma = \rho\alpha + \rho'\beta$ whence $i\gamma = \alpha$, $i'\gamma = \beta$. $\qquad\qquad\qquad\qquad\qquad\qquad\qquad\qquad\qquad\square$

Noting Observation 6.4, the zero maps in $\mathcal{P}$ are the only null maps. As in 6.5, we say a morphism $i : K \longrightarrow X$ is the *kernel* $Ker(\alpha)$ of $\alpha : X \longrightarrow Y$ if $i\alpha = 0$ and if, whenever $t\alpha = 0$, t factors uniquely through i. We have

11 COROLLARY *In a preadditive category, if* $(X, P, i, \rho, P', i', \rho')$ *is a coproduct system then* $i = Ker(\rho')$.

Proof That $i\rho' = 0$ is known. Now let $\alpha : W \longrightarrow X$ satisfy $\alpha\rho' = 0$. We must find unique $\psi : W \longrightarrow P$ such that $\alpha = \psi i$. Uniqueness is clear since i is (split)

mono. For existence, define $\psi = \alpha\rho i$. Then $\alpha = \alpha(\rho i + \rho' i') = \alpha\rho i + 0 = \alpha\rho i$.

$\square$

We now turn to finding sufficient conditions for a preadditive category to be Boolean. Since the category of real vector spaces is not Boolean, we will have to impose some properties which do not hold in all abelian categories. While the second condition below is occasionally true for an abelian category, the first never is.

12 PROPOSITION   *Let $\mathcal{P}$ be a preadditive category. Then $\mathcal{P}$ is Boolean if and only if the following two conditions hold:*

1. *For all summable $\alpha, \beta : X \longrightarrow Y$, if $\alpha + \beta = 0$ then $\alpha = 0 = \beta$; and,*

2. *For all $\alpha : X \longrightarrow Y$, $Ker(\alpha)$ exists and is a summand of X.*

Proof   The necessity of (2) is clear and that of (1) will be deferred until **10.5** where it will be proved independently. We turn to sufficiency. If T is a trivial object it admits at most one morphism to each object but also admits at least one such morphism since there is a zero object, so T is a zero object. To see $[\alpha]Q$ exists, $j : Q \longrightarrow Y = Ker(\rho')$ for appropriate ρ' by 11. Define $i : [\alpha]Q \longrightarrow X = Ker(\alpha\rho')$ which exists and is a summand of X by hypothesis. Consider the diagram

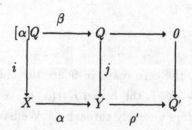

where β is still to be constructed. The right hand square is a pullback by the definition of "kernel", as is the outer rectangle, so β with $\beta j = i\alpha$ exists and this left hand square is a pullback by Proposition **5.20**. For the final axiom, peruse the diagram

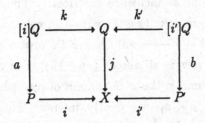

where the bottom row is a coproduct and $j : Q \longrightarrow X$ is a summand. The squares are pullbacks so it completes the proof to show that the top row is a coproduct. We do this using 8(2), **10**, **11**. Let $\rho : X \longrightarrow P$, $\rho' : X \longrightarrow P'$ be the coproduct projections and write $j = Ker(\eta')$ for appropriate η'. As $0 = j\eta' = j(\rho i + \rho' i')\eta' = j\rho i\eta' + j\rho' i'\eta'$, it follows from the hypothesis that $j\rho i\eta' = 0 = j\rho' i'\eta'$. Thus there exist unique morphisms $r, r' : Q \longrightarrow Q$ with, respectively, $rj = j\rho i$, $r'j = j\rho' i'$. Since $k : [i]Q \longrightarrow Q = Ker(j\eta')$ by the construction above (use **5.20**) and since $rj\eta' = j\rho i\eta' = 0$, there exist unique $\theta : Q \longrightarrow [i]Q$ with $\theta k = r$ and, similarly, unique $\theta' : Q' \longrightarrow [i']Q$ with $\theta' k' = r'$. Now i is monic because $i\rho = id_P$ so k, being the pullback of i, is monic. As j is a summand, j is monic so kj is monic. Also $kj = kj(\rho i + \rho' i') = kj\rho i$ since $kj\rho' i' = ai\rho' i' = 0$. Thus $(k\theta)kj = k(\theta k)j = krj = kj\rho i = kj \Rightarrow k\theta = id_{[i]Q}$. From $kj\rho' i' = 0$ just seen, $(k\theta')k'j = k(\theta' k')j = kr'j = kj\rho' i' = 0$, so $k\theta' = 0$ as $k'j$ is mono. Similarly, $k'\theta' = id_{[i']Q}$, $k'\theta = 0$. If $j\delta = id_Q$, $id_Q = j(\rho i + \rho' i')\delta = j\rho i\delta + j\rho' i'\delta = rj\delta + r'j\delta = r + r'$, so $\theta k + \theta' k'$ exists and is id_Q. $\qquad\square$

We can now establish the long-promised

13 COROLLARY *For R a positive partial semiring (1.3), the matrix category* **Mat**$_R$ *(1.4) is a Boolean Category.*

Proof $\emptyset$ is a zero object. The zero morphism $X \longrightarrow \emptyset \longrightarrow Y$, the composition of the X–by–0 matrix with the 0–by–Y matrix, is not empty but has entries consisting of empty sums and so is $[\alpha_{xy}]$ with each $\alpha_{xy} = 0$. The usual disjoint union provides coproducts (represent functions as incidence matrices.) Thus the coproduct injection $in_X : X \longrightarrow X+Y$ has x-th row ($x \in X$) with 1 in column x and 0 elsewhere. The coproduct projection $\rho_X : X+Y \longrightarrow X$ has x-th row with 1 in column x and 0 elsewhere whereas the y-th row is all zeroes ($y \in Y$.) For an arbitrary matrix $\alpha : Z \longrightarrow X+Y$, the x-th column is the x-th column of $\alpha\rho_X$ whereas the y-th column is the y-th column of $\alpha\rho_Y$ so ρ_X, ρ_Y are jointly monic. This shows that $\mathbf{Mat}_R$ is a semiadditive category. We need only show, then, that the conditions of the previous theorem hold.

Now $\sigma = <id_Y, id_Y> : Y+Y \longrightarrow Y$ is obtained by putting one Y-by-Y identity matrix beneath another. If $\alpha, \beta : X \longrightarrow Y$ are matrices and if $F : X \longrightarrow Y+Y$ satisfies $F\rho_1 = \alpha$, $F\rho_2 = \beta$, then F is the block-array $F = [\alpha\,|\,\beta]$. Thus α, β are summable if and only if such F is a matrix according to **1.4**, specifically,

14      $\forall x \in X \ \sum_y (\alpha_{xy} + \beta_{xy})$ exists.

Evaluation of the matrix product $F\sigma$ then shows that if α, β are summable then

15      $(\alpha + \beta)_{xy} = \alpha_{xy} + \beta_{xy}.$

Condition **12**(1) is then clear since R satisfies the additive positivity property **1.3f**. Now let $\alpha : X \longrightarrow Y$ and define $K = \{x \in X : \forall y \ \alpha_{xy} = 0\}$. Let $[i_{kx}]$ be the corresponding summand, $i_{kx} = 1$ if $k = x$, and $= 0$ otherwise. That $i\alpha = 0$ is clear. Suppose $\beta : W \longrightarrow X$ satisfies $\beta\alpha = 0$. We must find $\gamma : W \longrightarrow K$ such that $\gamma i = \beta$. Define $\gamma_{wk} = \beta_{wk}$. Then γi has w–x entry $\sum_k \gamma_{wk} i_{kx}$ and this is α_{wx} if $x \in K$ and is otherwise 0. Thus we must show that $\beta_{wx_0} = 0$ if $x_0 \notin K$. Indeed there exists y_0 with $\alpha_{x_0 y_0} \neq 0$. But as $\beta\alpha = 0$, $0 = \sum_x \beta_{wx}\alpha_{xy_0}$ so each $\beta_{wx}\alpha_{xy_0} = 0$ and, in particular, $\beta_{wx_0}\alpha_{x_0 y_0} = 0$. As $\alpha_{x_0 y_0} \neq 0$, $\beta_{wx_0} = 0$ by the multiplicative positivity property of R (**1.3h**.) $\square$

16 **EXAMPLE** It is easy to give examples of preadditive categories satisfying (1) but not (2) of Proposition 12. Consider the full subcategory $\mathcal{C}$ of **Pfn** of all sets of finite even cardinality. This is preadditive and even ω–complete, but it is not Boolean. Consider $\alpha : \{a, b\} \longrightarrow \{c, d\}$ with $a\alpha = \{c\}$, $b\alpha$ undefined. The $\mathcal{C}$–summands of

$\{a, b\}$ are $\emptyset$, $\{a, b\}$ and neither provides a kernel.

We conclude this section with a straightforward generalization of **3.31**.

17 LEMMA   *Consider* $F : X \longrightarrow X + Y$, $\overline{F} : \overline{X} \longrightarrow \overline{X} + \overline{Y}$ *in a preadditive category and write* $\alpha = F \rho_X$, $\beta = F \rho_Y$, $\overline{\alpha} = \overline{F} \rho_X$, $\overline{\beta} = \overline{F} \rho_Y$. *Then*

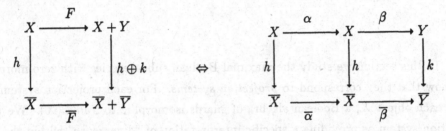

Proof   Exactly the same proof as in Lemma **3.31** works. By virtue of Proposition **12**, the same matrix calculus is available in a preadditive category save that $F \mapsto (\alpha, \beta)$ is now only injective rather than bijective, that is, not every "$[\alpha, \beta]$" is legal.   □

8   PROJECTIONS AND GUARDS

In this section we study the maximal Boolean subcategories with zero morphisms and show that they correspond to *projection systems*. For each projection system there is, for each object X, a Boolean algebra of guards isomorphic to $Summ(X)$. We view a projection system as providing a specific interpretation of "divergence" within the larger category. Further results in the balance of the paper support the feeling that a well-behaved Boolean category should have at least one projection system. Indeed, each polymorphic iterate induces one.

In this section, $\mathcal{B}$ is a Boolean category.

1   DEFINITION   If $\mathcal{C} \subset \mathcal{B}$ is a Boolean extension (Definition **4.14**) and if $\mathcal{C}$ has a family of zero morphisms then $\mathcal{C}$ is a *zero-subcategory of* $\mathcal{B}$.

We note at once that if $\mathcal{C}$ is a zero-subcategory of $\mathcal{B}$ then the $\mathcal{C}$-zeroes $X \longrightarrow Y$ are null morphisms and form an X-sink in $\mathcal{B}$ (as defined in the introduction.) This is clear from the initiality of the object 0 in both $\mathcal{B}$ and $\mathcal{C}$ since the zero morphism $X \longrightarrow Y$ factors as $X \longrightarrow 0 \longrightarrow Y$ with $X \longrightarrow 0$ the $\mathcal{C}$-zero.

Let $\mathcal{C}$ be a zero-subcategory of $\mathcal{B}$ and denote the zero morphism $X \longrightarrow Y$ by 0. It follows easily from the definitions (**4.14** and **1**) that a finite diagram in $\mathcal{B}$ is a coproduct in $\mathcal{C}$ if and only if it is a coproduct in $\mathcal{B}$. As in the preadditive case **7.1**, whenever $P \in Summ(X)$ there is a canonical "projection" $\rho_{XP} : X \longrightarrow P$ defined in $\mathcal{C}$ by

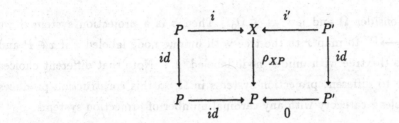

2

In this section, we will axiomatize such projection systems (ρ_{XP}) and show that there is a bijective correspondence between projection systems and maximal zero-subcatgories. (Not every Boolean category has a zero-subcategory —Set surely doesn't.) We will also show that every zero-subcategory is canonically contained in a maximal one, so we have made a good start toward understanding the zero-subcategories.

3   DEFINITION   A *projection system for* $\mathcal{B}$ is a family $\rho = (\rho_{XP})$ (for $i : P \longrightarrow X$ a summand representative —it would be more accurate to write ρ_{XPi}) where $\rho_{XP} : X \longrightarrow P$ and the following two axioms hold:

1. For all objects X, taking $i : P \longrightarrow X$ $= id_X$ gives $\rho_{XX} = id_X$.

2. For all summand representatives $i : P \longrightarrow X$, $j : Q \longrightarrow X$ and for all representatives of $P \bigcap Q$ (considered as a summand of P by Proposition 5.5), the following square commutes:

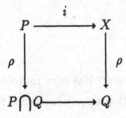

(Here we use the convention that the subscripts of ρ need not be shown if context makes them clear.) A morphism of form ρ_{XP} will be called a ρ–*projection*.

4   EXAMPLE   **Mfn** and **Pfn** have a unique projection system (by Proposition 8 below.) In both cases, ρ_{XP} is the partial function $x \mapsto x$ with domain P.

5   EXAMPLE   Consider Ω and let $\perp \in \Omega_0$. Then ρ is a projection system if we define $\rho_{XP} : X \longrightarrow P$ to map x to the tree with unique node labeled x if $x \in P$ and otherwise maps x to the tree with unique node labeled $\perp$. Note that different choices of $\perp \in \Omega_0$ give rise to different projection systems in Ω, so this construction produces an example of a Boolean category with any cardinal number of projection systems.

6   DEFINITION   Let ρ be a projection system for $\mathfrak{B}$. Given any pair of objects X, Y we denote by $0 : X \longrightarrow Y$ the morphism $X \overset{\rho}{\longrightarrow} 0 \longrightarrow Y$. A morphism of this form is obviously a null map and will be called a ρ-*null* map, so there is a unique ρ-null map $X \longrightarrow Y$ for all X, Y. Further, a morphism $\alpha : X \longrightarrow Y$ is ρ-*nulling* if for all ρ-null $0 : Y \longrightarrow Z$, $\alpha 0 = 0 : X \longrightarrow Z$.

We can now recapture the intuition of **2**:

7   PROPOSITION   *If ρ is a projection system then for $P \in Summ(X)$, $Dom(\rho_{XP})$ $= P$ and ρ_{XP} is determined by diagram **2**.*

Proof   The left hand square commutes by **3(2)** letting $Q = P$. The right hand square obtains similarly with P', P for P, Q. Since identity morphisms are total and ρ-null maps are null, it follows from the uniqueness of kernel-domain decomposition **(6.13)** that $Dom(\rho_{XP}) = P$. $\square$

A preadditive Boolean category has zero morphisms and projections defined by **2** (see **7.2**.) It follows from the next proposition, then, that such projections constitute a projection system.

8   PROPOSITION   *A Boolean category with zero morphisms has a unique projection system.*

Proof   As there is only one null morphism $P' \longrightarrow P$, the diagram of 2 defines the only possible candidate for the ρ_{XP}. That $\rho_{XX} = id_X$ is clear. For the remaining axiom, since $i : P \longrightarrow X$ is crisp, it pulls back the coproduct Q, Q' to yield a commutative diagram

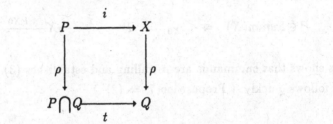

whose top row is a coproduct. Thus to establish the commutativity of

$$
\begin{array}{ccc}
P & \xrightarrow{\ \ i\ \ } & X \\
{\scriptstyle \rho}\downarrow & & \downarrow{\scriptstyle \rho} \\
P \cap Q & \xrightarrow{\ \ t\ \ } & Q
\end{array}
$$

it suffices to verify this preceded by k and k'. To this end, use 7 (with P for X and $P \cap Q$ for Q.) We have $k(\rho t) = (k\rho)t = t$ whereas $k(i\rho) = (ki)\rho = (tj)\rho = t(j\rho)$ $= t$ and $k'\rho t = 0t = 0$ whereas $k'i\rho = uj'\rho = u0 = 0$. $\square$

If ρ is a projection system it is obvious that $0\alpha = 0$ for any α so that the ρ-null maps form a family of zeroes if and only if every morphism is ρ-nulling. As the following lemma records, there are always a goodly number of ρ-nulling morphisms.

9 LEMMA   *Let ρ be a projection system. The following hold.*

    1. (See **6**) *Given X and $\alpha : Y \longrightarrow Z$,*

$$
X \xrightarrow{\ 0\ } Y \xrightarrow{\ \alpha\ } Z \ = \ X \xrightarrow{\ 0\ } Z.
$$

    2. *If $\alpha : X \longrightarrow Y$ is any of: ρ-null, a summand, a ρ-projection*

or an isomorphism, then α is ρ–nulling.

3.   *Given $\alpha : X \longrightarrow Y$, $\beta : Y \longrightarrow Z$, if α, β are ρ–nulling then so
     is $\alpha\beta$; if β is a summand and $\alpha\beta$ is ρ–nulling then α is ρ–nulling;
     if β is a summand and $\alpha\beta$ is ρ–null then α is ρ–null.*

4.   *If $P \xrightarrow{\ i\ } X \xleftarrow{\ i'\ } P'$ is a coproduct then, given $\alpha : X \longrightarrow Y$,
     α is ρ–null if and only if $i\alpha$ and $i'\alpha$ are ρ–null; and, α is ρ–nulling
     if and only if $i\alpha$ and $i'\alpha$ are ρ–nulling.*

5.   *For all $\alpha : X \longrightarrow Y$, α is ρ–null if and only if α is null and ρ–nulling.*

Proof   Axiom 3(2) with $Q = 0$ gives

10       $P \in Summ(X) \;\Rightarrow\; \rho_{X0} \;=\; P \xrightarrow{\quad i \quad} X \xrightarrow{\ \rho_{X0}\ } 0.$

This shows that summands are ρ–nulling and establishes (3) (use $i = \beta$) and (4). The
rest follows quickly (Proposition 7 $\Rightarrow$ (2) .) $\square$

We can now give the promised connection between projection systems and zero-
subcategories.

11   THEOREM   *If ρ is a projection system for $\mathcal{B}$, the $\mathcal{B}$–objects and ρ–nulling maps
constitute a maximal zero-subcategory $\mathcal{B}_\rho$ of $\mathcal{B}$ and the passage $\rho \mapsto \mathcal{B}_\rho$ establishes a
bijection between projection systems and maximal zero-subcategories. Further, if $\mathcal{C}$ is
any zero-subcategory of $\mathcal{B}$ then $\mathcal{C} \subset \mathcal{B}_\rho$ for ρ the unique projection system for $\mathcal{C}$ of
Proposition 8.*

Proof   Let ρ be a projection system for $\mathcal{B}$. It follows from Lemma 9 that $\mathcal{B}_\rho$ is a
subcategory, that a coproduct diagram of $\mathcal{B}$ is one of $\mathcal{B}_\rho$ as well and that the pullback
diagram associated with $[\alpha]Q$ is a pullback in $\mathcal{B}_\rho$ when α is in $\mathcal{B}_\rho$. It is then clear that
$\mathcal{B}_\rho$ is a wide Boolean subcategory. Since ρ acts as a projection system for $\mathcal{B}_\rho$ and since
every morphism of $\mathcal{B}_\rho$ is ρ–nulling by construction, $\mathcal{B}_\rho$ is a zero-subcategory. If $\mathcal{B}_\rho \subset \mathcal{C}$

with $\mathcal{C}$ a zero-subcategory then both subcategories share the same zero object and so the ρ-null maps form the zeroes of $\mathcal{C}$; but then every $\mathcal{C}$-morphism is ρ-nulling, so $\mathcal{C} = \mathcal{B}_\rho$. So far we have shown that for each ρ, $\mathcal{B}_\rho$ is a maximal zero-subcategory of $\mathcal{C}$. Continuing, $\rho \mapsto \mathcal{B}_\rho$ is injective by Proposition 7. To complete the proof, it suffices to show that if $\mathcal{C}$ is any zero-subcategory with unique projection system ρ as in 8 (which is clearly also a projection system for $\mathcal{B}$) then $\mathcal{C} \subset \mathcal{B}_\rho$. But, as just argued above, every morphism in $\mathcal{C}$ is ρ-nulling. □

For the balance of the section we study the structure of a Boolean category equipped with a projection system.

12 LEMMA *Let ρ be a projection system and let $P \subset Q$ in $Summ(X)$. Then*
$$X \xrightarrow{\ \rho\ } Q \xrightarrow{\ \rho\ } P \ = \ X \xrightarrow{\ \rho\ } P.$$

Proof X is the three-component coproduct of $i : P \longrightarrow X$, $t : P' \cap Q \longrightarrow X$, and $u : P' \cap Q' \longrightarrow X$ so we must show that $z\rho_{XQ}\rho_{QP} = z\rho_{XP}$ for $z \in \{i, t, u\}$. We have

$$
\begin{array}{ccccc}
P' \cap Q & \xrightarrow{\ a\ } & P' & \xleftarrow{\ a'\ } & P' \cap Q' \\
{\scriptstyle k'}\downarrow & & {\scriptstyle i'}\downarrow & & \downarrow{\scriptstyle b} \\
Q & \xrightarrow{\ j\ } & X & \xleftarrow{\ j'\ } & Q'
\end{array}
$$

where $ai' = t = k'j$ and $a'i' = u = bj'$. Then, using 7, $t\rho_{XQ}\rho_{QP} = k'id_X\rho_{QP}$ $= k'\rho_{QP} = 0$ (the last obtains because the coproduct complement of k' is $k :$ $P \longrightarrow Q$) whereas $t\rho_{XP} = ai'\rho_{XP} = a0 = 0$ (summands are ρ-nulling.) Similarly, $u\rho_{XP} = 0$ and also $u\rho_{XQ}\rho_{QP} = a'i'\rho_{XQ}\rho_{QP} = a'0\rho_{QP} = 0$. Finally, we have $i\rho_{XP} = id_P$ whereas $i = kj$ for $j : Q \longrightarrow X$ so $i\rho_{XQ}\rho_{QP} = k(j\rho_{XQ})\rho_{QP} = k\rho_{QP} = id_P$. □

As promised, we now introduce guards.

13 DEFINITION   In any Boolean category, a *guard* is an endomorphism which fixes its domain, that is, a morphism $p : X \longrightarrow X$ with the property that $ip = i$ where $i : D \longrightarrow X = Dom(p)$.

Intuitively, "p guards D. If $x \in D$, $xp = x$ whereas x is mapped by a null morphism for $x \notin D$ since D' is the kernel of p".

14 DEFINITION   If ρ is a projection system, say that an endomorphism of X is a ρ-*guard* if it is a guard which is ρ-null on its kernel. Denote the set of all ρ-guards $X \longrightarrow X$ by $Guard_\rho(X)$.

15 THEOREM   *Let ρ be a projection system and let X be an object. Then the passages*

$$Summ(X) \overset{\Gamma}{\longrightarrow} Guard_\rho(X) \qquad\qquad Guard_\rho(X) \overset{\Delta}{\longrightarrow} Summ(X)$$
$$P \mapsto p \qquad\qquad\qquad\qquad p \mapsto Dom(p)$$

where $P\Gamma = p$ is defined by the diagram

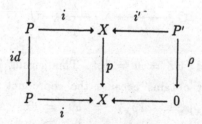

are mutually-inverse bijections. Moreover, if $p = P\Gamma$, $q = Q\Gamma$, then $(P \bigcap Q)\Gamma = pq$.

Proof   If $p = P\Gamma$, P',P is a kernel-domain decomposition of p so $P\Gamma\Delta = P$ by Proposition 6.13. If $i : P \longrightarrow X = p\Delta$ with complement $i' : P' \longrightarrow X$ then, as $p \in Guard_\rho(X)$, $ip = i$ and $i'p = 0$ so $p\Delta\Gamma = p$. For $P = Dom(p)$, $Q = Dom(q)$ it remains to show that pq is a guard with $Dom(pq) = P \bigcap Q$. To this end, first note

16 OBSERVATION *The ρ-guard corresponding to the summand $i : P\longrightarrow X$, namely $P\Gamma$, is given as* $X\xrightarrow{\ \rho\ }P\xrightarrow{\ i\ }X$. *This is immediate from the definition of* Γ *and* **7, 9** *since* $i(\rho_{XP}i) = (i\rho_{XP})i = i$ *and* $i'(\rho_{XP}i) = (i'\rho_{XP})i = 0i = 0$. $\qquad\square$

To complete the proof of the theorem, apply **3**(2), **12** and **16** to the diagram

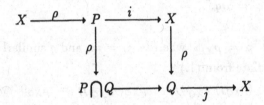

observing that the upper path is pq and the lower is the guard of $P\bigcap Q$. $\qquad\square$

17 NOTATIONS Rather than retain the symbols Γ, Δ of **15**, we use the simpler convention that upper case denotes summands and corresponding lower case denotes guards. Thus, given $P \in Summ(X)$,

$\qquad P\Gamma$ *is denoted p and, given q, $q\Delta$ is denoted Q.*

By virtue of Theorem **15**, $Guard_\rho(X)$ is a Boolean algebra with Γ, Δ Boolean isomorphisms. The ρ-null map $0 : X\longrightarrow X$ is indeed the Boolean zero and id_X is the greatest element. Thus $p \wedge q = pq = (p' \vee q')'$ etc.

The following lemma and observation will be useful in the next section.

18 LEMMA *Let ρ be a projection system. Let* $\alpha, \beta : X\longrightarrow Y$, $i : P\longrightarrow X$ $\in Summ(X)$, $j : Q\longrightarrow Y$ $\in Summ(Y)$. *Then the following hold:*

1. $i\alpha = i\beta \Leftrightarrow p\alpha = p\beta$.

2. $\alpha\, \rho_{YQ} = \beta\, \rho_{YQ} \Leftrightarrow \alpha q = \beta q$.

3. If $p\alpha = p\beta$ and $p'\alpha = p'\beta$ then $\alpha = \beta$.

4. $qq' = 0 = q0$ (so that ρ-guards are ρ-nulling.)

5. $i : P \longrightarrow X$ is the equalizer of id_X, $p : X \longrightarrow X$ in $\mathfrak{B}$.

6. $p'\alpha = 0 \Leftrightarrow p\alpha = \alpha$.

7. If α is ρ-nulling then $\alpha q'\rho$-null $\Leftrightarrow \alpha = \alpha q$. In general, $\alpha q'$ null $\Leftrightarrow \alpha = \alpha q$.

Proof   (1,2): $p = \rho_{XP}i$ whereas $i = ip$, and q similarly.

(3): Immediate from (1.)

(4): $qq' = (\rho_{XQ}j)(\rho_{XQ'})j' = \rho_{XQ}(j\rho_{XQ'})j' = \rho_{XQ}0$ which is 0 by Lemma 9(2). Similarly, $q0 = 0$ as q is the composition of a projection and a summand.   We pause for

19 OBSERVATION

19 OBSERVATION Let $j : Q \longrightarrow Y$ be a summand. Then with respect to any projection system, j is the kernel of its complementary guard, $j = Ker(q')$. This observation follows from 7 and 16 since, because j' is a monomorphism, $Ker(q') = Ker(\rho_{YQ'}j') = j$.   □

(5): By 19, $i = Ker(p')$. For any γ, if $\gamma p = \gamma$ then $\gamma p' = \gamma pp' = \gamma 0$ is a null morphism (not necessarily ρ-null) so factors through $Ker(q')$.

(6): If $p\alpha = \alpha$, $p'\alpha = p'p\alpha = 0\alpha = 0$. For the converse, in general we have $ip\alpha = i\alpha$ and $i'p\alpha = 0$, so we must show $p'\alpha = 0 \Rightarrow i'\alpha = 0$ and this is immediate from (4) since $i' = i'p'$.

(7): If $\alpha q = \alpha$, $\alpha q' = \alpha qq' = \alpha 0$ is null and is 0 if α is ρ-nulling. Conversely, $j = Ker(q')$ by 19 so if $\alpha q' = 0$, there exists β with $\beta j = \alpha$ and $\alpha q = \beta jq = \beta q = \alpha$.

□

In **3.21** we introduced the "infinite loop" morphisms associated with a pre-polymorphic iterate. The next result relates this construction to the theory of this section.

20   THEOREM *Let $\mathfrak{B}$ be a Boolean category and let $(-)^{\dagger}$ be a pre-polymorphic iterate on $\mathfrak{B}$ (as defined in* **3.19.**) *Denote by $0 : X \longrightarrow Y$ the morphism $in_X^{\dagger}$ of* **3.21.** *Then the following statements hold.*

1. *The system ρ defined by* **2** *using $0 : X \longrightarrow Y$ as above is a projection system on $\mathfrak{B}$, and $\mathfrak{B}_{\rho}$ consists precisely of the $\dagger$–pure morphisms of* **3.23.**

2. *If $(-)^{\dagger}$ is a polymorphic iterate then $\xi \in \mathfrak{B}_{\rho} \Rightarrow \xi^{\dagger} \in \mathfrak{B}_{\rho}$ and the restriction of $(-)^{\dagger}$ to $\mathfrak{B}_{\rho}$ is an unrestricted polymorphic iterate.*

Proof   It is an immediate consequence of **2** that $\rho_{XX} = id_X$ and that the diagram

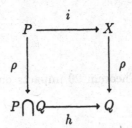

commutes restricted to $h : P \bigcap Q \longrightarrow Q$ as both paths $P \bigcap Q \longrightarrow Q$ are h. As $P \bigcap Q \longrightarrow P \longleftarrow^{k} P \bigcap Q'$ is a coproduct it remains to show that the square commutes restricted to k. This in turns requires that $k0 = 0h$, that is, that $0h = 0$ and this is true by Proposition **3.20** which asserts that all summands are $\dagger$–pure, whereas $\dagger$–pure is ρ–nulling by definition. This establishes the first statement. For the second, observe that each 0 is $\dagger$–pure and so belongs to $\mathfrak{B}_{\rho}$. Since $0 \oplus 0 :$ $X + Y \longrightarrow 0 + 0 = 0$ can be constructed in $\mathfrak{B}_{\rho}$ where 0 is a zero object, this morphism is 0. But then if $\xi : X \longrightarrow X + Y$ is $\dagger$–pure we have that both $0 \, in_1$ and $\xi(0 \oplus 0)$ are $0 : X \longrightarrow 0 + 0$ so that $\xi^{\dagger}0 = 0$ because $0 \in \mathcal{H}_{\dagger}$. Here the codomains of the 0 are the object 0 but it then follows at once that $\xi^{\dagger}0 = 0$ where the 0 have arbitrary codomain, so $\xi^{\dagger}$ is $\dagger$–pure. The rest is routine. $\square$

In the proof of Proposition **3.28** we postponed until now the proof that $< id_X, id_X > \in \mathcal{H}_\dagger$.

21 COROLLARY *Let $(-)^\dagger$ be a polymorphic iterate on $\mathcal{B}$ with canonical projection system ρ. Then the following hold.*

1. *If* $\alpha : X \longrightarrow Z, \quad \beta : Y \longrightarrow Z \quad \in \mathcal{H}_\dagger, \quad < \alpha, \beta > : X + Y \longrightarrow Z$ $\in \mathcal{H}_\dagger$.

2. *All ρ-guards belong to $\mathcal{H}_\dagger$.*

3. *All ρ-null morphisms belong to $\mathcal{H}_\dagger$.*

Proof These and other related properties are immediate because $\mathcal{H}_\dagger \subset \mathcal{B}$ is an extension. $\square$

We pause to explore how Theorem **20** impacts on the Main and Black category of **3.24**.

22 EXAMPLE Continuing with the discussion of **3.24**, It is easy to show that every isomorphism in **Mfn**$_\perp$ is a bijective total function (just show that if α, β are inverse then $\perp \notin x\alpha$, $\perp \notin y\beta$ and then use the calculations provided by the diligent reader in establishing that **Mfn** was Boolean in Example **4.4**.) It follows that the inclusions of subsets are the only summands of X. It is then easy to see that $[\alpha]Q = \{x \in X : x\alpha \subset Q + \{\perp\}\}$ provides the needed pullbacks and the remaining details that **Mfn**$_\perp$ is Boolean are routine. Notice that **Mfn** $\subset$ **Mfn**$_\perp$ is a Boolean extension.

Define two projection systems on **Mfn**$_\perp$, ρ and θ, as follows. For $P \in Summ(X)$,

22a $\qquad X \xrightarrow{\rho} P, \; x \mapsto x$ if $x \in P$, $\emptyset$ otherwise;

22b $\qquad X\xrightarrow{\ \theta\ }P, \ x \ \mapsto \ x$ if $x \in P, \ \perp$ otherwise.

Verification of the axioms of **3** for ρ is routine, whereas θ is the projection system of **20** for the (in fact polymorphic —verify!) iterate of **3.24**. The ρ–null maps are always empty whereas θ–null maps diverge (and do nothing else.) The ρ–guard of P is undefined if $x \notin P$ whereas the θ–guard diverges for $x \notin P$. The zero subcategories of nulling maps are as follows.

22c $\qquad X\xrightarrow{\ \alpha\ }Y \ \in \ (\mathbf{Mfn}_{\perp})_\rho \ \Leftrightarrow \ \forall x \ \perp \ \notin x\alpha;$

22d $\qquad X\xrightarrow{\ \alpha\ }Y \ \in \ (\mathbf{Mfn}_{\perp})_\theta \ \Leftrightarrow \ \forall x \ \ x\alpha \neq \emptyset.$

Thus $(\mathbf{Mfn}_{\perp})_\rho \ \cong \ \mathbf{Mfn}$ under the embedding described above. As an abstract Boolean category, $(\mathbf{Mfn}_{\perp})_\theta$ is also isomorphic to $\mathbf{Mfn}$ if we reinterpret $\perp$ as "undefined".

23 EXAMPLE For $\perp \in \Omega_0$, the zero-subcategory $\Omega_{\perp}$ of Ω induced by the projection system corresponding to $\perp$ of Example **5** in the manner of Theorem **11** is an ω–complete category as defined in **3.9** if $\alpha \leq \beta$ is the pointwise order in $\Omega_{\perp}(X,Y)$ induced by the partial order on $Y\Omega$ described in **1.12**. We leave it as an exercise for the reader to generalize the *while-do* in **1.12** to a polymorphic iterate for Ω whose restriction to $\Omega_\rho = \Omega_{\perp}$ as in **20** is just the one described above.

We conclude with

24 PROPOSITION *Let $i : P\longrightarrow X$ be a summand in a preadditive Boolean category and let p be the ρ–guard of P for the unique projection system ρ. Then $p + p'$ exists and is id_X. Moreover, for $\alpha, \beta : X\longrightarrow Y$, $if_P(\alpha, \beta) = p\alpha + p'\beta$.*

Proof Choose a coproduct $X\xrightarrow{\ j\ }X+X\xleftarrow{\ j'\ }X$ so that $p = \rho j, \ p' = \rho' j'$ by **16**. Then $p + p' = id_X$ by **7.10** and, in turn, $p\alpha + p'\beta$ exists by **7.8(2)**. If $I = if_P(\alpha, \beta)$, I is defined by $iI = i\alpha, \ i'I = i'\beta$. Indeed, $i(p\alpha + p'\beta) = (ip)\alpha + (ip')\beta = i\alpha + 0 = i\alpha$ and by the same means $i'(p\alpha + p'\beta) = i'\beta$. $\qquad\qquad\square$

9 HOARE ASSERTIONS AND WHILE-DO

The primary intuitive meaning of the Hoare-style assertion $\{P\}\ \alpha\ \{Q\}$ is that for $x \in P$, all halting states (if any) of $x\alpha$ are in Q [Hoare 1969]. We define this for $\alpha :$ $X \longrightarrow Y$, $P \in Summ(X)$, $Q \in Summ(Y)$ in an arbitrary Boolean category, and establish a number of standard properties. The guards introduced in the previous section provide the tool to prove the *while-do* rule

Let $\mathcal{B}$ be a Boolean category.

1 DEFINITION AND PROPOSITION *Given* $\alpha : X \longrightarrow Y$, $i : P \longrightarrow X$ $\in Summ(X)$, $j : Q \longrightarrow Y \in Summ(Y)$ *the following four conditions are equivalent. If they hold we write* $\{P\}\ \alpha\ \{Q\}$ *and call such an assertion a* Hoare assertion.

1. *The P–restriction of α factors through Q, that is, there exists (necessarily unique) β with $\beta j = i\alpha$ as shown:*

$$
\begin{array}{ccc}
P & \overset{\beta}{\dashrightarrow} & Q \\
\downarrow{\scriptstyle i} & & \downarrow{\scriptstyle j} \\
X & \underset{\alpha}{\longrightarrow} & Y
\end{array}
$$

2. $P \subset [\alpha]Q$.

3. *If* $Y \overset{in_1}{\longrightarrow} Y + Y \overset{in_2}{\longleftarrow} Y$ *is a coproduct with corresponding*

fanout $F : Y \longrightarrow Y + Y$ *for* Q *as in 2.21 then* $i\alpha F = i \alpha \, in_1$.

4. *For all objects* Z *and morphisms* $t, u : Y \longrightarrow Z$,
   $v : X \longrightarrow Z$, $if_P(\alpha t, v) = if_P(\alpha \, if_Q(t, u), v)$ *(where,*
   as in 2.21–23, $if_P(a, b) = F < a, b > .)$

Proof That $1 \Leftrightarrow 2$ is obvious from the pullback property of $[\alpha]Q$. Proposition 5.15 gives $1 \Leftrightarrow 3$. The equation of (4), by restricting to the injections $i : P \longrightarrow X$ and i' $: P' \longrightarrow X$, reduces to $i\alpha t = i\alpha \, if_Q(t, u)$ (since $i'\alpha v = i'\alpha v$ is surely always true) which in turn, using F as in (3), reduces to $i\alpha t = i\alpha F < t, u >$. Thus if (3) holds, $i\alpha F < t, u > = i\alpha in_1 < t, u > = i\alpha t$ as needed. Conversely, if (4) holds, apply $i\alpha t$ $= i\alpha F < t, u >$ for t, u the coproduct injections of $Y + Y$ to get $i\alpha F =$ $i\alpha F < in_1, in_2 > = i \alpha \, in_1$. $\qquad\qquad\Box$

An immediate corollary is: $[\alpha]Q = eq(\alpha F, \alpha \, in_1)$.

Further characterizations of $\{P\} \, \alpha \, \{Q\}$ exist using guards for a Boolean category with projection system, as is seen below in Proposition 7.

If $\mathcal{C}$ is a Boolean subcategory of $\mathcal{B}$ and if $P \in Summ(X)$, $\alpha : X \longrightarrow Y$, $Q \in Summ(Y)$ in $\mathcal{C}$, then $\{P\} \, \alpha \, \{Q\}$ in $\mathcal{C}$ if and only if $\{P\} \, \alpha \, \{Q\}$ in $\mathcal{B}$. This is immediate from 1(2), but there is a subtle point: if $P, R \in Summ(X)$ in $\mathcal{C}$, a summand inclusion $P \longrightarrow R$ in $\mathcal{B}$ is necessarily in $\mathcal{C}$ since it can be written as the pullback of $[P \to X]Q$.

2 REMARK In [Bloom and Ésik, 1988] a class of categories (not Boolean in general) is studied with objectives similar to those of this book. In this framework they create Boolean algebras whose elements are maps $T : X \longrightarrow X + X$ in the style of Proposition 2.32, but they cannot pull back the injections to a coproduct decomposition of X. They define $\{T\} \, \alpha \, \{U\}$ by the equation

$$X \xrightarrow{\quad T \quad} X + X \xrightarrow{\quad \alpha \oplus id_X \quad} Y + X$$

$$T \downarrow \qquad\qquad\qquad\qquad\qquad\qquad \downarrow U \oplus id_X$$

$$X + X \xrightarrow[\alpha \oplus id_X]{} Y + X \xrightarrow[in_{13}]{} Y + Y + X$$

In a Boolean category, one can form the coproduct decomposition $P \xrightarrow{\ i\ } X \xleftarrow{\ i'\ } P'$ corresponding to T and break this into two equations by restricting to i and i'. The $i'-$restriction always commutes so the entire equation reduces to 1(3) above (using the fact that in_{13} is monomorphic.)

Some of the basic properties of Hoare assertions are summed up in the following proposition.

3 PROPOSITION   *The following statements are valid.*

1. $P \subset P_1 \iff \{P\}\, id_X\, \{P_1\}$ *for* $P, P_1 \in Summ(X)$.

2. $\{0\}\, \alpha\, \{Q\}$ *for* $\alpha : X \longrightarrow Y$, $Q \in Summ(Y)$.

3. $\{P\}\, \alpha\, \{Y\}$ *for* $P \in Summ(X)$, $\alpha : X \longrightarrow Y$.

4. *If* $P_1 \subset P$ *and* $Q \subset Q_1$ *with* $P, P_1 \in Summ(X)$, $\alpha : X \longrightarrow Y$ *and* $Q, Q_1 \in Summ(Y)$ *then* $\{P\}\, \alpha\, \{Q\} \Rightarrow \{P_1\}\, \alpha\, \{Q_1\}$.

5. *(Composition rule)* *If* $X \xrightarrow{\ \alpha\ } Y \xrightarrow{\ \beta\ } Z$, $P \in Summ(X)$, $Q \in Summ(Y)$, $R \in Summ(Z)$, *then* $\{P\}\, \alpha\, \{Q\}$ *and* $\{Q\}\, \beta\, \{R\}$ $\Rightarrow \{P\}\, \alpha\beta\, \{R\}$.

6. *(Interpolation property)* *If* $X \xrightarrow{\ \alpha\ } Y \xrightarrow{\ \beta\ } Z$, $P \in Summ(X)$, $R \in Summ(Z)$ *then if* $\{P\}\, \alpha\beta\, \{R\}$ *there exists* $Q \in Summ(Y)$ *with* $\{P\}\, \alpha\, \{Q\}$ *and* $\{Q\}\, \beta\, \{R\}$.

7. $\{P\}\, \alpha\, \{Q \bigcap R\} \iff \{P\}\, \alpha\, \{Q\} \wedge \{P\}\, \alpha\, \{R\}$ *for* $P \in Summ(X)$, $Q, R \in Summ(Y)$ *and* $\alpha : X \longrightarrow Y$.

8. $\{P \bigcup Q\} \, \alpha \, \{R\} \iff \{P\} \, \alpha \, \{R\} \; \wedge \; \{Q\} \, \alpha \, \{R\}$ for $P, Q \in$ $Summ(X)$, $R \in Summ(Y)$ and $\alpha : X \longrightarrow Y$.

9. *(Hoare conditional rule)* For $P, Q \in Summ(X)$, $\beta : X \longrightarrow Y$, $R \in Summ(Y)$, and $if_P(\alpha, \beta)$ as described before **5.13**,

$$\{Q\} \; if_P(\alpha, \beta) \; \{R\} \iff \{P \bigcap Q\} \, \alpha \, \{R\} \; \wedge \; \{P' \bigcap Q\} \, \beta \, \{R\}.$$

10. For $P \in Summ(X_1 + \cdots + X_n)$, $\alpha_i : X_i \longrightarrow Y$
    $(i = 1, \ldots, n)$, $Q \in Summ(Y)$,

$$\{P\} \; <\alpha_1, \ldots, \alpha_n> \; \{Q\} \iff \{P \bigcap X_i\} \, \alpha_i \, \{Q\} \; \text{for all } i = 1, \ldots, n.$$

11. If α is a null map, $\{P\} \, \alpha \, \{Q\}$ holds for all $P \in Summ(X)$, $Q \in Summ(Y)$.

Proof $1, \ldots, 5$ are obvious from $1(1)$. For (6) set $Q = [\beta]R$ and use the pullback property. (7) is immediate from the fact that intersections in $Summ(Y)$ are pullbacks. In (8), $\Rightarrow$ follows from (4). To prove $\Leftarrow$ consult the diagrams below. Since $P \xrightarrow{a} P \bigcup Q \xleftarrow{b} P' \bigcap Q$ is a coproduct by Theorem 5.11,

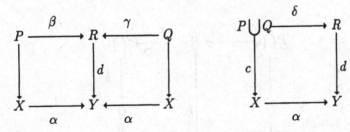

if β, γ exist define δ by $a\delta = \beta$, $b\delta = P' \bigcap Q \longrightarrow Q \xrightarrow{\gamma} R$; $\delta d = c\alpha$ because this is true preceded by a and by b. Now for (9). Recall that $if_P(\alpha, \beta)$ is defined by

4

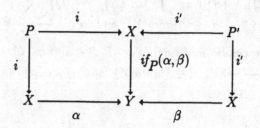

By Theorem 5.11, $P \bigcap Q \xrightarrow{\quad a \quad} Q \xleftarrow{\quad b \quad} P' \bigcap Q$ is a coproduct. Now $\{Q\}\, if_P(\alpha, \beta)$ $\{R\}$ holds if and only if there exists γ as shown in the diagram

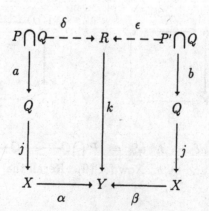

whereas $\{P \bigcap Q\}\, \alpha\, \{R\}$ and $\{P' \bigcap Q\}\, \beta\, \{R\}$ are equivalent to the existence of δ, ϵ in the following diagram:

If γ exists, define $\delta = a\gamma$, $\epsilon = b\gamma$ whence $\delta k = a\gamma k = a\, j\, if_P(\alpha,\beta) = c\, i\, if_P(\alpha,\beta)$ $= ci\alpha = aj\alpha$ and $\epsilon k = bj\beta$ similarly. Conversely, if δ, ϵ exist define γ by $a\gamma = \delta$, $b\gamma = \epsilon$. Then $a\gamma k = \delta k = aj\alpha = ci\alpha = c\, i\, if_P(\alpha,\beta) = a\, j\, if_P(\alpha,\beta)$ and $b\gamma k = b\, j\, if_P(\alpha,\beta)$ similarly so $\gamma k = j\, if_P(\alpha,\beta)$. To prove (10), we use (8) applied to $P = \bigcup(P \bigcap X_i)$ as follows. Write $X = X_1 + \cdots + X_n$, and $\alpha = <\alpha_1,...,\alpha_n>$ and consider the diagram

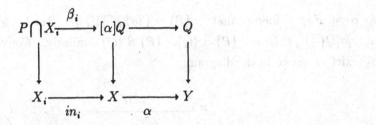

Then $\{P\}\, \alpha\, \{Q\} \Leftrightarrow \forall i\; \{P \bigcap X_i\}\, \alpha\, \{Q\} \Leftrightarrow \forall i\; \beta_i$ exists $\Leftrightarrow \forall i\; \{P \bigcap X_i\}\, \alpha_i\, \{Q\}$. Finally, we prove (11) by noting that $[\alpha]Q = X$ when α is null. Write $\alpha = X \xrightarrow{\beta} 0 \longrightarrow Y$. Since any summand of 0 is a trivial object, $[0 \to Y]Q = 0$. Then, using **5.20**, and noting that β is null, $[\alpha]Q = [\beta]0 = Ker(\beta) = X$. $\qquad\square$

It follows from 3(11) that all null morphisms $X \longrightarrow Y$ are indiscernible in the sense of Definition 5.21. Thus if Dijkstra's dictum that an action is determined by its predicate transformer were adhered to, we could not distinguish between divergence and failing in a Boolean category.

5 PROPOSITION *In a preadditive Boolean category, if* $\alpha, \beta : X \longrightarrow Y$ *and* $\alpha + \beta$ *exists then* $\{P\}\, \alpha + \beta\, \{Q\} \Leftrightarrow \{P\}\, \alpha\, \{Q\} \wedge \{P\}\, \beta\, \{Q\}$ *for all* $P \in Summ(X)$, $Q \in Summ(Y)$.

Proof Let $F : X \longrightarrow Y + Y$ with $F\rho_1 = \alpha$, $F\rho_2 = \beta$ so that $F\sigma = \alpha + \beta$. We will use Y_m, $m = 1, 2$, to denote the summand $in_m : Y \longrightarrow Y + Y$. First suppose $\{P\}\, F\sigma\, \{Q\}$ so that $\{P\}\, F\, \{[\sigma]Q\}$. Letting $\rho : [\sigma]Q \longrightarrow [\sigma]Q \bigcap Y_1$ denote the coproduct projection, it follows from the basic projection-system axiom (see the remark preceding 8.8) that

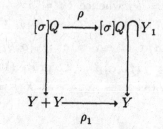

As $\alpha = F\rho_1$, it follows that $\{P\} \alpha \{ [\sigma]Q \bigcap Y_1 \}$. But by 3(10) with $\alpha_1 = id_Y = \alpha_2$, $[\sigma]Q \bigcap Y_1 \subset Q$, so $\{P\} \alpha \{Q\}$. $\{P\} \beta \{Q\}$ similarly. Conversely, assume that γ_1, γ_2 exist as shown in the diagram

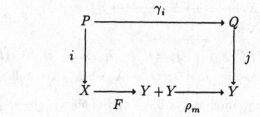

Observe that $\gamma_1 + \gamma_2$ exists since, using Proposition **7.10** and the projection $\theta :$ $Y \longrightarrow Q$, $iF = iF\rho_1 in_1 + iF\rho_2 in_2 = \gamma_1 j\, in_1 + \gamma_2 j\, in_2$ whence $iF\sigma\theta = \gamma_1 + \gamma_2$. The desired result follows because then $i(\alpha + \beta) = iF\sigma = \gamma_1 j + \gamma_2 j = (\gamma_1 + \gamma_2)j$ so $\{P\} \alpha + \beta \{Q\}$. $\qquad\qquad\qquad\qquad\qquad\qquad\qquad\qquad\qquad\qquad\qquad\qquad\qquad$ □

6 PROPOSITION *If ρ is a projection system for $\mathfrak{B}$ and if $p : X \longrightarrow X$ is a ρ-guard then for all $\alpha : X \longrightarrow Y$, $Q \in Summ(X)$, $R \in Summ(Y)$,*

$$\{Q\}\, p\alpha\, \{R\} \Leftrightarrow \{P \bigcap Q\}\, \alpha\, \{R\} \ .$$

Proof Consider the diagram

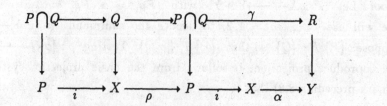

in which the middle square is an instance for the projection system axioms. If γ exists (that is to say if $\{P \bigcap Q\}\ \alpha\ \{R\}$), paste on the middle square to see $\{Q\}\ p\alpha\ \{R\}$, noting that $p = \rho i$. Conversely, if the rectangle consisting of the perimeter of the rightmost two squares is given (i.e. if $\{Q\}\ p\alpha\ \{R\}$), paste on the leftmost square to get the assertion $\{P \bigcap Q\}\ \alpha\ \{R\}$, recalling that $ip = i$.   □

The interesting thing about the next proposition is that it makes use of a projection system ρ but applies to arbitrary morphisms and (not necessarily $\rho-$) null maps.

7 PROPOSITION *Let ρ be a projection system for $\mathcal{B}$ and recall the notational conventions for guards of 8.17. Given $i : P \longrightarrow X\ \in Summ(X)$, $\alpha : X \longrightarrow Y$ and $j : Q \longrightarrow Y\ \in Summ(Y)$, the following statements are equivalent:*

1. $\{P\}\ \alpha\ \{Q\}$.
2. $i\alpha q'$ is null ($\Leftrightarrow p\alpha q'$ is null.)
3. $i\alpha = i\alpha q$ ($\Leftrightarrow p\alpha = p\alpha q$.)

Proof The alternate versions of (2,3) follows from 8.18. For $1 \Leftrightarrow 2$, $\{P\}\ \alpha\ \{Q\} \Leftrightarrow i\alpha$ factors through $j \Leftrightarrow i\alpha q' = 0$ (the last because by 8.19, $j = Ker(q')$.) For $2 \Leftrightarrow 3$ use 8.18(7).   □

Since $i\alpha q'$ is null if and only if it is ρ-null when α is ρ-nulling (8.9(5)), restricted to the zero-subcategory $\mathcal{B}_\rho$, $\{P\}\ \alpha\ \{Q\} \Leftrightarrow p\alpha q'$ ρ-null. One could also consider the assertion "$p\alpha q'$ ρ-null" for a given projection system ρ applied to a general $\mathcal{B}$-morphism α. The next example illustrates.

8 EXAMPLE Consider the category $Mfn_\perp$ of strict multi-valued functions of Examples **3.25, 8.22**, and its two projection systems ρ, θ. [Main and Black 1989] emphasize the Hoare-style assertion $[P]\ \alpha\ [Q] \Leftrightarrow p\alpha q'$ is ρ-null; here, as usual, p, q are the ρ-guards correponding to P, Q. It is easily verified that this assertion holds if and only if $x \in P \Rightarrow \bot \notin x\alpha \subset Q$. This appears more like total correctness than partial correctness since non-divergence is guaranteed. But abortion may still occur since the assertion is true if $x \in P$ and $x\alpha = \emptyset$. Contrast with the alternate assertion $[P]\,\alpha\,[Q]$ $\Leftrightarrow p\alpha q'$ is θ-null (where now p, q are the corresponding θ-guards.) This holds if and only if $x \in P \Rightarrow \emptyset \neq x\alpha \subset Q \bigcup \{\bot\}$, so abortion cannot occur but divergence is possible. In both cases, "$p\alpha q'$ is null" is equivalent to $x\alpha \subset Q$ by 7.

The remainder of this section is devoted to defining *while-do* and establishing standard proof-rules for it. We assume that the Boolean category $\mathfrak{B}$ is equipped with a polymorphic iterate $(-)^\dagger$ as in **3.26**. Let ρ be the canonical projection system of Theorem **6.20**. We are thus free to use the characterizations of $\{P\}\,\alpha\,\{Q\}$ of Proposition 7.

9 DEFINITION   With respect to the polymorphic iterate $(-)^\dagger$, for $P \in Summ(X)$, $\alpha : X \longrightarrow X$, define   *while P do α*   to be $\beta^\dagger : X \longrightarrow X$ where $\beta :$ $X \longrightarrow X + X$ is defined by

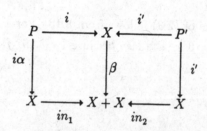

For brevity we introduce the alternate notation $W_P(\alpha)$ for *while P do α*. It is an easy exercise (use the polymorphic axiom with $h = k = id_X$)   that $W_P(\alpha)$ is independent of the choice of coproduct $X + X$.

All the examples of *while-do* in **1.12** arise this way. (For Ω, see Example **8.25**.) For $\mathbf{Mat}_R$ we leave it as an exercise for the reader to generalize Example **3.10**.

We begin with a lemma which holds for any Boolean category equipped with projection system ρ, so long as h is ρ–nulling. This generalizes the first square in **7.9**.

10 LEMMA   *If $h : X \longrightarrow \overline{X}$, $k : Y \longrightarrow \overline{Y}$ with h †–pure, the following square commutes.*

$$
\begin{array}{ccc}
X+Y & \xrightarrow{\ \rho_X\ } & X \\
\scriptstyle h \oplus k \downarrow & & \downarrow \scriptstyle h \\
\overline{X}+\overline{Y} & \xrightarrow[\ \rho_{\overline{X}}\ ]{} & \overline{X}
\end{array}
$$

Symmetrically, a similar square commutes for the Y–projections.

Proof   We have $in_X(\rho_X h) = h$, $in_X((h \oplus k)\rho_{\overline{X}}) = h\, in_{\overline{X}}\, \rho_{\overline{X}} = h$. Also, since h is ρ–nulling, $in_Y((h \oplus k)\rho_{\overline{X}}) = h\, in_{\overline{Y}}\, \rho_{\overline{X}} = 0$. $\square$

The next result, in the style of Lemmas **3.12**, **7.16** characterizes the polymorphic hypothesis for *while-do* in terms of guards. In the absence of a matrix calculus, we are forced to work a little harder.

11 PROPOSITION   *Let $\alpha : X \longrightarrow X$, $\overline{\alpha} : \overline{X} \longrightarrow \overline{X}$, $P \in Summ(X)$, $\overline{P} \in Summ(\overline{X})$ and define $\beta, \overline{\beta}$ by*

$$
\begin{array}{ccccc}
P & \xrightarrow{\ i\ } & X & \xleftarrow{\ i'\ } & P' \\
\scriptstyle i\alpha \downarrow & & \scriptstyle \beta \downarrow & & \downarrow \scriptstyle i' \\
X & \xrightarrow[\ in_1\ ]{} & X+X & \xleftarrow[\ in_2\ ]{} & X
\end{array}
\qquad
\begin{array}{ccccc}
\overline{P} & \xrightarrow{\ \overline{i}\ } & \overline{X} & \xleftarrow{\ \overline{i}'\ } & \overline{X} \\
\scriptstyle \overline{i}\,\overline{\alpha} \downarrow & & \scriptstyle \overline{\beta} \downarrow & & \downarrow \scriptstyle \overline{i}' \\
\overline{X} & \xrightarrow[\ \overline{in}_1\ ]{} & \overline{X}+\overline{X} & \xleftarrow[\ \overline{in}_2\ ]{} & \overline{X}
\end{array}
$$

so that while P do α is $\beta^{\dagger}$ and similarly $\overline{\beta}^{\dagger}$ is while $\overline{P}$ do $\overline{\beta}$. Let $h, k : X \longrightarrow \overline{X}$.

Then

$$
\begin{array}{ccc}
X & \xrightarrow{\ \beta\ } & X+X \\
{\scriptstyle h}\Big\downarrow & (A) & \Big\downarrow{\scriptstyle h\oplus k} \\
\overline{X} & \xrightarrow[\ \overline{\beta}\ ]{} & \overline{X}+\overline{X}
\end{array}
\qquad \Leftrightarrow \qquad
\begin{array}{ccccc}
X & \xrightarrow{\ p\alpha\ } & X & \xrightarrow{\ p'\ } & X \\
{\scriptstyle h}\Big\downarrow & (B) & {\scriptstyle h}\Big\downarrow & (C) & \Big\downarrow{\scriptstyle k} \\
\overline{X} & \xrightarrow[\ \overline{p}\,\overline{\alpha}\ ]{} & \overline{X} & \xrightarrow[\ \overline{p}'\ ]{} & \overline{X}
\end{array}
$$

Proof Consider the diagrams

$$
\begin{array}{ccccccc}
P & \xrightarrow{\ i\ } & X & \xrightarrow{\ h\ } & \overline{X} & \xrightarrow{\ \overline{p}\ } & \overline{X} \\
{\scriptstyle i\alpha}\Big\downarrow & & {\scriptstyle \beta}\Big\downarrow & (A) & {\scriptstyle \overline{\beta}}\Big\downarrow & (D) & \Big\downarrow{\scriptstyle \overline{\alpha}} \\
X & \xrightarrow[\ in_1\ ]{} & X+X & \xrightarrow[\ h\oplus k\ ]{} & \overline{X}+\overline{X} & \xrightarrow[\ \overline{\rho_1}\ ]{} & \overline{X}
\end{array}
$$

$$
\begin{array}{ccccccc}
P & \xrightarrow{\ i'\ } & X & \xrightarrow{\ h\ } & \overline{X} & \xrightarrow{\ id\ } & \overline{X} \\
{\scriptstyle i'}\Big\downarrow & & {\scriptstyle \beta}\Big\downarrow & (A) & {\scriptstyle \overline{\beta}}\Big\downarrow & (E) & \Big\downarrow{\scriptstyle \overline{p}'} \\
X & \xrightarrow[\ in_2\ ]{} & X+X & \xrightarrow[\ h\oplus k\ ]{} & \overline{X}+\overline{X} & \xrightarrow[\ \overline{\rho_2}\ ]{} & \overline{X}
\end{array}
$$

Then $in_1(h\oplus k)\rho_1 = h\,\overline{in_1}\,\overline{\rho_1} = h$ and, similarly, $in_2(h\oplus k)\overline{\rho_2} = k$. Also (D,E) commute by Corollary **6.21**, Lemma **10** and **8.16** (as $\beta = i\alpha \oplus i'$, $\overline{\beta} = \overline{i\alpha}\oplus\overline{i}'$); in detail, $\overline{\beta}\,\overline{\rho_1} = \overline{\rho_1}\,\overline{i}\,\overline{\alpha} = \overline{p}\,\overline{\alpha}$, $\overline{\beta}\,\overline{\rho_2} = \overline{\rho_2}\,\overline{i}' = \overline{p}'$.

First assume (A) commutes. To show (B), we have from $ip = i$ and the perimeter of the topmost diagram in the proof so far above that $ip\alpha h = i\alpha h = ih\overline{p}\,\overline{\alpha}$; and, $i'h\overline{p}\,\overline{\alpha} = i'\beta(h\oplus k)\overline{\rho_1} = i'\beta\rho_1 h = i'p\alpha h$ (similar to (D)) so as i, i' constitute a coproduct we have (B). To get (C), $ip'k = 0$ and (consult both diagrams) $ih\overline{p}' = ih\overline{\beta}\,\overline{\rho_2} = i\alpha\,in_1(h\oplus k)\overline{\rho_2} = i\alpha\,(h\oplus k)\overline{in_1}\,\overline{\rho_2} = i\alpha(h\oplus k)0 = 0$.

Conversely, let us assume (B,C) and show that (A) holds. We have $i\,\beta(h\oplus k)$
$= i\,\alpha\,in_1(h\oplus k) \quad = i\,\alpha\,h\,\overline{in_1} \quad = \quad (ip)\,\alpha\,h\,\overline{in_1} = i\,h\,\overline{p}\,\overline{\alpha}\,in_1 = i\,h\,\overline{\beta}\,\overline{p_1}\,\overline{in_1}.$ \quad But
$i\,h\,\overline{\beta}\,\overline{p_2}\,\overline{in_2} = i\,h\,\overline{p'}\,\overline{in_2} = i\,p'k\,\overline{in_2} = 0\,k\,\overline{in_2} = 0$ \; so by Lemma $\mathbf{8.18}(1,6)$ \; $i\beta(h\oplus k)$
$= ih\overline{\beta}$. Continuing, $i'\beta(h\oplus k) = i'\,in_2(h\oplus k) = i'\,k\,\overline{in_2} = (i'p')k\,\overline{in_2} = i'\,h\,\overline{p'}\,\overline{in_2} =$
$i'\,h\overline{\beta}\,\overline{p_2}\,\overline{in_2}$. But $i'\,h\,\overline{\beta}\,\overline{p_1}\,\overline{in_1} = i'\,h\,\overline{p}\,\overline{\alpha}\,\overline{in_1} = i'\,p\,\alpha\,h\,\overline{in_1} = 0$ so, by Lemma \qquad $\mathbf{8.18}(6)$
again, $i'\beta(h\oplus k) = i'h\overline{\beta}$ and we are done. \hfill $\square$

We can now prove

12 PROPOSITION \quad *The following while-do rule holds in a Boolean category with polymorphic iterate. For* $\alpha: X\longrightarrow X$, $P,Q \in Summ(X)$,

$$\{P\textstyle\bigcap Q\}\,\alpha\,\{Q\} \quad \Rightarrow \quad \{Q\}\ while\ P\ do\ \alpha\ \{Q\textstyle\bigcap P'\}.$$

Proof \quad Consider

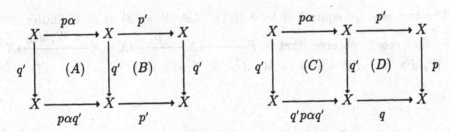

Using Theorem **8.15**, (B,D) commute. If $\{P\bigcap Q\}\,\alpha\,\{Q\}$ then $qp\alpha q' = 0$ by Proposition 5. It follows from 8.18(6) that (A,C) commute; note that $q'q' = q'$ since $Q'\bigcap Q' = Q'$. By Proposition 9, Corollary 6.21 and the polymorphic axiom we have (E,F) as shown:

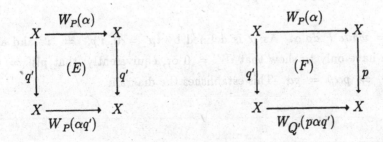

By (E), $q\,W_P(\alpha)\,q' = 0$, so $\{Q\}\,W_P(\alpha)\,\{Q\}$. Using (F), $q\,W_P(\alpha)\,p = 0$ which gives $\{Q\}\,W_P(\alpha)\,\{P'\}$. Now use **3**(7).   □

13 PROPOSITION   *For* $i : P \longrightarrow X \in Summ(X)$, $\alpha : X \longrightarrow X$ *in a Boolean category with polymorphic iterate, the Elgot fixed point equation for* $W = $ *while P do α is tantamount to the pair of equations*

$$iW = i\alpha W$$
$$i'W = i'$$

or equivalently (with respect to the guards of the unique projection system)

$$pW = p\alpha W$$
$$p'W = p'\,.$$

Proof   The two sets are equivalent by **8.18**(1). Let $W = \beta^{\dagger}$ as in Definition **9**. To complete the proof, observe that $P \xrightarrow{\ \ i\ \ } X \xrightarrow{\ \ \beta\ \ } X + X \xrightarrow{\ <W,id>\ } X = i\,\alpha\,in_1 < W, id > \ = i\alpha W$ and $i'\beta < W, id > \ = i'\,in_2 < W, id > \ = i'$.   □

It is possible to define guards using *while-do*. The next proposition shows that $P = $ *while P' do id_X*.

14 PROPOSITION   *For $i : P \longrightarrow X \in Summ(X)$, $\alpha : X \longrightarrow X$, if* $\{P\}\,\alpha\,\{P\}$ *then* *while P do α* $=\ p'$.

Proof   Let $W = $ *while P do α*. As p' is defined by $ip' = 0$, $i'p' = i'$ and as $i'W = i'$ by **11**, we have only to show that $iW = 0$ or, equivalently, that $pW = 0$. By **7**(3), $\{P\}\,\alpha\,\{P\} \Leftrightarrow p\alpha p = p\alpha$. This establishes the diagram

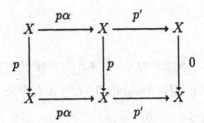

and the proposition follows from **12**, Corollary **6.21** and the polymorphic property of *while-do*.   □

10   PREDICATE TRANSFORMERS

The inverse predicate transformers were defined in **5.16**. Many of their basic properties follow from those of $\{P\}\ \alpha\ \{Q\}$ because of the interexpressibility results of **5.17**. For *ranged Boolean categories* we define the direct transformers $P[\alpha]$, $P < \alpha >$ and $sp(P, \alpha)$ which are interexpressible with the inverse ones. A ranged Boolean category has zero morphisms if and only if each of its morphisms has a cokernel and such cokernels can be used to describe $P < \alpha >$.

In Propositions 7 and 8 below we are able to establish that despite the dependence of *while P do α* and α^* on the choice, respectively, of polymorphic iterate or Kleene-∗, the predicate transformers of these constructions are independent of such choices.

We work in a Boolean category $\mathcal{B}$.

Pointy brackets have two independent uses —as the predicate transformer and for coproduct-induced maps. While both uses may occur together (see 1(8)) there is little worry about confusion. The first proposition records basic properties of $[\alpha](-)$ and

$< \alpha > (-)$.

1 PROPOSITION *Let* $\alpha : X \longrightarrow Y$. *The following statements are valid.*

1. *For* $P \in Summ(X)$, $Q \in Summ(Y)$, $\{P\}\, \alpha\, \{Q\} \Leftrightarrow P \subset [\alpha]Q$.

2. $[\alpha]Y = X$, $< \alpha > 0 = 0$.

3. $[\alpha]0 = Ker(\alpha)$, $< \alpha > Y = Dom(\alpha)$.

4. *For* $\beta : Y \longrightarrow Z$, $R \in Summ(Z)$, $[\alpha\beta]R = [\alpha]([\beta]R)$.

5. *For* $Q, R \in Summ(Y)$, $[\alpha](Q \bigcap R) = [\alpha]Q \bigcap [\alpha]R$, $< \alpha > (Q \bigcup R)$
   $= < \alpha > Q \bigcup < \alpha > R$.

6. *For* $P \in Summ(X)$, $\beta : X \longrightarrow Y$, $R \in Summ(Y)$,
   $[if_P(\alpha, \beta)]R = (P' \bigcup [\alpha]R) \bigcap (P \bigcup [\beta]R)$
   $< if_P(\alpha, \beta) > R = (P \bigcap < \alpha > R) \bigcup (P' \bigcap < \beta > R)$.

7. *If* α *is null and* $Q \in Summ(Y)$, $[\alpha]Q = X$ *and* $< \alpha > Q = 0$.

8. *Given a coproduct* $X_i \xrightarrow{\; in_i \;} X_1 + \cdots + X_n$, $\alpha_i : X_i \longrightarrow Y$ *and*
   $Q \in Summ(Y)$, $[\alpha_i]Q \longrightarrow [< \alpha_1, ..., \alpha_n >]Q$
   and $< \alpha_i > Q \longrightarrow < < \alpha_1, ..., \alpha_n > > Q$ *are coproducts.*

9. *If* $p : X \longrightarrow X$ *is a guard (Definition 8.13), then if* $P = Dom(p)$
   and $Q \in Summ(X)$, $[p]Q = P \Rightarrow Q$ *and* $< p > Q = P \bigcap Q$. *(As
   usual, $P \Rightarrow Q$ abbreviates $P' \bigcup Q$.)*

10. *If* $i : P \longrightarrow X$ *is a summand then for* $Q \in Summ(X)$, $[i]Q =$
    $< i > Q = P \bigcap Q$.

Proof Excepting (8), all statements for $< \alpha > (-)$ follow from those for $[\alpha](-)$ by De
Morgan duality. (1,...,7,10) are either obvious or immediate from earlier results (**5.11,
5.20, 6.7, 9.1, 9.3**), noting that "$P \subset [\alpha]Q \Leftrightarrow \{P\}\, \alpha\, \{Q\}$" determines $[\alpha]Q$; e.g., for
(6), refer to **9.3**(9) and observe that the largest Q with $P \bigcap Q \subset [\alpha]R$ is $Q = P' \bigcup [\alpha]R$.

It is a trivial exercise that a crisp morphism pulls back arbitrary finite
coproducts, not just binary, so the first part of (8) obtains by pulling back the
coproduct $in_i : X_i \longrightarrow X$ (where we abbreviate $X = X_1 + \cdots + X_n$) along the

summand $[<\alpha_1,...,\alpha_n>]Q\longrightarrow X$; the resulting summand is indeed $[\alpha_i]Q$ by
5.20 because $in_i<\alpha_1,...,\alpha_n> = \alpha$. For the second half of (8) set $P = [<\alpha_1,...,\alpha_n>]Q'$. Then $<\alpha_i>Q = <in_i>([<\alpha_1,...,\alpha_n>]Q')' = <in_i>P' = X_i - [in_i]P = X_i - P\bigcap X_i = P'\bigcap X_i \in Summ(X_i)$. Now pull back the coproduct
along the summand $P'\longrightarrow X$ as before to get that $<\alpha_i>Q\longrightarrow P'$ is a coproduct
as desired. Finally we prove (9). Let $P = Dom(p)$, $i: P\longrightarrow X$, $i':$
$Ker(\alpha)\longrightarrow X$. Then $[p]Q\bigcap Dom(\alpha) = [ip]Q$ (5.20) $= [i]Q$ (as $ip = i$) $=$
$P\bigcap Q$ whereas $[p]Q\bigcap Ker(\alpha) = [i'p]Q = 0$ (by (7)) so $[p]Q = P\bigcap Q$.

$\square$

We next present the basic properties of the weakest precondition operator.
Notice that the "composition rule" analogous to 1(4) is missing. This will be discussed
further in Section 12.

2 PROPOSITION *The following statements are valid.*

1. *For* $Q \in Summ(X)$, $wp(id_X, Q) = Q$.

2. *For* $\alpha: X\longrightarrow Y$, $wp(\alpha, Y) = Dom(\alpha)$.

3. *For* $\alpha: X\longrightarrow Y$, $wp(\alpha, 0) = 0$.

4. *For* $\alpha: X\longrightarrow Y$, $Q, R \in Summ(Y)$, $wp(\alpha, Q\bigcap R) =$
   $wp(\alpha, Q) \bigcap wp(\alpha, R)$.

5. $wp(if_P(\alpha, \beta), R)) = (P\bigcap wp(\alpha, R)) \bigcup (P'\bigcap wp(\beta, R))$ *for* $P \in Summ(X)$, $\alpha, \beta: X\longrightarrow Y$, $R \in Summ(Y)$.

6. *With respect to the coproduct* $X_i: in_i\longrightarrow X_1 + \cdots + X_n$ *and*
   $\alpha_i: X_i\longrightarrow Y$, $Q \in Summ(Y)$, $wp(\alpha_i, Q)\longrightarrow wp(<\alpha_1,...,\alpha_n>, Q)$
   is a coproduct.

7. *If* $\alpha: X\longrightarrow Y$ *is null and* $Q \in Summ(Y)$ *then* $wp(\alpha, Q) = 0$.

8. *If* $p: X\longrightarrow X$ *is a guard then if* $P = Dom(p)$ *and* $Q \in Summ(X)$, $wp(p, Q) = P\bigcap Q$.

9. *If* $i: P\longrightarrow X$ *is a summand then, for* $Q \in Summ(X)$,
   $wp(i, Q) = P\bigcap Q$.

Proof Since $wp(\alpha, Q) = Dom(\alpha) \bigcap [\alpha]Q$, these are all clear from **5.11** and Proposition 1. $\square$

3 COROLLARY *For* $\alpha, \beta : X \longrightarrow Y$, $P \in Summ(X)$, $Dom(if_P(\alpha, \beta)) = (P \bigcap Dom(\alpha)) \bigcup (P' \bigcap Dom(\beta))$. $\square$

The following identity from [Segerburg 1977] asserts "if $x\alpha \subset Q$ and $x\alpha \bigcap R \neq \emptyset$ then $x\alpha \bigcap Q \bigcap R \neq \emptyset$".

4 PROPOSITION *For* $\alpha : X \longrightarrow Y$, $Q, R \in Summ(Y)$, $[\alpha]Q \bigcap <\alpha> R \subset <\alpha> (Q \bigcap R)$.

Proof We have $([\alpha]Q \bigcap <\alpha> R) \bigcap (<\alpha> (Q \bigcap R))'$
$$
\begin{aligned}
&= <\alpha> R \bigcap [\alpha]Q \bigcap [\alpha](Q' \bigcup R') \\
&= <\alpha> R \bigcap [\alpha](Q \bigcap (Q' \bigcup R')) \\
&= <\alpha> R \bigcap [\alpha](Q \bigcap R') \\
&= ([\alpha]R')' \bigcap [\alpha]R' \bigcap [\alpha]Q \\
&= 0.
\end{aligned}
$$
$\square$

The next result completes the proof of Proposition 7.12.

5 PROPOSITION *In a preadditive Boolean category, if* $\alpha + \beta$ *exists for* $\alpha, \beta : X \longrightarrow Y$ *then for* $Q \in Summ(Y)$,

$$
\begin{aligned}
[\alpha + \beta]Q &= [\alpha]Q \bigcap [\beta]Q \\
<\alpha + \beta> Q &= <\alpha> Q \bigcup <\beta> Q \\
wp(\alpha + \beta, Q) &= (wp(\alpha, Q) \bigcap [\beta]Q) \bigcup ([\alpha]Q \bigcap wp(\beta, Q))
\end{aligned}
$$

Further, if $\alpha + \beta = 0$ *then* $\alpha = 0 = \beta$.

Proof The first statement is clear from **9.5** and the second is its De Morgan dual. A special case of the second gives

$$6 \qquad Dom(\alpha + \beta) \; = \; Dom(\alpha) \bigcup Dom(\beta)$$

whence the third is a routine calculation. For the last statement, $X \; = \; Ker(\alpha + \beta)$

$$= \; [\alpha + \beta]0 \; = \; [\alpha]0 \bigcap [\beta]0 \; = \; Ker(\alpha) \bigcap Ker(\beta), \;\; \text{so} \;\; Ker(\alpha) = X = Ker(\beta).$$

$\square$

7 PROPOSITION *In a Boolean category with polymorphic iterate the following statements hold for* $\alpha : X \longrightarrow X$, $P, Q \in Summ(X)$.

1. $[while\ P\ do\ \alpha]Q$ *is the greatest solution S of the fixed-point-equation*
$$S \; = \; (P \bigcap [\alpha]S) \bigcup (P' \bigcap Q).$$

2. $< while\ P\ do\ \alpha > Q$ *is the least solution of the fixed-point-equation*
$$S \; = \; (P' \bigcup <\alpha> S) \bigcap (P \bigcup Q).$$

Proof We need prove only (1) since (2) is the De Morgan dual. Write $W \; = \; while\ P\ do\ \alpha$. To show $[W]Q$ satisfies the fixed-point-equation, use **9.13**: $P \bigcap [W]Q \; = \; [iW]Q$ (where $i : P \longrightarrow X$) $= \; [i\alpha W]Q \; = \; P \bigcap [\alpha]([W]Q)$ whereas $P' \bigcap [W]Q \; = \; [i'W]Q$ $= \; [i']Q \; = \; P' \bigcap Q$ so $[W]Q \; = \; (P \bigcup P') \bigcap [W]Q \; = \; (P \bigcap [\alpha]([W]Q)) \bigcup (P' \bigcap Q)$. Continuing, if S is any solution, $S \; = \; (P \bigcap [\alpha]S) \bigcup (P' \bigcap Q)$, then $P \bigcap S = P \bigcap [\alpha]S \subset [\alpha]S$ so $\{P \bigcap S\}\,\alpha\,\{S\}$ and, by the while rule **9.12**, $\{S\}\,W\,\{S \bigcap P'\}$. But $S \bigcap P' \; = \; P' \bigcap Q \subset Q$ so $\{S\}\,W\,\{Q\}$ and $S \subset [W]Q$ as desired. $\square$

The proof of (3) in the next proposition is adapted from [Pratt 1980, Lemma 1]; regarding (5), see [Bloom and Ésik 1988, Prop. 5.9, Cor. 5.10]. These results show that in a Boolean category, the predicate transformer of a polymorphic iterate is completely determined.

8 PROPOSITION   *Let* $(-)^*$ *be a Kleene-$*$ on a semiadditive Boolean category. Then for* $\alpha : X \longrightarrow X$, $P,Q \in Summ(X)$, *the following statements are valid.*

1. $[\alpha^*]Q$ *is the greatest solution of the fixed-point-equation* $S = Q \bigcap [\alpha]S$.

2. $< \alpha^* > Q$ *is the least solution of the fixed-point-equation*
   $$S = Q \bigcup < \alpha > S.$$

3. [Segerburg 1977]   *"If* $x \in P$ *and if* $(y \in P \bigcap x\alpha^* \Rightarrow y\alpha \subset P)$ *then* $y\alpha^*$
   $\subset P$" *or, more precisely put,* $P \bigcap [\alpha^*](P \Rightarrow [\alpha]P) \subset [\alpha^*]P$ *where, as usual,* $P \Rightarrow Q$ *abbreviates* $P' \bigcup Q$.

Further, given $\xi : X \longrightarrow X + Y$ *and* $Q \in Summ(X)$ *in any Boolean category with polymorphic iterate* $(-)^\dagger$, *the following two statements hold.*

4. $[\xi^\dagger]Q$ *is the greatest solution of the fixed-point-equation* $S = [\xi](S + Q)$ *(where the coproduct* $S + Q \in Summ(X + Y)$ *as in Lemma 5.5.)*

5. *(Invariant guard property)   If* $\{P\} \xi^\dagger \{Q\}$ *then there exists* $R \supset P$ *with* $\{R\} \xi \{R + Q\}$.

Proof   For the first statement, $[\alpha^*]Q = [id_X + \alpha\alpha^*]Q = [id_X]Q \bigcap [\alpha\alpha^*]Q = Q \bigcap [\alpha]([\alpha^*]Q)$ so $[\alpha^*]Q$ is a solution. Now suppose $S \subset Q \bigcap [\alpha]S$; we shall not need the reverse inclusion to prove that $S \subset [\alpha^*]Q$ as follows. As $S \subset [\alpha]S$, $\{S\} \alpha \{S\}$. As $S \subset Q$, $\{S\} \alpha^* \{Q\}$ so $S \subset [\alpha^*]Q$. The second statement is De Morgan dual to the first. Finally, we use (1) and 5 to establish the Segerburg induction axiom as follows. Let $S = P \bigcap [\alpha^*](P \Rightarrow [\alpha]P)$. We must show $P \bigcap [\alpha]S \subset S$. Indeed

$$
\begin{aligned}
P \bigcap [\alpha]S &= P \bigcap [\alpha](P \bigcap [\alpha^*](P \Rightarrow [\alpha]P)) \\
&= P \bigcap (P' \bigcup ([\alpha]P \bigcap [\alpha\alpha^*](P \Rightarrow [\alpha]P))) \\
&= P \bigcap (P \Rightarrow [\alpha]P) \bigcap (P' \bigcup [\alpha\alpha^*](P \Rightarrow [\alpha]P)) \\
&= P \bigcap [id_X + \alpha\alpha^*](P \Rightarrow [\alpha]P) = S.
\end{aligned}
$$

For the fourth statement, we use the Elgot equation and $1(4,8)$ as follows.

$$[\xi^\dagger]Q = [\xi][< \xi^\dagger, id_Y >]Q = [\xi]([\xi^\dagger]Q + Q) .$$

If also $S = [\xi](S + Q)$ then we have a pullback

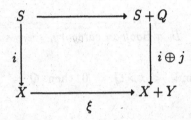

As summands are †–pure (Proposition **3.20**), it follows from the polymorphic axiom that $i\xi^\dagger$ factors through Q which gives $\{S\}\,\xi^\dagger\,\{Q\}$ so that $S \subset [\xi^\dagger]Q$.

For the last statement, let $R = [\xi^\dagger]Q$. Then $\{P\}\,\xi^\dagger\,\{Q\} \Leftrightarrow P \subset R$. As $R = [\xi](R + Q)$, $R \subset [\xi](R + Q)$ so $\{R\}\,\xi\,\{R + Q\}$. ☐

We now introduce some new "surjectivity" notions for Boolean categories.

9 DEFINITION A morphism $\alpha : X \longrightarrow Y$ is *surjective* if for all $Q \in Summ(Y)$, $<\alpha>Q = 0 \Rightarrow Q = 0$. We say α is *cototal* if for all $\beta : Y \longrightarrow Z$ $\alpha\beta$ null $\Rightarrow \beta$ null. Examples are shown in Table **10**.

Category	$\alpha : X \longrightarrow Y$ is surjective if
Set	α is onto
Pfn	$\forall y \in Y \; \exists x \in X \;\; x\alpha = y$
Mfn	$\forall y \in Y \; \exists x \in X \;\; y \in x\alpha$
$\mathbf{Mat}_R$	$\forall y \in Y \; \exists x \in X \;\; \alpha_{xy} \neq 0$
Ω	$\forall y \in Y \; \exists x \in X \;\; y$ is a leaf in $x\alpha$
$\mathbf{Pfn}_M$	$\forall y \in Y \; \exists x \in X \; \exists t \in M \;\; x\alpha = (y, t)$

Table 10 : Examples of surjective maps.

In **Set**, the only null maps are $\emptyset \longrightarrow X$ so that almost all morphisms are (vacuously) cototal.

11 PROPOSITION *In a Boolean category, every split epimorphism is surjective.*

Proof If $\alpha\beta = id$ and $<\beta>Q = 0$ then $Q = <id>Q = <\alpha>(<\beta>Q) = <\alpha>0 = 0$. □

12 PROPOSITION   *In any Boolean category, the following hold.*

1. *Given $\alpha : X \longrightarrow Y$, $\beta : Y \longrightarrow Z$, if α, β are surjective then $\alpha\beta$ is surjective; if $\alpha\beta$ is surjective then β is surjective.*

2. *Given a pullback*

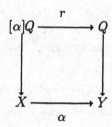

if α is surjective then so is r.   □

13 PROPOSITION   *In any Boolean category a surjective morphism is cototal.*

Proof Let $\alpha : X \longrightarrow Y$ be surjective and let $\beta : Y \longrightarrow Z$ with $\alpha\beta$ null. As $Dom(\alpha\beta) = 0$, $X = Ker(\alpha\beta) = [\alpha](Ker(\beta)) = (<\alpha>Dom(\beta))'$ so it follows that $<\alpha>(Dom(\beta)) = 0 \Rightarrow Dom(\beta) = 0 \Rightarrow \beta$ is null. □

The abelian categories discussed in the introduction have *image factorization*: each morphism factors uniquely (up to isomorphism) as an epimorphism followed by a monomorphism. Let us define a *surjective-summand* factorization of α to be a factorization $\alpha = si$ with s surjective and i a summand. We now study these in

Boolean categories.

14 PROPOSITION *Given* $\alpha : X \longrightarrow Y$ *in a Boolean category, the following three statements are equivalent.*

1. α *has a surjective-summand factorization.*
2. *There exists a least summand of Y through which α factors.*
3. *There exists a minimal summand of Y through which α factors.*

Proof $1 \Rightarrow 2$. Let $\alpha = X \xrightarrow{\ \ s\ \ } R \xrightarrow{\ \ j\ \ } Y$ with s surjective and j a summand. Suppose also that $\alpha = tk$ with k a summand. Define $P = R \bigcap S'$. Then $P' = R' \bigcup S \supset S$. As $\{X\} \alpha \{S\}$ also $\{X\} \alpha \{P'\}$ and so $X = [\alpha]P'$. We then have $0 = ([\alpha]P')' = \ <\alpha> P\ = \ <sj> P\ = \ <s> <j> P\ = \ <s> (R \bigcap P)$ $= \ <s> P$. As s is surjective, $P = 0$, so $R \subset S$.

$3 \Rightarrow 1$. Let $\alpha = tj$ with $j : R \longrightarrow Y$ a summand and such that α factors through no summand properly contained in R. Let $0 \neq Q \in Summ(R)$. As $Q' \neq R$, $\{X\} S \{Q'\}$ is false. Thus $[t]Q' \neq X$, so $<t> Q \neq 0$. This proves that t is surjective. $\square$

15 PROPOSITION *In a Boolean category, the following hold.*

1. *Any two surjective-summand factorizations of a morphism α are isomorphic.*
2. *If a summand $i : P \longrightarrow X$ is surjective, i is an isomorphism.*

Proof The first statement is clear since both factorizations yield the least summand through which α factors. The second follows from $1(10)$: if $P' \neq 0$ then $0 \neq$ $<i> P' = P \bigcap P'$, the desired contradiction. $\square$

16 DEFINITION The least summand through which α factors, if it exists, is called the *range* of α, denoted $Ran(\alpha)$. A Boolean category in which every morphism has a range (that is, every morphism satisfies any of the three equivalent conditions of Proposition 15) is called a *ranged* Boolean category. In a ranged Boolean category we can define direct predicate transformers. For $P \in Summ(X)$, $\alpha : X \longrightarrow Y$, define

$$P[\alpha] \;=\; Ran(P\xrightarrow{\;i\;}X\xrightarrow{\;\alpha\;}Y)$$

$$P<\alpha> \;=\; (P'[\alpha])'$$

$$sp(P,\alpha) \;=\; Ran(\alpha)\bigcap P<\alpha> \quad (\textit{strongest postcondition}).$$

If $\mathcal{B},\mathcal{C}$ are ranged Boolean categories, a Boolean functor $F:\mathcal{B}\longrightarrow\mathcal{C}$ is *range-preserving* if for all $\alpha:X\longrightarrow Y$ in $\mathcal{B}$, $(Ran(\alpha))F = Ran(\alpha F)$ in $Summ(YF)$ or, equivalently, F preserves surjective morphisms. Clearly such F preserves $P[\alpha]$ and so $P<\alpha>$ and $sp(P,\alpha)$ as well. A Boolean extension $\mathcal{B}\subset\mathcal{C}$ is *ranged* if $\mathcal{B},\mathcal{C}$ are ranged Boolean categories and the inclusion functor preserves ranges.

17 EXAMPLE $\mathbf{Mat}_R$ is a ranged Boolean category. For $\alpha:X\longrightarrow Y$,

$$
\begin{aligned}
Ran(\alpha) &= \{y\in Y : \exists x\in X,\ \alpha_{xy}\neq 0\}\\
P[\alpha] &= \{y\in Y : \exists x\in P,\ \alpha_{xy}\neq 0\}\\
P<\alpha> &= \{y\in Y : \text{if } \alpha_{xy}\neq 0 \text{ then } x\in P\}\\
sp(P,\alpha) &= \{y\in Y : \emptyset\neq\{x:\alpha_{xy}\neq 0\}\subset P\}
\end{aligned}
$$

Mfn and **Pfn** are special cases of $\mathbf{Mat}_R$. For **Mfn**,

$$
\begin{aligned}
P[\alpha] &= \bigcup(x\alpha : x\in P)\\
P<\alpha> &= \{y\in Y : \text{if } y\in x\alpha \text{ then } x\in P\}\\
sp(P,\alpha) &= \{y\in Y : \emptyset\neq\{x: y\in x\alpha\}\subset P\}
\end{aligned}
$$

and, for **Pfn**,

$$
\begin{aligned}
P[\alpha] &= \{x\alpha : x\in P\}\\
P<\alpha> &= \{y\in Y : y = x\alpha \Rightarrow x\in P\}\\
sp(P,\alpha) &= \{y\in Y : \emptyset\neq\{x: y = x\alpha\}\subset P\}\,.
\end{aligned}
$$

18 EXAMPLE Ω is a ranged Boolean category. The direct transformers are

$$P[\alpha] \;=\; \{y \in Y : \exists x \in P \text{ with } y \text{ a leaf of } x\alpha\}$$
$$P<\alpha> \;=\; \{y \in Y : \text{if } y \text{ is a leaf of } x\alpha \text{ then } x \in P\}$$
$$sp(P,\alpha) \;=\; \{y \in Y : \emptyset \neq \{x : y \text{ is a leaf of } x\alpha\} \subset P\}.$$

19 EXAMPLE Pfn_M is a ranged Boolean category. We have

$$P[\alpha] \;=\; \{y \in Y : \exists x \in P \text{ with } x\alpha \text{ of form } (y,s)\}$$
$$P<\alpha> \;=\; \{y \in Y : \text{if } x\alpha \text{ has form } (y,s),\; x \in P\}$$
$$sp(P,\alpha) \;=\; \{y \in Y : \emptyset \neq \{x : x\alpha \text{ has form } (y,s)\} \subset P\}\,.$$

20 PROPOSITION   *Given* $\alpha : X \longrightarrow Y$, $P \in Summ(X)$, $Q \in Summ(Y)$ *in any ranged Boolean category,*

$$P \subset [\alpha]Q \;\Leftrightarrow\; \{P\}\,\alpha\,\{Q\} \;\Leftrightarrow\; P[\alpha] \subset Q\,.$$

Further, the six predicate transformers $[\alpha]Q$, $<\alpha>Q$, $wp(\alpha,Q)$, $P[\alpha]$, $P<\alpha>$, $sp(P,\alpha)$ *are mutually interexpressible.*

Proof   The first equivalence is an old result and the second is clear from Proposition 15 because $i\alpha$ factors through Q if and only if $\{P\}\,\alpha\,\{Q\}$. That $P[\alpha]$ and $P<\alpha>$ are interexpressible is obvious. To see that $P<\alpha>$ and $sp(P,\alpha)$ are interexpressible first observe that $P'[\alpha] \subset Ran(\alpha) \Rightarrow (Ran(\alpha))' \subset P<\alpha>$ and that because $0[\alpha] = 0$, $(sp(X,\alpha))' = (Ran(\alpha))'$. Thus $P<\alpha> = (sp(X,\alpha))' \cup sp(P,\alpha)$; the other direction is immediate as $sp(P,\alpha) = (0<\alpha>)' \cap P<\alpha>$. This shows that the direct transformers are interexpressible and we know the inverse ones are by 5.17. To make the crossover, observe that $P[\alpha]$ is the least Q with $P \subset [\alpha]Q$ and $[\alpha]Q$ is the largest P with $P[\alpha] \subset Q$. $\square$

The reader familiar with image factorization systems in a category will recognize that $\mathbf{E}$ = surjectives, $\mathbf{M}$ = summands forms such a system in a ranged Boolean category. There is some discrepancy in the literature as to whether the axioms on such a system should require morphisms in $\mathbf{E}$ should be epimophisms and morphisms in $\mathbf{M}$ should be monomorphisms. The latter statement is true in our case, but not necessarily so for the former. For example, a non-Boolean topos provides a counterexample as the following shows.

21 PROPOSITION *In a ranged Boolean category with equalizers, every surjective morphism is an epimorphism if and only if every equalizer is a summand.*

Proof First assume every equalizer is a summand, and let $\alpha : X \longrightarrow Y$ be surjective and let $t, u : Y \longrightarrow Z$ with $\alpha t = \alpha u$. To prove α is an epimorphism we must show $t = u$. To this end, form the equalizer $i : E \longrightarrow X$ of t, u. Since α factors through i, i is surjective by **12**. But i is a summand by hypothesis so it follows from **15** that i is an isomorphism whence $t = u$. Conversely, let $i : E \longrightarrow X$ be the equalizer of $\alpha, \beta : X \longrightarrow Y$. Let $j : R \longrightarrow X = Ran(i)$ so that $i = sj$ with s surjective. Since s is an epimorphism by hypothesis, $j\alpha = j\beta$ which induces unique $\psi : R \longrightarrow E$ with $\psi i = j$. As i, j are monomorphisms, j is an isomorphism so that i is a summand. □

For abelian categories, epimorphisms coincide with cokernels (which are about to be defined.) While the role of cokernels in ranged Boolean categories cannot be described so simply, it turns out that cokernels are useful precisely when there is a family of zero morphisms. We round out this section by explaining this point.

22 DEFINITION For $\alpha : X \longrightarrow Y$ in a Boolean category, a *cokernel of* α is a morphism $\beta : Y \longrightarrow C$ with $\alpha\beta$ null and universal with that property, that is, if $\alpha\gamma$ is null then there exists unique ψ with $\beta\psi = \gamma$.

Thus cokernels are dual to kernels and so are unique up to isomorphism. We denote the cokernel of α, if it exists, by $Cok(\alpha)$. A morphism which is the cokernel of some morphism is said to be *a cokernel*.

23 LEMMA *In any Boolean category, the following hold.*

1. *Every cokernel is an epimorphism.*

2. *If there exists a null epimorphism $X \longrightarrow Y$, $Y = 0$.*

Proof Let $\theta = Cok(\alpha)$ and suppose $\theta\beta = \delta = \theta\gamma$. As $\alpha\delta = (\alpha\theta)\beta$ is null, both β, γ are the unique ψ with $\theta\psi = \delta$, so $\beta = \gamma$. For the second statement, recall the basic fact that in any category an equalizer which is an epimorphism must be an isomorphism. To apply this, consider a typical null morphism

$$\alpha \ = \ X \xrightarrow{\quad\beta\quad} 0 \xrightarrow{\quad\quad} Y$$

and suppose such α is epi. Thus $0 \xrightarrow{\quad\quad} Y$ is both epi and an equalizer (5.15.) $\square$

24 PROPOSITION *Let $\mathcal{B}$ be a ranged Boolean category. Then the following two statements are equivalent.*

1. *$\mathcal{B}$ has a family of zero morphisms.*

2. *Every morphism has a cokernel.*

Proof $1 \Rightarrow 2$. Given $\alpha : X \longrightarrow Y$ there exists a coproduct $R \xrightarrow{\ i\ } Y \xleftarrow{\ i'\ } R'$ and a factorization $\alpha = si$ with s surjective. Let $\theta : Y \longrightarrow R'$ be the projection with respect to the unique projection system of Proposition 8.8, so that θ is defined by $i\theta = 0$, $i'\theta = id$. We will show that $\theta = Cok(\alpha)$. We have $\alpha\theta = si\theta = s0 = 0$. Now let $\gamma : Y \longrightarrow W$ satisfy $\alpha\gamma = 0$. Define $\psi : R' \longrightarrow W$ by $\psi = i'\gamma$. It suffices to show that $\theta\psi = \gamma$ since uniqueness follows from the fact that θ is (split) epi. To verify the equation it is equivalent to verify it preceded by the coproduct injections i, i'. We have $i\theta\psi = 0\psi = 0$ whereas also $i\gamma = 0$ because $si\gamma = 0$ is given and s, being surjective, is cototal by **13**. Finally, $i'\theta\psi = \psi = i'\gamma$.

$2 \Rightarrow 1$. Given X, let $\rho_X : X \longrightarrow W = Cok(id_X)$. Such ρ_X is null so it follows from both parts of Lemma **23** that $W = 0$. Define the desired family of zero morphisms by

$$0_{XY} \; = \; X \xrightarrow{\quad \rho_X \quad} 0 \xrightarrow{\qquad} Y \; .$$

Let $\alpha : W \longrightarrow X$, $\beta : Y \longrightarrow Z$. That $0_{XY}\beta = 0_{XZ}$ is obvious. Since $\alpha 0_{XY}$ is null and $\rho_W = Cok(id_W)$, ρ_W factors through $\alpha 0_{XY}$ which shows $\alpha 0_{XY} = 0_{WY}$. $\square$

The proof construction of the previous Proposition gives a rather striking fact: In a ranged Boolean category with zero morphisms, the cokernel of a map is identified with a summand of its codomain, namely the complement of the range (though one must remember that it is the projection to the summand and not the inclusion that comprises the cokernel.) This contrasts sharply with what happens with abelian categories.

25 PROPOSITION *For* $\alpha : X \longrightarrow Y$ *in a ranged Boolean category with zero morphisms, the following statements are equivalent.*

1. α *is surjective.*

2. α *is cototal.*

3. $Cok(\alpha) = 0$.

4. $Ran(\alpha) = Y$.

Proof $1 \Rightarrow 2$ holds by **13**. For $2 \Rightarrow 3$, set $\theta : Y \longrightarrow C = Cok(\alpha)$. Then as $\alpha\theta = 0$ also $\theta = 0$ and it follows from **23** that $C = 0$ as needed. As just discussed above, $Ran(\alpha)$ and $Cok(\alpha)$ are complementary summands so the equivalence of (3) and (4) is clear. Finally, for $4 \Rightarrow 1$, $\alpha = \alpha \, id_Y$ is a surjective-summand factorization; now use Proposition **14**. $\square$

We saw in **11** that every split epimorphism is surjective. In a ranged Boolean category with zero morphisms, every cokernel is the projection to a summand and so is a split epimorphism. It is not always true that every surjective morphism is a cokernel, even in **Mfn**; we leave it as a routine exercise to construct a split epimorphism some of whose values are sets with more than one element.

There is no scarcity of ranged Boolean categories with zero morphisms as is shown by the concluding proposition for this section.

26 PROPOSITION *If* $\mathcal{B}$ *is a ranged Boolean category and* ρ *is a projection system for* $\mathcal{B}$ *with canonical zero-subcategory* $\mathcal{B}_\rho$ *then* $\mathcal{B}_\rho \subset \mathcal{B}$ *is a ranged Boolean extension.*

Proof   Let $\alpha : X \longrightarrow Y$ be ρ-nulling and let

$$\alpha \quad = \quad X \xrightarrow{\quad s \quad} R \xrightarrow{\quad i \quad} Y$$

be a surjective-summand factorization of α in $\mathcal{B}$. It suffices to show that s is ρ-nulling. Denoting the projection to the zero summand by $\rho_W : W \longrightarrow 0$, we are given $\alpha\rho_Y = \rho_X$ and must show that $s\rho_R = \rho_X$. By 8.9(2), i is ρ-nulling so $i\rho_Y = \rho_R$. Thus $s\rho_R = si\rho_Y = \alpha\rho_Y = \rho_X$. $\qquad\qquad\square$

PART III   METATHEORY

Part III initiates the study of a few issues concerned with the first-order theory
of Boolean categories. "Formulas" are summands expressible in the language **PBC** of
Boolean categories introduced in Section 11. The fundamental completeness theorem
11.15 asserts that a formula is universally valid if and only if it is true in the classical
example of **Mfn**. A similar result holds for ranged Boolean categories. Using a
completion by ideals developed in Section 13, the forward predicate transformers are
seen to be categorically dual to the inverse ones, at least in the preadditive case.
Section 14 provides the equational theory for 3-valued *if-then-else* in a Boolean category.

11   REPRESENTATIONS BY RELATIONS

In this section we will introduce the typed formal language **PBC** for the
Propositional logic of Boolean Categories which may be regarded as loop-free
propositional dynamic logic with data types. The main result is that the set of formulas
valid in all Boolean categories coincides precisely with the set of formulas true in **Mfn**.
We give two proofs. The first works only for atomic Boolean categories, but the
construction is very straightforward. The second, general proof uses ultrafilters and

follows that of [Kozen 1980] for dynamic algebras.

The language **PDL** of [Fischer and Ladner 1979] defines programs and formulas by mutual recursion as follows (where we have made notational changes to conform to previous sections of this paper):

Atomic programs are programs; $\emptyset$ is a program; if α, β are programs and P is a formula then $\alpha\beta$, $\alpha + \beta$, α^* and p (the guard corresponding to P) are programs.

Atomic formulas are formulas; true and false are formulas; if P,Q are formulas and α is a program then $P\bigcup Q$, P' and $<\alpha>P$ are formulas.

The Kripke model semantics which is standard for **PDL** is, essentially, **Mfn** so that $\alpha + \beta = \alpha\bigcup\beta$ and α^* are available. In particular, *if-then-else* can be expressed as in 8.24. The identity program is expressible as 0^*.

While **PBC** is necessarily more complicated because we wish to express the Boolean category building blocks, namely coproducts and $[\alpha]Q$ as pullbacks, we can still write it down directly as follows. (Though morphisms in a Boolean category are not always to be interpreted as "programs" we will use that metaphor in this section and keep the Fisher-Ladner terminology.)

1 DEFINITION The typed language **PBC** has three types: *objects; programs from X to Y $Prog(X,Y)$* for X,Y objects; and *formulas on X $Form(X)$* for X an object. These are defined by mutual recursion as follows:

Atomic objects are objects; 0 is an object; if X,Y are objects, $X + Y$ is an object; if P is a formula, $|P|$ is an object.

Atomic programs from X to Y are in $Prog(X,Y)$; $0_X \in Prog(0,X)$ and $id_X \in Prog(X,X)$; if $\alpha \in Prog(X,Y)$ and $\beta \in Prog(Y,Z)$ then $\alpha\beta \in Prog(X,Z)$; if $P \in Form(X)$ then $inc_P \in Prog(|P|,X)$; if $P \in Form(X)$, $\alpha \in Prog(|P|,Y)$ and $\beta \in Prog(|P'|,Y)$ then $<\alpha,\beta> \in Prog(X,Y)$; if $\alpha \in Prog(X,Y)$ and $Q \in Form(Y)$ then $res_{\alpha,Q} \in Prog(|[\alpha]Q|,|Q|)$ ("restriction of α to $[\alpha]Q$.")

Atomic formulas on X are in $Form(X)$; $true_X \in Form(X)$; if $P, Q \in Form(X)$ then P' and $P \bigcap Q$ $\in Form(X)$; if $\alpha \in Prog(X,Y)$, $Q \in Form(Y)$ then $[\alpha]Q \in Form(X)$; if X, Y are objects then $copr_{X,Y} \in Form(X+Y)$; if $R \in Form(X)$, $P \in Form(|R|)$ then P_TR ("P through R") $\in Form(X)$.

The meaning of the constructions of **PBC** is explicated by the intended semantics. The following definition assumes that a Boolean category is provided with chosen representatives of structures that are determined, in general, only up to isomorphism. This allows interpretations to extend from atomic formulas to formulas in the traditional way. We do this to show precisely how such a program could be carried out, but immediately abandon this approach as is discussed immediately after.

2 DEFINITION Let $\mathfrak{B}$ be a Boolean category with a chosen initial object and in which each equivalence class of summands of an object has a chosen representative (e.g. in the examples of Section 1 it is natural to choose subset inclusions.) We say a coproduct is *chosen* if both of its summands are and if its summands are ordered, that is, one is first and the other is second (in the standard diagrammatic representation of a coproduct, the leftmost summand is "first".) We assume that the coproduct $X \xrightarrow{id} X \longleftarrow 0$ is chosen. More generally, we assume that for each pair (X,Y) of objects there exists a chosen coproduct of form $X \xrightarrow{i} X + Y \xleftarrow{j} Y$.

An *interpretation* $(-)^{\bullet}$ of **PBC** in $\mathfrak{B}$ assigns objects $X^{\bullet}$ of $\mathfrak{B}$ to each atomic object X, assigns morphisms $\alpha^{\bullet} : X^{\bullet} \longrightarrow Y^{\bullet}$ to each atomic program from X to Y and assigns chosen coproduct decompositions of $X^{\bullet}$ to each atomic formula on X.

An interpretation $(-)^{\bullet}$ is extended to all objects, programs and formulas as follows. $0^{\bullet}$ is the chosen initial object; $0_X^{\bullet} = 0^{\bullet} \longrightarrow X^{\bullet}$; $id_X^{\bullet} = id_{(X^{\bullet})}$; $(\alpha\beta)^{\bullet} = \alpha^{\bullet}\beta^{\bullet}$; $true_X^{\bullet}$ is the coproduct $X^{\bullet} \xrightarrow{id} X^{\bullet} \longleftarrow 0^{\bullet}$; $(P')^{\bullet}$ is obtained by reversing the order of the ordered coproduct $P^{\bullet}$; $inc_P^{\bullet} : |P|^{\bullet} \longrightarrow X^{\bullet}$ is defined as the first summand of $P^{\bullet}$; $<\alpha,\beta>^{\bullet} = <\alpha^{\bullet},\beta^{\bullet}>$; $(P \bigcap Q)^{\bullet}$ has first summand the chosen summand representing the intersection of the first summands of $P^{\bullet}$ and $Q^{\bullet}$, the second summand then being

forced.   Given (X, Y), define $copr_{X,Y}$ to be the chosen coproduct
$X^\bullet \longrightarrow (X + Y)^\bullet \longleftarrow Y^\bullet$, defining $(X + Y)^\bullet$ as well. For $\alpha \in Prog(X, Y)$,
$Q \in Form(Y)$, there exists a unique pullback square

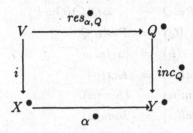

with $i : V \longrightarrow X^\bullet$ a chosen summand, and this defines $res_{\alpha,Q}^\bullet$. Finally, given $R \in$
$Form(X)$, $P \in Form(|R|)$, with the chosen coproducts $P^\bullet = A \overset{i}{\longrightarrow} B \overset{i'}{\longleftarrow} A'$,
$R^\bullet = B \overset{j}{\longrightarrow} X \overset{j'}{\longleftarrow} B'$, define $copr_{A',B'} = A' \overset{t}{\longrightarrow} C \overset{u}{\longleftarrow} B'$. Following the
construction of the proof of Lemma 5.5, define $(P\tau R)'$ to be the coproduct obtained by
replacing the summands of $A \overset{ij}{\longrightarrow} X \overset{<i'j, j'>}{\longleftarrow} C$ with the chosen ones.

The chosen summands and coproducts on $\mathfrak{B}$ above allow unique extensions for
interpretations as is conventional. The theory makes just as much sense if we choose
arbitrary summands and coproducts in the extension process above having started with
any Boolean category with no choices made. Indeed it is clear that every Boolean
functor maps interpretations to interpretations but only a "chosen functor" would
preserve the unique extensions above. For these reasons we prefer to present the
metatheory for arbitrary Boolean categories and arbitrary Boolean functors. This
wholly embraces the "unique only up to isomorphism" principle which underlies the
philosophy of working in a category.

3 DEFINITION A formula P is *valid* in $\mathfrak{B}$ if for every interpretation $(-)^\bullet$ in $\mathfrak{B}$
$inc_P^\bullet$ is an isomorphism. A formula is *universally-valid* if it is valid in every Boolean
category.

4 ABBREVIATIONS IN PBC   (We avoid subscripts to the fullest extent possible.)

$$false = true'$$
$$P \bigcup Q = (P' \bigcap Q')'$$
$$P \Rightarrow Q = P' \bigcup Q$$
$$P \Leftrightarrow Q = (P \Rightarrow Q) \bigcap (Q \Rightarrow P)$$
$$\{P\}\, \alpha\, \{Q\} = P \Rightarrow [\alpha] Q$$
$$Ker(\alpha) = [\alpha] false$$
$$null(\alpha) = Ker(\alpha)$$
$$Dom(\alpha) = (Ker(\alpha))'$$
$$total(\alpha) = Dom(\alpha)$$
$$<\alpha> Q = ([\alpha] Q')'$$
$$wp(\alpha, Q) = Dom(\alpha) \bigcap [\alpha] Q$$
$$if_P(\alpha, \beta) = <inc_P \alpha, inc_{P'} \beta>$$
$$deterministic(\alpha) = [\alpha] Q \bigcup [\alpha] Q'$$
$$crisp(\alpha) = total(\alpha) \bigcap deterministic(\alpha)$$
$$X = 0 = Ker(id_X) \Leftrightarrow Dom(id_X) .$$

Note that there is no mathematical distinction between $null(\alpha)$ and $Ker(\alpha)$. In practice, we think of $Ker(\alpha)$ as a subformula whereas $null(\alpha)$ is an assertion, true for $\alpha : X \longrightarrow Y$ if $Ker(\alpha) = X$. Similar comments apply to $total(\alpha)$. The theorems of the next section will show that α is deterministic if and only if $deterministic(\alpha)$ is valid, and similarly for $crisp(\alpha)$.

5 EXAMPLE   The following are examples of universally-valid formulas. Notice that the variables α, β, γ etc. are implicitly universally quantified since the definition of universal validity requires truth in all interpretations.

1. $[\alpha\beta] R \Leftrightarrow [\alpha]([\beta] R).$

2. $\{Q\}\, if_P(\alpha, \beta)\, \{R\} \Leftrightarrow (\{P \bigcap Q\}\, \alpha\, \{R\}) \bigcap (\{P' \bigcap Q\}\, \beta\, \{R\}.)$

3. $total(\alpha\beta) \Rightarrow total(\alpha).$

4. For $\alpha \in Prog(X, Y)$, $Q \in Form(Y)$, $total(\alpha) \Rightarrow ((total(res_{\alpha, Q}))\, \tau\, true_X)$

5. For $\alpha \in Prog(X,X)$, $X = 0 \Leftrightarrow \ < if_{<\alpha>}{}_Q(\alpha, id_X) > ([\alpha]Q)$.

Before turning to representations by relations, we briefly study some properties of strict Boolean functors.

6 PROPOSITION   Let $\mathcal{B}, \mathcal{C}$ be Boolean categories and let $F : \mathcal{B} \longrightarrow \mathcal{C}$ be a strict Boolean functor. Then the following statements hold.

1. $0F = 0$.

2. The passage $P \mapsto PF$ is an injective Boolean homomorhism
   $Summ(X) \longrightarrow Summ(XF)$.

3. F preserves kernel-domain decompositions. In particular, for α
   in $\mathcal{B}$, $(Ker(\alpha))F = Ker(\alpha F)$ and $(Dom(\alpha))F = Dom(\alpha F)$.

4. For α in $\mathcal{B}$, α is null if and only if αF is null.

5. For α in $\mathcal{B}$, α is total if and only if αF is total.

6. For $p : X \longrightarrow X$ in $\mathcal{B}$, if p is a guard so is pF.

Proof Since F preserves id_X and the coproduct $X \xrightarrow{\ id\ } X \longleftarrow 0$, $0F = 0$. As F preserves coproducts and $[\alpha]Q$, $Summ(X) \longrightarrow Summ(XF)$ preserves $\bigcap$ and $(-)'$ so is a Boolean homomorphism; and the kernel of this homomorphism is trivial precisely because F is strict. Strictness is also used for the $\Leftarrow$ directions in (4,5.) The remaining details are easy. $\qquad\qquad\square$

7 METATHEOREM   If $F : \mathcal{B} \longrightarrow \mathcal{C}$ is a strict Boolean functor then every **PBC**– formula valid in $\mathcal{C}$ is also valid in $\mathcal{B}$.

Proof If P is a formula interpreted as $P^{\bullet}$ in $\mathcal{B}$ and if P is valid in $\mathcal{C}$ then $(inc_P^{\bullet})F$ is an isomorphism, that is, $P^{\bullet}F = XF$ in $Summ(XF)$. By 6(2), $P = X$ in $Summ(X)$, that is, $inc_P^{\bullet}$ is an isomorphism and P is valid in $\mathcal{B}$. $\qquad\qquad\square$

In the above context, it is clear that if $inc_{P\bullet}$ is an isomorphism then so is $(inc_{P\bullet})F$, but this is not enough to argue "P valid in $\mathcal{B} \Rightarrow P$ valid in $\mathcal{C}$". The problem is that an interpretation of P in $\mathcal{C}$ may not be the F–image of an interpretation of P in $\mathcal{B}$.

8 EXAMPLE Define $F : \mathbf{Bag} \longrightarrow \mathbf{Mfn}$ as follows. $XF = X$. Recall that if $\alpha : X \longrightarrow Y$, $\alpha = [\alpha_{xy}]$ is an array each of whose entries is a natural number or is "∞". Define $x(\alpha F) = \{y : \alpha_{xy} > 0\}$. It is easily checked that F is a strict Boolean functor. If $\alpha : X \longrightarrow X$ is defined by $\alpha_{xy} = 0$ when $y \neq x$ but $\alpha_{xx} = 2$ then α is not a guard but αF is a guard being the identity relation. This proves that "$guard(\alpha)$" is not expressible in **PBC**.

We now define the central notion of this section.

9 DEFINITION Let $\mathcal{B}$ be a Boolean category. A *representation by relations for* $\mathcal{B}$ is a strict Boolean functor $F : \mathcal{B} \longrightarrow \mathbf{Mfn}$ which is *reduced* in the sense that for X a $\mathcal{B}$–object and $x, y \in XF$, $x \neq y \Rightarrow \mathcal{U}_x \neq \mathcal{U}_y$ where

10 $\qquad \mathcal{U}_x = \{P \in Summ(X) : x \in PF\}.$

(Here we identify PF with its image in XF.) The term "reduced" directly generalizes a well-known concept for representations of Boolean algebras [Koppelberg 1989, 7.12]. It is natural to require a representation to be reduced since $\mathcal{U}_x$ reflects all that can be said about x using formulas.

The next result motivates our approach toward showing that every Boolean category admits a representation by relations. We will discuss it after the proof.

11 PROPOSITION Let $F : \mathcal{B} \longrightarrow \mathbf{Mfn}$ be a strict Boolean functor and let $\alpha : X \longrightarrow Y$. Then for $x \in XF$,

$$x(\alpha F) \ \subset \ \{y \in YF : \forall V \in \mathcal{U}_y \ <\alpha> V \in \mathcal{U}_x\}$$

If αF is a partial function and F is reduced (and hence a representation by relations) then

$$x(\alpha F) \ = \ \{y \in YF : \forall V \in \mathcal{U}_y \ <\alpha> V \in \mathcal{U}_x\}$$

(and, in particular, the right hand side has at most one element.)

Proof Let $y \in x(\alpha F)$, $V \in \mathcal{U}_y$. By definition of $\mathcal{U}_y$, $y \in VF$ so $y \in VF \cap x(\alpha F)$. In **Mfn**, for $\beta : A \longrightarrow B$, $Q \subset B$, $<\beta> Q \ = \ \{a : a\beta \cap Q \neq \emptyset\}$ so $x \in <\alpha F>(VF) \ = \ (<\alpha> V)F$ and $<\alpha> V \in \mathcal{U}_x$. Now suppose αF is a partial function and that $<\alpha> V \in \mathcal{U}_x$ for all $V \in \mathcal{U}_y$. We have

$$x \in \ \bigcap((<\alpha> V)F : V \in \mathcal{U}_y) \ = \ \bigcap(<\alpha F>(VF) : V \in \mathcal{U}_y)$$

which means that $x(\alpha F) \cap VF \neq \emptyset$ for all $V \in \mathcal{U}_y$. Thus $x(\alpha F) \neq \emptyset$ so, α being a partial function, $x(\alpha F) = \{z\}$ with $z \in VF$ for all $V \in \mathcal{U}_y$ which says $\mathcal{U}_y \subset \mathcal{U}_x$. But we have

12 LEMMA *Each $\mathcal{U}_x$ is an ultrafilter on $Summ(X)$.*

Proof of 12 It is obvious from 6 that: $\mathcal{U}_x \neq \emptyset$; $P,Q \in \mathcal{U}_x \Rightarrow P \cap Q \in \mathcal{U}_x$; $P \in \mathcal{U}_x, P \subset Q \Rightarrow Q \in \mathcal{U}_x$; $P \in Summ(X) \Rightarrow P \in \mathcal{U}_x$ or $P' \in \mathcal{U}_x$. $\qquad\Box$

Returning to the main proof, as ultrafilters are maximal, $\mathcal{U}_y = \mathcal{U}_x$ and then, as F is reduced, $y = z$. Thus $x(\alpha F) = \{y\}$ as needed. $\qquad\Box$

If F is a representation by relations then $x \mapsto \mathcal{U}_x$ establishes an injection from XF to the set of ultrafilters on $Summ(X)$ so we have narrowed down how F must behave on objects. Proposition 11 also suggests what to look at in defining such F on morphisms. The two representation theorems we shall prove follow through on this program. The first, defined only for "atomic Boolean categories", sets XF as the set of all principal ultrafilters on $Summ(X)$. The second, which depends on the axiom of choice (or, at least, the ultrafilter theorem), works in general but defines XF as the set of all ultrafilters on XF. Both functors use the formula of 11 to define αF.

13 DEFINITION   A Boolean category is *atomic* if for all $\alpha : X \longrightarrow Y$ and $Q \in Summ(Y)$, if $<\alpha>Q \neq 0$ then there exists an atom y of the Boolean algebra $Summ(Y)$ with $y \subset Q$, $<\alpha>y \neq 0$.

Notice that $Summ(X)$ is an atomic Boolean algebra if $\mathcal{B}$ is atomic (consider $\alpha = id_X$.)

All of the examples of Boolean categories presented in this paper are atomic. It is hard to think of any Boolean category useful in semantics which is not atomic. It will not surprise us if non-atomic examples arise in future applications but the atomic case seems so common that it is worth a special representation theorem, and such is the following.

14 THEOREM   *Let $\mathcal{B}$ be an atomic Boolean · category.   Then $F : \mathcal{B} \longrightarrow$ Mfn defined by*

$$XF = At(X), \text{ the set of atoms of } Summ(X)$$
$$x (X \xrightarrow{\ \alpha\ } Y)F = \{y \in At(Y) : x \subset <\alpha>y\}$$

is a representation by relations for $\mathcal{B}$.

Proof   We first must show F is a functor. Now $y \in x(id_X) \Leftrightarrow x \subset <id_X>y \Leftrightarrow x \subset y$ $\Leftrightarrow x = y$ (x, y are atoms), so F preserves identities. For composition, let $y \in x(\alpha F)$, $z \in y(\beta F)$. Then $x \subset <\alpha>y$, $y \subset <\beta>z$ so $x \subset <\alpha>y \subset <\alpha>(<\beta>z) =$

$< \alpha \beta > z$, and $(\alpha F)(\beta F) \subset (\alpha \beta) F$. For the reverse inclusion, let x be an atom, $x \subset < \alpha \beta > z$. Then $< \alpha > (< \beta > z) \neq 0$. As $\mathcal{B}$ is atomic, there exists an atom $y \subset < \beta > z$ with $< \alpha > y \neq 0$. If $x \subset < \alpha > y$ then $z \in x(\alpha F)(\beta F)$ as desired. Otherwise $x \not\subset < \alpha > y$ and, as x is an atom, $x \subset (< \alpha > y)' = [\alpha]y'$. Now use the identity 10.4 with $Q = y'$ and $R = < \beta > z$ to get $x \subset [\alpha]y' \bigcap < \alpha \beta > z \subset < \alpha > (y' \bigcap < \beta > z)$. Thus there exists an atom y_1 with $y_1 \subset y' \bigcap < \beta > z$ with $x \subset < \alpha > y_1$ so we still get $z \in x(\alpha F)(\beta F)$.

Now that F is a functor we must prove it is strict Boolean. By 10.1(10) if $i : P \longrightarrow X$ is a summand then iF is the obvious inclusion $At(P) \subset At(X)$. If $P \in Summ(X)$ and $x \in At(X)$, consideration of $x \bigcap (P \bigcup P')$ shows that exactly one of $x \subset P$, $x \subset P'$ occurs and this shows that $At(X)$ is the disjoint union of $At(P)$ and $At(P')$. Thus F preserves coproducts. Even the two-element Boolean algebra has an atom (an atom is a minimal nonzero element) so if $XF = \emptyset$, $X = 0$ in $Summ(X)$. This shows F is strict. Next, we must show F preserves $[\alpha]Q$, that is, if $x \in At(X)$ then

$$x \subset [\alpha]Q \quad \Leftrightarrow \quad (\forall y \in At(Y),\ x \subset < \alpha > y \Rightarrow y \in Q).$$

If $x \in [\alpha]Q \bigcap < \alpha > y$ then $x \subset < \alpha > (Q \bigcap Y)$ (10.4) $\Rightarrow Q \bigcap y \neq 0 \Rightarrow y \in Q$. Conversely, assume $x \subset < \alpha > y \Rightarrow y \in Q$. Suppose $x \subset < \alpha > Q'$. Consider the summand $i : x \longrightarrow X$. By 10.1(10), $<i>(< \alpha > Q') = x \bigcap < \alpha > Q'$ so $< i \alpha > Q = x$ and, since $\mathcal{B}$ is atomic, there exists an atom $y \subset Q'$ with $< i \alpha > y \neq 0$ so, as x is an atom, $x \subset < \alpha > y$. Thus, by the hypothesis on x, $y \subset Q$ which is impossible as $y \subset Q'$ and $y \neq 0$. As $x \subset < \alpha > Q'$ is false we have $x \subset (< \alpha > Q')' = [\alpha]Q$ as needed. Finally, observe that $\mathcal{U}_x = \{P \in Summ(X) : x \subset P\}$ so it is clear that $x = \bigcap \mathcal{U}_x$ which shows F is reduced.

$\square$

Notice that if $\mathcal{B} = \mathbf{Mfn}$ then the functor F of the previous theorem is essentially the identity functor. This is not true for the next theorem. The atomic theorem is tighter when available.

The main result of this section is

15 THEOREM   *Every Boolean category admits a representation by relations. Hence* (by Metatheorem 7) *the universally-valid* **PBC**-*formulas are precisely the set of such formulas valid in* **Mfn**.

Proof Define XK to be the set of all ultrafilters on $Summ(X)$ and, for α : $X \longrightarrow Y$, define

16 $\mathcal{U}(\alpha K) \;=\; \{\mathcal{V} \in YK : V \in \mathcal{V} \Rightarrow \;<\alpha> V \in \mathcal{U}\}.$

We refer the reader to [Kozen 1980, 3.8'] for a proof that $(\alpha\beta)K = (\alpha K)(\beta K)$ since virtually no changes are needed to adapt this to a category. That $id_X K = id_{XK}$ is obvious. We call K the *Kozen functor*.

If $X \neq 0$ then $0, X$ are distinct elements of $Summ(X)$ so that (using the ultrafilter theorem) $XK \neq \emptyset$, and this shows K is strict. K preserves coproducts as follows. Let $P \overset{i}{\longrightarrow} X \overset{j}{\longleftarrow} Q$ be a coproduct in $\mathfrak{B}$. Let $\mathcal{U} \in PK$ and define $\mathcal{U}^P$ $= \{R \in Summ(X) : P \bigcap R \in \mathcal{U}\}$. $\mathcal{U}^P$ is obviously a filter and is, in fact, an ultrafilter because for any $R \in Summ(X)$ one of $P \bigcap R$, $P \bigcap R'$ must belong to $\mathcal{U}$. Now observe that by **10.1**(10), $\mathcal{V} \in \mathcal{U}(iK) \Leftrightarrow (V \in \mathcal{V} \Rightarrow <i> V \in \mathcal{U}) \Leftrightarrow (V \in \mathcal{V} \Rightarrow$ $P \bigcap V \in \mathcal{U}) \Leftrightarrow \mathcal{V} \subset \mathcal{U}^P \Leftrightarrow \mathcal{V} = \mathcal{U}^P$ (maximality!) so iK is a total function mapping $\mathcal{U}$ to $\mathcal{U}^P$. If $\mathcal{U} \neq \mathcal{U}_1$ in PK there exists $U \in \mathcal{U}$, $U \notin \mathcal{U}_1$. Since U (considered in $Summ(X)$ as in Lemma **5.5**) $= P \bigcap U, U \in \mathcal{U}^P$. But no subset of U belongs to $\mathcal{U}_1$ so $U \notin \mathcal{U}_1^P$. This shows that iK is injective. Clearly no $\mathcal{V} \in XK$ contains both a subset of P and a subset of Q so the images of iK, jK do not intersect. Let $\mathcal{V} \in XK$ be arbitrary. As P, Q partition $Summ(X)$, $\mathcal{V}$ contains exactly one of P, Q. If $P \in \mathcal{V}$ then $\mathcal{U} = \{P \bigcap V : V \in \mathcal{V}\}$ is routinely checked to be an ultrafilter in PK and $\mathcal{V} \subset \mathcal{U}^P \Rightarrow$ $\mathcal{V} = \mathcal{U}^P$. Otherwise $Q \in \mathcal{V}$ and $\mathcal{V}$ has the form $\mathcal{U}^Q$. Thus the images of iK, jK cover XK. This completes the proof that K preserves coproducts. For $\mathcal{V} \in XK$, $\mathcal{U}_\mathcal{V} = \{P \in Summ(X) : \mathcal{V} \in PK\} = \{P \in Summ(X) : P \in \mathcal{V}\}$ (for we just saw above that $\mathcal{V}$ has form $\mathcal{U}^P$ if and only if $P \in \mathcal{V})$ $= \mathcal{V}$ so $x \mapsto \mathcal{U}_x$ is seen to be the identity function and this establishes that K is reduced.

To complete the proof we must demonstrate that K preserves $[\alpha]Q$. We rely on the following lemma whose proof (which requires the ultrafilter theorem), once again, is unchanged by moving to the category setting:

17 LEMMA   [Kozen 1980, Lemma 3.4(iii).] Let $\alpha : X \longrightarrow Y$, $\mathcal{U} \in XK$ and let $R \in Summ(Y)$ with $<\alpha>R \in \mathcal{U}$. Then there exists $\mathcal{V} \in \mathcal{U}(\alpha K)$ with $R \in \mathcal{V}$.

$\square$

Returning to the main proof, let $\alpha : X \longrightarrow Y$, $Q \in Summ(Y)$. As K is a coproduct-preserving functor (and so maps summands to summands) we have $([\alpha]Q)K \subset [\alpha K](QK)$ and need to show the reverse inclusion. Let $\mathcal{U} \in [\alpha K](QK)$. To show: $[\alpha]Q \in \mathcal{U}$. If $<\alpha>Q' \in \mathcal{U}$ it follows from Lemma 17 that there exists $\mathcal{V} \in \mathcal{U}(\alpha K)$ with $Q' \in \mathcal{V}$. On the other hand, as $\mathcal{U} \in [\alpha K](QK)$ it follows from the **Mfn**-construction "for $\beta : A \longrightarrow B$, $R \subset B$, $[\beta]R = \{a : a\beta \subset R\}$" that $\mathcal{V} \in \mathcal{U}(\alpha K) \Rightarrow Q \in \mathcal{V}$. Since both Q, Q' cannot be in $\mathcal{V}$ it must be false that $<\alpha>Q' \in \mathcal{U}$, so $(<\alpha>Q')' = [\alpha]Q \in \mathcal{U}$.

$\square$

18 OBSERVATION   *The Boolean category $\mathfrak{B}$ is faithful (in the sense of Definition 5.21) if and only if its Kozen functor $K : \mathfrak{B} \longrightarrow$ **Mfn** is a faithful functor.* For let $\alpha, \beta : X \longrightarrow Y$. If $<\alpha>V = <\beta>V$ for all V, it is obvious from **16** that $\alpha K = \beta K$ so K faithful $\Rightarrow \mathfrak{B}$ faithful. Conversely, suppose there exist α, β, V with $<\alpha>V - <\beta>V \neq 0$ (where $P - Q$ means $P \bigcap Q'$.) It suffices to find $\mathcal{U} \in X\beta$, $\mathcal{V} \in Y\beta$ with $\mathcal{V} \in \mathcal{U}(\alpha K)$, $\mathcal{V} \notin \mathcal{U}(\alpha K)$. As any nonzero element belongs to an ultrafilter, there exists $\mathcal{V} \in Y\beta$ with $V \in \mathcal{V}$ and there exists $\mathcal{U} \in X\beta$ with $<\alpha>V \in \mathcal{U}$, $<\beta>V \notin \mathcal{U}$, exactly as needed.

A similar observation applies to the atomic case. We leave the details to the reader.

The following characterizes those strict Boolean functors which are bijective on summands.

19 PROPOSITION   *Let* $F : \mathfrak{B} \longrightarrow \mathfrak{C}$ *be a strict Boolean functor.   The following three statements are equivalent.*

1. *For all* X, $Summ(X) \longrightarrow Summ(XF)$ *is surjective.*

2. *If* $G : \mathfrak{C} \longrightarrow \mathbf{Mfn}$ *is a representation by relations, then so is* FG.

3. *If* $K : \mathfrak{C} \longrightarrow \mathbf{Mfn}$ *is the Kozen functor then* FK *is a representation by relations.*

Proof $1 \Rightarrow 2$: Let $x \neq y \in XFG$. As G is reduced, there exists $Q \in Summ(XF)$ with $x \in QG$, $y \notin QG$. As $Summ(X) \longrightarrow Summ(Y)$ is surjective, there exists $P \in Summ(X)$ with $PF = Q$. As $x \in PFG$, $y \notin PFG$, FG is reduced.

$3 \Rightarrow 1$: Let N be the image of $Summ(X) \longrightarrow Summ(XF)$ so that N is a Boolean subalgebra of $Summ(XF)$. If $N \neq Summ(XF)$ it follows from [Koppelberg 1989, Lemma 5.32] that there exist $\mathcal{U} \neq \mathcal{V} \in XFK$ with $\mathcal{U} \bigcap N = \mathcal{V} \bigcap N$. This directly contradicts the assumption that FK is reduced, so N must be all of $Summ(XF)$ after all.   □

We conclude this section by extending the metatheory to ranged Boolean categories.

20 DEFINITION The typed language **PRBC** (for Propositional Ranged Boolean Categories) extends **PBC** as follows:

$$If \ \alpha \in Prog(X,Y) \ then \ Ran(\alpha) \in Form(Y) \ and \ sf_\alpha \in Prog(X, |\, Ran(\alpha)\,|).$$

sf_α is for "surjective factor of α". The semantics should be clear. If $(-)^\bullet$ is an interpretation as in 2, let $(Ran(\alpha))^\bullet$ be the (chosen) least sumand through which $\alpha^\bullet$ factors and let $(sf_\alpha)^\bullet$ be the unique s with $\alpha^\bullet = s\, inc^\bullet_{Ran(\alpha)}$.

21   ABBREVIATIONS IN PRBC

$$P[\alpha] = Ran(inc_P \alpha)$$
$$surjective(\alpha) = Ran(\alpha)$$
$$P<\alpha> = (P'[\alpha])'$$
$$sp(P,\alpha) = Ran(\alpha) \bigcap P<\alpha>.$$

22   METATHEOREM   *Let $\mathfrak{B},\mathfrak{C}$ be ranged Boolean categories and let $F : \mathfrak{B} \longrightarrow \mathfrak{C}$ be a strict Boolean functor which preserves ranges. Then every PRBC–formula valid in $\mathfrak{C}$ is also valid in $\mathfrak{B}$.*   □

23   THEOREM   *The Kozen functor $K : \mathfrak{B} \longrightarrow \mathbf{Mfn}$ of a ranged Boolean category $\mathfrak{B}$ is range-preserving. Hence the PRBC–formulas valid in all ranged Boolean categories are precisely those valid in $\mathbf{Mfn}$.*

Proof   Let $\alpha : X \longrightarrow Y$ be surjective in $\mathfrak{B}$. We must show that αK is onto. Let $\mathcal{V} \in YK$. To find: $\mathcal{U} \in XK$ such that $V \in \mathcal{V} \Rightarrow <\alpha>V \in \mathcal{U}$. Equivalently, we must demonstrate that $\{<\alpha>V : V \in \mathcal{V}\}$ has the finite intersection property. Let $V_1,...,V_n \in \mathcal{V}$, and set $V = V_1 \bigcap ... \bigcap V_n$. As α is surjective and $V \neq 0$, also $<\alpha>V \neq 0$. But $<\alpha>V \subset <\alpha>V_1 \bigcap ... \bigcap <\alpha>V_n$.   □

The next is an analogue to Proposition **10.20** which demonstrates the power of the previous theorem.

24   COROLLARY   *Let $P \in Summ(X)$, $\alpha : X \longrightarrow Y$, $Q \in Summ(Y)$ in a ranged Boolean category. Then*

$$P<\alpha> \supset Q \iff \{P'\} \alpha \{Q'\} \iff P \supset <\alpha>Q .$$

Proof   Check in **Mfn**   □

We conclude with an atomic form of Proposition 23.

25 PROPOSITION *Let* $\mathcal{B}$ *be a ranged Boolean category in which the Boolean algebra* $Summ(X)$ *is atomic for each* X. *Then* $\mathcal{B}$ *is an atomic Boolean category and the representation* $F : \mathcal{B} \longrightarrow \mathbf{Mfn}$ *of 14 is range-preserving.*

Proof Let $\alpha : X \longrightarrow Y$, $Q \in Summ(X)$ with $<\alpha>Q \neq 0$. We must find an atom $y \in Summ(Y)$ with $h \subset Q$, $<\alpha>y \neq 0$. Let $R = Ran(\alpha)$. As $[\alpha]Q' \neq X$, $\{X\} \alpha \{Q'\}$ is false so $R \subset Q'$ is false and $R \bigcap Q \neq 0$. As $Summ(Y)$ is atomic, there exists an atom $y \subset R \bigcap Q$. As $R \subset y'$ is false, $\{X\} \alpha \{y'\}$ is false so $[\alpha]y' \neq X$ and $<\alpha>y \neq 0$. This shows $\mathcal{B}$ is atomic. Now let α be surjective. For any atom y of $Summ(Y)$, $<\alpha>y \neq 0$ so there exists an atom $x \subset <\alpha>y$. This shows that αF is onto, so F preserves surjectives as needed. □

12 DETERMINISTIC MORPHISMS

In this section we study further the deterministic morphisms introduced in **2.13**. We give several characterizations and show that crisp ⇔ total and deterministic. Dijkstra's "composition rule" $wp(\alpha\beta, R) = wp(\alpha, wp(\beta, R))$, conspicuously absent from Proposition **10.2**, is seen (for fixed α and arbitrary β) to characterize "α is deterministic" in all Boolean categories with a projection system, **Mfn** included. When all morphisms are deterministic, $Dom(\alpha)$ is characterized by a universal property analogous to that of the kernel. The deterministic maps in a Boolean category $\mathcal{B}$ constitute a Boolean subcategory $\mathcal{B}_{det}$.

We work in a Boolean category $\mathcal{B}$. We shall make free use of the calculus of predicate transformers developed in preceding sections. We begin with a lemma.

1 LEMMA   *The following hold:*

1. *Given* $\alpha : X \longrightarrow Y$, $Q \in Summ(Y)$, $Ker(\alpha) \subset [\alpha]Q$.

2. *Given* $\alpha : X \longrightarrow Y$, $\beta : Y \longrightarrow Z$, $Dom(\alpha\beta) \subset Dom(\alpha)$.

Proof   For the first statement, $Ker(\alpha) = [\alpha]0$ and $[\alpha](-)$ is monotone. For the second, $t\alpha$ null $\Rightarrow t\alpha\beta$ null so $Ker(\alpha) \subset Ker(\alpha\beta)$; now take complements. $\square$

2 PROPOSITION   *For any* $\alpha : X \longrightarrow Y$, *the following statements are equivalent.*

1. *α is deterministic, that is,* $\forall Q \in Summ(Y)$ $\exists P \in Summ(X)$ *with*
   $\{P\}\,\alpha\{Q\}$, $\{P'\}\,\alpha\,\{Q'\}$.

2. For $Q, R \in Summ(Y)$, $[\alpha](Q \bigcup R) = [\alpha]Q \bigcup [\alpha]R$.

3. [Dijkstra 1976] For $Q, R \in Summ(Y)$, $wp(\alpha, Q \bigcup R) = wp(\alpha, Q) \bigcup wp(\alpha, R)$.

4. [Fischer and Ladner 1979, p. 194] For $Q \in Summ(Y)$, $<\alpha> Q \subset [\alpha]Q$.

5. For $Q \in Summ(Y)$, $[\alpha]Q \bigcup [\alpha]Q' = X$.

6. For $Q, R \in Summ(Y)$, $<\alpha> (Q \bigcap R) = <\alpha> Q \bigcap <\alpha> R$.

7. For $Q \in Summ(Y)$, $\{([\alpha]Q)'\} \, \alpha \, \{Q'\}$.

Proof 1$\Rightarrow$4: We assume $P \subset [\alpha]Q$, $P' \subset [\alpha]Q'$. Thus $<\alpha> Q = ([\alpha]Q')' \subset P \subset [\alpha]Q$.

4$\Rightarrow$7: $([\alpha]Q')' = <\alpha> Q' \subset [\alpha]Q'$.

7$\Rightarrow$1: Set $P = [\alpha]Q$.

2$\Rightarrow$3: Use the distributive law in $Summ(X)$.

3$\Rightarrow$2: By 1(1), $[\alpha](Q \bigcup R)$ and $[\alpha]Q \bigcup [\alpha]R$ have the same intersection with $Ker(\alpha)$ and so are equal if and only if they intersect equally with $Dom(\alpha)$ and this is precisely the hypothesis.

4$\Leftrightarrow$5: Since $[\alpha]Q' = (<\alpha> Q)'$, 5 $\Leftrightarrow$ $([\alpha]Q)' \subset (<\alpha> Q)' \Leftrightarrow$ 4.

4,5 $\Rightarrow$ 2: $X = [\alpha](Q \bigcup R) \bigcup [\alpha](Q' \bigcap R') = [\alpha](Q \bigcup R) \bigcup ([\alpha]Q' \bigcap [\alpha]R') = [\alpha](Q \bigcup R) \bigcup (<\alpha> Q \bigcup <\alpha> R)'$ so $[\alpha](Q \bigcup R) \subset <\alpha> Q \bigcup <\alpha> R \subset [\alpha]Q \bigcup [\alpha]R$. The reverse inclusion follows from the monotonicity of $[\alpha](-)$.

As 2$\Rightarrow$5 is trivial and 2$\Leftrightarrow$6 by De Morgan duality, we are done. $\square$

Notice that $\{[\alpha]Q\} \, \alpha \, \{Q\}$ is always true so that 2(7) amounts to the original definition in **2.13**.

We saw in Corollary **6.10** that a crisp map is total and it was clear from the beginning that crisp $\Rightarrow$ deterministic. The following provides a sharper statement.

3 COROLLARY *A morphism is crisp if and only if it is total and deterministic. Indeed, for $\alpha : X \longrightarrow Y$ the following hold:*

1. α is deterministic $\Leftrightarrow$ for $Q \in Summ(Y)$, $<\alpha> Q \subset [\alpha]Q$.

2. α is total $\Leftrightarrow$ for $Q \in Summ(Y)$, $<\alpha> Q \supset [\alpha]Q$.

3. α is crisp $\Leftrightarrow$ for $Q \in Summ(Y)$, $<\alpha> Q = [\alpha]Q$.

4. α is crisp $\Leftrightarrow$ $Q \mapsto [\alpha]Q$ is a Boolean algebra homomorphism
$Summ(Y) \longrightarrow Summ(X)$.

Proof The first statement is just 2(4). For the second, $Ker(\alpha) = [\alpha]0 = [\alpha]Q \cap$ $[\alpha]Q'$ so α is total $\Leftrightarrow Ker(\alpha) = 0 \Leftrightarrow [\alpha]Q \subset ([\alpha]Q')' = <\alpha>Q$. Turning to statement 3, in retrospect the original definition of "crisp" in **4.3** is equivalent to the assertion that $([\alpha]Q)' = [\alpha]Q'$ which is the same as saying $<\alpha>Q = [\alpha]Q$. Having said this, the fourth statement is clear since $[\alpha](-)$ preserves $\cap$ and $[\alpha]Y = X$ for any α. $\qquad\qquad\qquad\qquad\qquad\qquad\qquad\qquad\qquad\qquad\qquad\qquad\qquad\square$

From the viewpoint of [Dijkstra 1976] semantics is either by partial functions or multivalued functions and so each morphism α is indiscernible, that is, is determined by $wp(\alpha, -)$. Indeed, $x\alpha = \emptyset$ if $x \notin wp(\alpha, Y)$ and otherwise $x\alpha = \bigcap(Q : x \in wp(\alpha, Q))$. Thus Dijkstra *defined* program-chaining $\alpha\beta$ by the natural-appearing rule $wp(\alpha\beta, Q) = wp(\alpha, wp(\beta, Q))$. However, consider the following example:

4 EXAMPLE In **Mfn**, if $X = \{a\}$, $Y = \{b, c\}$, and if we define two morphisms by $\alpha : X \longrightarrow Y$, $a\alpha = Y$; $\beta : Y \longrightarrow Y$, $b\beta = \{b\}$, $c\beta = \emptyset$ then $wp(\alpha, wp(\beta, Q))$ $= \emptyset$ for all Q whereas $wp(\alpha\beta, Y) = X$. Therefore the Dijkstra composition rule is false in **Mfn**.

The discrepancy is explained by observing that the composition defined by the Dijkstra rule is not the usual one in **Mfn** but is rather that of the pathological category of Example 4.12. Still, the rule is very compelling and it seems natural to ask what it means for Boolean categories. We now turn to that investigation.

5 LEMMA *The following hold for arbitrary $\alpha : X \longrightarrow Y$, $\beta : Y \longrightarrow Z$:*

1. *For all $R \in Summ(Y)$, $wp(\alpha\beta, R) = wp(\alpha, Dom(\beta)) \cap [\alpha\beta]R$.*

2. *$wp(\alpha, Dom(\beta)) \subset Dom(\alpha\beta)$.*

Proof For the first statement,

$$wp(\alpha, wp(\beta, R)) = Dom(\alpha) \bigcap [\alpha](Dom(\beta) \bigcap [\beta]R)$$
$$= Dom(\alpha) \bigcap [\alpha](Dom(\beta)) \bigcap [\alpha]([\beta]R)$$
$$= wp(\alpha, Dom(\beta)) \bigcap [\alpha\beta]R.$$

For the second, consider the diagram

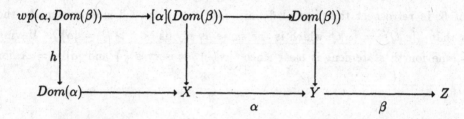

Since $wp(\alpha, Dom(\beta)) \longrightarrow Dom(\alpha)$ and $Dom(\alpha) \longrightarrow Y$ are total, so is $wp(\alpha, Dom(\beta)) \longrightarrow Dom(\beta)$ by **6.3**. But $Dom(\beta) \longrightarrow Z$ is total so that $wp(\alpha, Dom(\beta))$ is a summand of X restricted to which $\alpha\beta$ is total. Now use Proposition **6.11**.   □

We then have the following result which shows that, in **Mfn**, the Dijkstra composition rule characterizes determinism:

6 PROPOSITION   *For $\alpha : X \longrightarrow Y$ in $\mathfrak{B}$, statements 1, 2 are equivalent and are true if α is deterministic:*

1. *For all $\beta : Y \longrightarrow Z$, $R \in Summ(Y)$, $wp(\alpha\beta, R) = wp(\alpha, wp(\beta, R))$.*

2. *For all $\beta : Y \longrightarrow Z$, $Dom(\alpha\beta) = wp(\alpha, Dom(\beta))$.*

If $\mathfrak{B}$ has a projection system, these statements hold if and only if α is deterministic.

Proof   To see that the first statement implies the second, $Dom(\alpha\beta) = Dom(\alpha\beta) \bigcap [\alpha\beta]Z = wp(\alpha\beta, Z) = wp(\alpha, wp(\beta, Z)) = wp(\alpha, Dom(\beta))$.   The converse is immediate from Lemma 5(1). If α is deterministic, then

$$wp(\alpha, Dom(\beta)) = Dom(\alpha) \bigcap [\alpha](Dom(\beta))$$
$$= <\alpha>Y \bigcap [\alpha](<\beta>Z)$$

$$\supset \ <\alpha>Y \bigcap <\alpha>(<\beta>Z)$$
$$= \ <\alpha>(Y \bigcap <\beta>Z)$$
$$= \ <\alpha\beta>Z \ = \ Dom(\alpha\beta)$$

and the reverse inclusion follows from Lemma 5(2). Finally, let ρ be a projection system for $\mathfrak{B}$, assume α satisfies (2), let $j : Q \longrightarrow Y$ be a summand and consider the diagram

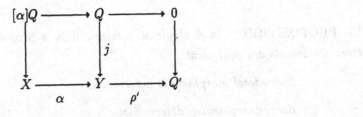

By 8.19, $j = Ker(\rho')$ so the right hand square is a pullback. By pullback-pasting 5.20, $[\alpha]Q = Ker(\alpha\rho')$ so $([\alpha]Q)' = Dom(\alpha\rho') = wp(\alpha, Dom(\rho')) \subset [\alpha]Q'$ and 2(5) holds. $\square$

7 EXAMPLE   Consider a Boolean category in which all morphisms are total, e.g. $\mathfrak{B}_{tot}$ (6.17) for any Boolean $\mathfrak{B}$. Then for all $\alpha : X \longrightarrow Y$, $\beta : Y \longrightarrow Z$, $wp(\alpha, Dom(\beta)) = Dom(\alpha) \bigcap [\beta]Y = X = Dom(\alpha\beta)$ so 6(2) is true. But not all morphisms need be deterministic;   consider, e.g., $\mathbf{Mfn}_{tot}$. This shows that the assumption about the existence of a projection system in Proposition **6** cannot be dropped.

8 OBSERVATION   We remarked just following Definition **6.14** that for a general Boolean category, $\mathfrak{B} \longrightarrow \mathfrak{B}_{part}$ need not be functorial. *A sufficient condition for functoriality is that   the composition rule* **6(1)** *holds.* For if $i : D \longrightarrow X$ = $Dom(\alpha)$, $j : E \longrightarrow X$ = $Dom(\beta)$ so that $\alpha \mapsto [D, i\alpha]$, $\beta \mapsto [E, j\beta]$ then as a summand of D, $Dom(\alpha\beta) = wp(\alpha, E) = D \bigcap [\alpha]E = [i\alpha]E$. Thus $t(i\alpha) = uj$ is a pullback square if $t : Dom(\beta) \longrightarrow D$, $u : Dom(\alpha\beta) \longrightarrow E$ so that $[D, i\alpha][E, j\beta]$ = $[Dom(\alpha\beta), uj\beta]$.   But $(ti)\alpha\beta = t(i\alpha)\beta = uj\beta$ which shows that $\alpha\beta \mapsto$ $[Dom(\alpha\beta), uj\beta]$ as well. $\square$

9   DEFINITION   For $\alpha : X \longrightarrow Y$ in a Boolean category, a *totalizer* of α is a morphism $\tau : W \longrightarrow X$ such that $\tau\alpha$ is total and τ is universal with this property, that is, whenever $\beta : V \longrightarrow X$ with $\beta\alpha$ total then β factors uniquely through τ, $\psi\tau = \beta$ for unique ψ.

Notice the analogy with the universal property for the kernel —just replace "null" with "total".

10   PROPOSITION   *In a Boolean category with a projection system the following three statements are equivalent.*

1. *Every total morphism is deterministic.*

2. *Every morphism is deterministic.*

3. *For all* $\alpha : X \longrightarrow Y$, $Dom(\alpha) \longrightarrow X$ *is a totalizer of* α.

Proof $1 \Rightarrow 3$:   Given $\alpha : X \longrightarrow Y$, let $\beta : W \longrightarrow X$ with $\beta\alpha$ total.   Then β is total (**6.3(2)**), hence deterministic by hypothesis.   By Proposition **6**, $W = Dom(\beta\alpha)$ $= wp(\beta, Dom(\alpha)) = Dom(\beta) \bigcap [\beta](Dom(\alpha)) = [\beta](Dom(\alpha))$,   and there exists a pullback of form

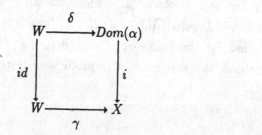

Thus δ provides the desired factorization and such δ is unique because i is mono.

$3 \Rightarrow 2$:   Let $\alpha : X \longrightarrow Y$, $\beta : Y \longrightarrow Z$ and consider the diagram

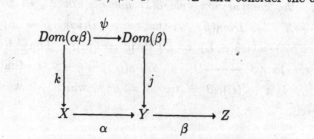

where ψ exists by hypothesis since $k\alpha\beta$ is total. Then

$$
\begin{aligned}
Dom(\alpha\beta) &= Dom(\alpha) \bigcap Dom(\alpha\beta) \quad \text{(Lemma 1(2))} \\
&\subset Dom(\alpha) \bigcap [\alpha](Dom(\beta)) \quad (\{Dom(\alpha\beta)\} \; \alpha \; \{Dom(\beta)\}) \\
&= wp(\alpha, Dom(\beta))
\end{aligned}
$$

so by 5(2) and 6, α is deterministic. $\qquad\qquad\qquad\qquad\qquad\qquad$ □

We can again invoke Example 7 to see that the existence of a projection system is necessary in 10, i.e. if $\alpha : X \longrightarrow Y$ is total then $id_X : X \longrightarrow X$ is a totalizer of α.

11 PROPOSITION *For any Boolean category $\mathcal{B}$, the deterministic morphisms constitute a wide Boolean subcategory $\mathcal{B}_{det}$ of $\mathcal{B}$. $\mathcal{B}_{det} \subset \mathcal{B}$ is a ranged Boolean extension if $\mathcal{B}$ is a ranged Boolean category.*

Proof $[id_X]Q = Q$ is union-preserving and $[\alpha\beta](-) = [\alpha]([\beta](-))$ is union-preserving if $[\alpha](-)$ and $[\beta](-)$ are, so $\mathcal{B}_{det}$ is a subcategory. Summands are crisp, hence deterministic, so if $P \xrightarrow{\;i\;} X \xleftarrow{\;j\;} Q$ is a coproduct in $\mathcal{B}$, the diagram lives in $\mathcal{B}_{det}$ and we must prove (what was promised in **5.13**) that

12 $\qquad\qquad$ If $\alpha : X \longrightarrow Y$, $\beta : Q \longrightarrow Y$ are deterministic then
$\qquad\qquad\qquad < \alpha, \beta > \; : X \longrightarrow Y$ also is.

It is immediate from **10.1(8)** and **5.5** that (pushed forward into $Summ(X)$) $[< \alpha, \beta >]Q$ $= [\alpha]Q \bigcup [\beta]Q$ so it is clear that $[< \alpha, \beta >](-)$ preserves unions if $[\alpha](-)$ and $[\beta](-)$ do. Thus $P \xrightarrow{\;i\;} X \xleftarrow{\;j\;} Q$ is a coproduct in $\mathcal{B}_{det}$.

By **10.1(7)**, $[\alpha](-)$ is constant if α is null so null maps are deterministic and, in particular, $0 \longrightarrow X$ is deterministic for every X. Thus 0 provides an initial object for $\mathcal{B}_{det}$. We pause for

13 LEMMA   *Given* $W \xrightarrow{\ \alpha\ } P \xrightarrow{\ i\ } X$ *with i a summand and αi deterministic, then α is deterministic.*

To see the lemma, for $Q \in Summ(P)$, $[\alpha]Q = [\alpha](P \bigcap Q) = [\alpha]([i]Q) = [\alpha i]Q$ so $[\alpha](-)$ is just the restriction of $[\alpha i](-)$ to P and so is union-preserving.   □

To apply the lemma, consider the $\mathcal{B}$–pullback

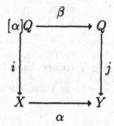

where α is deterministic. As βj is deterministic, so is β by the lemma. Again by the lemma, any $\psi : W \longrightarrow [\alpha]Q$ with ψi deterministic is itself deterministic, so we have shown that the square is a pullback in $\mathcal{B}_{det}$. Finally, $\mathcal{B}_{det} \subset \mathcal{B}$ is an extension because every isomorphism is crisp, deterministic in particular, and is a ranged extension if $\mathcal{B}$ is ranged since it is immediate from the Lemma that $\mathcal{B}_{det}$ is closed under surjective-summand factorizations.   □

14 EXAMPLE $Mfn_{det} = Pfn.$

15 OBSERVATION   *Excepting the trivial case when every object is initial, a semiadditive Boolean category always has a nondeterministic morphism.* For, given an object X, define $\alpha : X \longrightarrow X + X$ by $\alpha = in_1 + in_2$. By **10.5**, $<\alpha> Q = <in_1> Q \bigcup <in_2> Q$, and $[\alpha]Q = [in_2]Q \bigcap [in_2]Q$. By **3**, $<in_i> Q = [in_i]Q$. Thus, if α were deterministic we would have $[in_1]Q \bigcup [in_2]Q = [in_1]Q \bigcap [in_2]Q$, that is, $[in_1]Q = [in_2]Q$ for all $Q \in Summ(X + X)$. In particular, let Q be the first copy of X. Then $[in_1]Q = X$ whereas $[in_2]Q = 0$. Thus $X = 0$.   □

We now turn to a lemma and proposition relating $\alpha^\dagger$ to *while-do* when α is deterministic.

16 LEMMA *Let* $(-)^\dagger$ *be a polymorphic iterate in a preadditive Boolean category with canonical projection system* ρ. *Given a diagram*

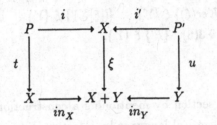

where the top row is a coproduct, $\xi^\dagger = (while\ P\ do\ \xi_X)\xi_Y$ *where* $\xi_X = \xi\,\rho_X$, $\xi_Y = \xi\,\rho_Y$.

Proof We use Lemma 7.17 and Proposition 7.10. Recall that for the coproduct system $(X, P, i, \theta, P', i', \theta')$, the guard p of P is θi and $p' = \theta'i'$ similarly. We have $i\xi_X = i\xi\,\rho_X = t\,in_X\,\rho_X = t = i\theta t$ and $i'\xi_X = i'\xi\,\rho_X = u\,in_Y\,\rho_X = 0 = i'\theta t$ so $\xi_X = \theta t$. By a similar calculation, $\xi_Y = \theta'u$. Thus $p\xi_X = (\theta i)(\theta t) = \theta t = \xi_X$ whereas $p'\xi_Y = \theta'i'\theta'u = \theta'u = \xi_Y$, yielding

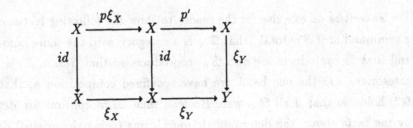

so that $\xi^\dagger = (while\ P\ do\ \xi_X)\xi_Y$. $\square$

This yields

17 PROPOSITION   *Let $(-)^\dagger$ be a polymorphic iterate in a preadditive Boolean category with canonical projection system ρ, and let $\xi : X \longrightarrow X + Y$ be deterministic. Define $\xi_X = \xi \, \rho_X$, $\xi_Y = \xi \, \rho_Y$. Let P be any element of $Summ(X)$ with $wp(\xi, X) \subset P \subset [\xi]X$. Then*

$$\xi^\dagger = (\ while\ P\ do\ \xi_X)\xi_Y.$$

Proof By the lemma it suffices to show that for any such P we have $\{P\} \, \xi \, \{X\}$ and $\{P'\} \, \xi \, \{Y\}$. If $P \subset [\xi]X$, $\{P\} \, \xi \, \{X\}$. Also $P' \subset (wp(\xi, X))' = Ker(\xi) \bigcup ([\xi]X)'$. As $\{Ker(\xi)\} \, \xi \, \{0\}$, $\{Ker(\xi)\} \, \xi \, \{Y\}$. $\{([\xi]X)'\} \, \xi \, \{Y\}$ because ξ is deterministic (Proposition 2(7).) By **9.3**(8), $\{P'\} \, \xi \, \{Y\}$. $\qquad\qquad\qquad\qquad\square$

We conclude the section by mentioning a construction of [Dijkstra and Scholten 1990] as expressed in categorical language by [Martin, Hoare and Jifeng 1991].

18 EXAMPLE Let $\mathcal{B}$ be a Boolean category with zero morphisms. Given the coproduct $P \xrightarrow{\;\;i\;\;} X \xleftarrow{\;\;i'\;\;} P'$ and $\alpha : X \longrightarrow Y$ define the *P-restriction of* α to be the morphism $P \triangleleft \alpha : X \longrightarrow Y$ defined by $i(P \triangleleft \alpha) = i\alpha$, $i'(P \triangleleft \alpha) = 0$. Define a new category $\mathcal{B}_\triangleleft$ with the same objects and morphisms as $\mathcal{B}$ but with the modified composition

$$\alpha * \beta = ([\alpha]Dom(\beta)) \triangleleft \alpha\beta .$$

We leave it as an exercise for the reader to show the following facts: $\alpha * \beta = \alpha\beta$ if α is a summand or if β is total; that $\mathcal{B}_\triangleleft$ is a category with the same isomorphisms as $\mathcal{B}$; and that $\mathcal{B}$-coproducts are also $\mathcal{B}_\triangleleft$–coproducts so that $Summ(X)$ is the same in both categories. On the one hand, we have redefined composition so that the condition in **6**(2) holds so that if all $\mathcal{B}_\triangleleft$ were Boolean then all morphisms are deterministic. But by the facts above, the deterministic morphisms (using the original definition **2.13**) are the same in both categories, so $\mathcal{B}_\triangleleft$ is not Boolean in general, in particular not if $\mathcal{B} = $ **Mfn**.

13 COMPLETION AND DUALITY

Particularly nice models of ranged Boolean categories are the semilattice-assertional categories of [Manes 1988] which we independently characterize here in terms of Boolean categories. The dual of a semilattice-assertional category is again such. The main result is that each preadditive ranged Boolean category admits a completion to a semilattice-asssertional one. This provides a categorical duality relating forward and inverse predicate transformers.

In this section, $\mathcal{B}$ is a preadditive Boolean category. We begin by relating ranges to the coproduct systems of **7.10**.

1 DEFINITION Given $\alpha : X \longrightarrow Y$ in a Boolean category, a *cokernel-range decomposition* of α is a coproduct system $(Y, C, i, \theta, R, i', \theta')$ such that $\alpha\theta$ is null and $\alpha\theta'$ is cototal.

The terminology is explained by the next proposition and corollary.

2 PROPOSITION Let $\alpha : X \longrightarrow Y$. Then α has a *surjective-summand factorization if and only if α has a cokernel-range decomposition.*

Proof First suppose $(Y, C, i, \rho, R, j, \theta)$ is a cokernel-range decomposition for α. As $\alpha\rho = 0$, $\alpha = \alpha(\rho i + \theta j) = (\alpha\theta)j$ is a cototal-summand factorization. But cototal is equivalent to surjective by Proposition 10.24. Conversely, let α have a cototal-summand factorization so that there exists a coproduct system $(Y, C, i, \rho, R, j, \theta)$ such that α factors through j and such that α factors through no summand properly contained in j. We shall show this system is a cokernel-range decomposition for α.

That $\alpha\rho = 0$ is clear since $j\rho = 0$ and α factors through j. Let $z : R \longrightarrow W$ with $\alpha\theta z = 0$. To show: $z = 0$. To this end let $k : S \longrightarrow R = Ker(z)$. Then $kj : S \longrightarrow Y \in Summ(Y)$ and $S \subset R$. We shall show that α factors through S, for then $Ker(z) = R$ and $z = 0$. By the universal property of $Ker(z)$, $\alpha\theta z = 0$ so that there exists $\psi : X \longrightarrow S$ with $\psi k = \alpha\theta$. Thus $\alpha = \alpha(\rho i + \theta j) = \alpha\theta j = \psi kj$ indeed factors through S. $\square$

3 COROLLARY *Let $\alpha : X \longrightarrow Y$. The following statements are valid.*

1. *Any two cokernel-range decompositions of α are isomorphic.*

2. *If $(Y, C, i, \theta, R, i', \theta')$ is a cokernel-range decomposition of α then $\theta = Cok(\alpha)$.*

3. *If $(X, P, i, \rho, P', i', \rho')$ is any coproduct system, $\rho' = Cok(i)$.*

Proof The first statement is clear from the uniqueness of surjective-summand factorizations and the second follows from the construction of cokernels in **10.23**. For the last statement, observe that $i\rho' = 0$ whereas $i\rho = id_P$ is cototal. $\square$

It can be shown that the semilattice-assertional categories about to be defined coincide with those of [Manes 1988, 3.21].

4 DEFINITION A *semilattice-assertional category* is a semiadditive category (**2.10**) such that

1. The abelian monoids $\mathcal{C}(X, Y)$ are in fact join-semilattices with least element 0; equivalently, $\alpha + \alpha = \alpha$ for all α.

2. For all $\alpha : X \longrightarrow Y$, $Ker(\alpha)$ exists and is a summand of X.

3. Every morphism has a cokernel-range decomposition.

By **7.12** and **2**, a semilattice-assertional category is a preadditive ranged Boolean category. From **12.15** we know that a semilattice-assertional category possesses morphisms which are not deterministic.

It is rare for the dual of a Boolean category to be Boolean. However,

5 PROPOSITION   *The dual of a semilattice-assertional category is semilattice-assertional.*

Proof   Let $\mathfrak{B}$ be semilattice-assertional. If $(X, P, i, \rho, Q, j, \theta)$ is a coproduct system in $\mathfrak{B}$, $(X, P, \rho, i, Q, \theta, j,)$ is a coproduct system in $\mathfrak{B}^{op}$. Summands in $\mathfrak{B}^{op}$ appears as the projections of summands in $\mathfrak{B}$. In particular, the construction of $Cok(\alpha)$ in **10.23** shows that in $\mathfrak{B}^{op}$, kernels exist as summands. Cokernel-range decompositions exist in $\mathfrak{B}^{op}$ being just the kernel-domain decompositions in $\mathfrak{B}$. Finally, in any semiadditive category, an alternate formula for $\alpha + \beta$ is

$$\alpha + \beta \quad = \quad X \xrightarrow{\;[id,id]\;} X + X \xrightarrow{\;<\alpha,\beta>\;} X$$

as is clear from the matrix calculus of Section 3; it follows that **4(1,2)** hold in $\mathfrak{B}^{op}$.□

6 EXAMPLE   Let R be a positive partial semiring whose additive structure is a complete semilattice. Then $\mathbf{Mat}_R$ is semilattice-assertional and $(\mathbf{Mat}_R)^{op} \cong \mathbf{Mat}_R$ via matrix transpose.

7 LEMMA   *For X in a semilattice-assertional category $\mathfrak{B}$, the passage from a summand to its corresponding projection is a Boolean isomorphism between $Summ(X)$ in $\mathfrak{B}$ and $Summ(X)$ in $\mathfrak{B}^{op}$.*

Proof   Let $(X, P, i, \rho, P', i', \rho')$ and $(X, Q, j, \theta, Q', j', \theta')$ be coproduct systems. By Corollary **7.11** and **3**, $j = Ker(\theta')$ and $\rho' = Cok(i)$. Thus

$$P \subset Q \in \mathfrak{B} \Leftrightarrow i \text{ factors through } j$$
$$\Leftrightarrow i\theta' = 0$$
$$\Leftrightarrow \theta' \text{ factors through } \rho'$$

$$\Leftrightarrow \; Q' \subset P' \text{ in } \mathcal{B}^{op}$$
$$\Leftrightarrow \; P \subset Q \text{ in } \mathcal{B}^{op}. \qquad\qquad \square$$

8 PROPOSITION   *Let* $P \in Summ(X)$, $\alpha : X \longrightarrow Y$, $Q \in Summ(Y)$ *in a semilattice-assertional category* $\mathcal{C}$. *Then the following duality relationships hold.*

1. $\{P\}\,\alpha\,\{Q\}$ *in* $\mathcal{B}$ $\Leftrightarrow$ $\{Q'\}\,\alpha\,\{P'\}$ *in* $\mathcal{B}^{op}$.

2. $P = [\alpha]Q \in \mathcal{B}$ $\Leftrightarrow$ $P = Q<\alpha>$ *in* $\mathcal{B}^{op}$.

3. $P =. <\alpha>Q$ *in* $\mathcal{B}$ $\Leftrightarrow$ $P = Q[\alpha]$ *in* $\mathcal{B}^{op}$.

4. $P = wp(\alpha, Q)$ *in* $\mathcal{B}$ $\Leftrightarrow$ $P = sp(Q, \alpha)$ *in* $\mathcal{B}^{op}$.

Proof   Let $(X, P, i, \rho, P', i', \rho')$ and $(X, Q, j, \theta, Q', j', \theta')$ be coproduct systems in $\mathcal{B}$. Following **9.7(3)**, $\{P\}\,\alpha\,\{Q\} \Leftrightarrow i\alpha q' = 0 \Leftrightarrow i\alpha\theta' = 0$ (as $q' = \theta'j'$ and j' is monic.) Viewed in $\mathcal{B}^{op}$, this reads $\theta'\alpha i = 0 \Leftrightarrow \{P'\}\,\alpha\,\{Q'\}$, and this proves the first statement. For the second, as $j : Q \longrightarrow Y = Ker(\theta') = [\theta']0$, it follows from pullback-pasting **(5.20)** that $[\alpha]Q = Ker(\alpha\theta')$. Thus $[\alpha]Q$ is dual to $Cok(i'\alpha)$ which is the definition of $Q<\alpha>$, so this finishes (2). (3,4) are similar. In $\mathcal{B}$, $<\alpha>Q = ([\alpha]Q')' = (Ker(\alpha\theta))' = Dom(\alpha\theta)$ which, in $\mathcal{B}^{op}$, is $Ran(\theta\alpha)$, the definition of $Q[\alpha]$; and $wp(\alpha, Q) = Dom(\alpha) \bigcap [\alpha]Q$ in $\mathcal{B}$ is $Ran(\alpha) \bigcap Q<\alpha> = sp(Q, \alpha)$ in $\mathcal{B}^{op}$.

$$\square$$

By Proposition 8, every statement in inverse predicate transformers has a dual one in direct transformers. For example, **10.4**

$$[\alpha]Q \bigcap <\alpha>R \; \subset \; <\alpha>(Q \bigcap R)$$

has dual

9          $$Q<\alpha> \bigcap R[\alpha] \; \subset \; (Q \bigcap R)[\alpha]$$

and the latter must be true in all semilattice-assertional categories since, quantifying over all such categories, it is exactly the same set of statements as the former.

We now turn to defining and constructing the desired completion.

10 DEFINITION   A *completion* of a ranged Boolean category $\mathcal{B}$ is a pair $(\mathcal{C}, \Psi)$ where $\mathcal{C}$ is a semilattice-assertional category and $\Psi : \mathcal{B} \longrightarrow \mathcal{C}$ is a strict range-preserving Boolean functor which is bijective on objects and is such that the boolean injections $Summ(X) \longrightarrow Summ(X\Psi)$ are bijective.

Note that such Ψ is not required to be a subcategory, that is, there can exist $\alpha, \beta : X \longrightarrow Y$ with $\alpha \neq \beta$ but $\alpha\Psi = \beta\Psi$. Such Ψ satisfies all properties in Proposition 11.6. The range-preserving hypothesis can be dropped from the definition since it follows from the other properties. To see this it suffices to show that α surjective $\Rightarrow \alpha\Psi$ surjective and this is done as follows: If $<\alpha\Psi>R = 0$ write $R = Q\Psi$; $\quad (<\alpha>Q)\Psi = 0\Psi \Rightarrow <\alpha>Q = 0 \Rightarrow R = 0$.   Thus Ψ preserves cokernels and ranges.

The existence of a completion for arbitrary ranged Boolean categories is an open question. We will, however, round out this section by showing that each *preadditive* ranged Boolean category has a universal completion $\mathcal{B}\hat{}$. Among other things, this provides many examples of semilattice-assertional categories. Such $\mathcal{B}\hat{}$ will be a "completion by ideals" so we begin by defining ideals.

11 DEFINITION   For X, Y in $\mathcal{B}$, an *ideal in* $\mathcal{B}(X, Y)$ is a subset I of $\mathcal{B}(X, Y)$ such that $0 \in I$ and with the following property: for summable $\alpha, \beta : X \longrightarrow Y$, $(\alpha \in I$ and $\beta \in I) \Leftrightarrow \alpha + \beta \in I$.

If we write $\alpha \leq \gamma$ to mean $\gamma = \alpha + \beta$ for some β, $\Leftarrow$ in **24** says that "if $\alpha \leq \gamma$ and $\gamma \in I$ then $\alpha \in I$". This justifies the term "ideal".

12 DEFINITION   For $A \subset \mathcal{B}(X, Y)$, define $I(A) = \bigcap \{J : J$ is an ideal, $A \subset J\}$.

Clearly, $I(A)$ is the smallest ideal containing A.

The next Lemma provides some of the technical properties needed to establish the universal completion.

13   LEMMA   *The following statements are valid:*

1. *If $\emptyset \neq B \subset \mathcal{B}(X,Y)$ and I is an ideal in $\mathcal{B}(X,Z)$ then*
   $\{Y \xrightarrow{\ \alpha\ } Z : B\alpha \subset I\}$ *is an ideal in $\mathcal{B}(Y,Z)$.*

2. *If $\emptyset \neq B \subset \mathcal{B}(X,Y)$ and I is an ideal in $\mathcal{B}(W,Y)$ then $J =$*
   $\{W \xrightarrow{\ \alpha\ } X : \alpha B \subset I\}$ *is an ideal in $\mathcal{B}(W,X)$.*

3. *If $A \subset \mathcal{B}(X,Y)$, $B \subset \mathcal{B}(Y,Z)$ then $I(AB) \supset I(A)I(B)$.*

4. *If A_1, $A_2 \subset \mathcal{B}(X,Y)$, B_1, $B_2 \subset \mathcal{B}(Y,Z)$ with $I(A_1) = I(A_2)$, $I(B_1) = I(B_2)$ then $I(A_1B_1) = I(A_2B_2)$.*

5. *Let $P \xrightarrow{\ i\ } X \xleftarrow{\ j\ } Q$ be a coproduct and let $\emptyset \neq A_n \subset \mathcal{B}(P,Y)$, $\emptyset \neq B_n \subset \mathcal{B}(Q,Y)$ with $I(A_1) = I(A_2)$, $I(B_1) = I(B_2)$. Define $C_n \subset \mathcal{B}(X,Y)$ by $C_n = \{<\alpha,\beta> : \alpha \in A_n, \beta \in B_n\}$. Then $I(C_1) = I(C_2)$.*

6. *Let $P \xrightarrow{\ i\ } X \xleftarrow{\ j\ } Q$ be a coproduct. Let $A_n \subset \mathcal{B}(W,P)$, $B_n \subset \mathcal{B}(W,Q)$ with $I(A_1) = I(A_2)$, $I(B_1) = I(B_2)$. Define $C_n \subset \mathcal{B}(W,X)$ by $C_n = \{\alpha i : \alpha \in A_n\} \bigcup \{\beta j : \beta \in B_n\}$. Then $I(C_1) = I(C_2)$.*

Proof (1,2): $B0 = 0 \in I \Rightarrow 0 \in J$. If $\alpha,\beta : Y \longrightarrow Z$ and $\alpha + \beta$ exists then for $\gamma \in B$, $\gamma(\alpha + \beta) = \gamma\alpha + \gamma\beta$, so it's clear that $\alpha + \beta \in J \Leftrightarrow \alpha,\beta \in J$. The proof of (2) is similar.

(3): Let $L = \{\alpha \in \mathcal{B}(X,Y) : \alpha B \subset I(AB)\}$. Then L is an ideal by (2) and $A \subset L$ so $I(A) \subset L$. Now let $M = \{\beta \in \mathcal{B}(Y,Z) : I(A)\beta \subset I(AB)\}$. Then M is an ideal containing B so $I(B) \subset M$ as desired.

(4): By (3), $I(A_1B_1) \supset I(A_1)I(B_1) = I(A_2)I(B_2) \supset A_2B_2$ so $I(A_1B_1) \supset I(A_2B_2)$.

(5): Define $D = \{P \xrightarrow{\ \alpha\ } Y : <\alpha,0> \in I(C_2)\}$. Since $<0,0> = 0$ by 6.2(5), $0 \in D$. Now let $\alpha,\beta : P \longrightarrow Y$ be summable. Then $<\alpha + \beta,0> = <\alpha,0> + <\beta,0>$ (since these agree preceded by the coproduct injections) so it is

clear that D is an ideal. $E = \{Q \xrightarrow{\beta} Y : \ <0,\beta> \ \in I(C_2)\}$ is an ideal similarly.
Now suppose $\alpha \in A_2$. As $B_2 \neq \emptyset$ by assumption, there exists $\beta \in B_2$. As $<\alpha,\beta>$
$\in C_2$ and $<\alpha,\beta> \ = \ <\alpha,0> + <0,\beta>$, $<\alpha,0> \ \in I(C_2)$. As D is an ideal
containing A_2, $A_1 \subset I(A_1) = I(A_2) \subset D$, so $<\alpha,0> \ \in I(C_2)$ if $\alpha \in A_1$. Similarly
$<0,\beta> \ \in I(C_2)$ if $\beta \in B_1$. Thus $<\alpha,\beta> \ \in I(C_2)$, so $I(C_1) \subset I(C_2)$.

(6): Define $D = \{W \xrightarrow{\alpha} P : \alpha i \in I(C_2)\}$, $E = \{W \xrightarrow{\beta} Q : \beta j \in I(C_2)\}$.
By (2), D, E are ideals. Clearly $A_2 \subset D$, $B_2 \subset E$. Thus $A_1 \subset I(A_1) = I(A_2) \subset$
D and $\alpha i \in I(C_2)$ if $\alpha \in A_1$. Similarly, $\beta j \in I(C_2)$ if $\beta \in B_1$. Thus $C_1 \subset I(C_2)$.
□

The promised completion is given by the following. Its universal property
guarantees that it is unique up to isomorphism of Boolean categories.

14 THEOREM *A preadditive ranged Boolean category $\mathcal{B}$ admits a completion Ψ :*
$\mathcal{B} \longrightarrow \mathcal{B}^\frown$ *which is universal in that for each Boolean functor $F : \mathcal{B} \longrightarrow \mathcal{C}$ with $\mathcal{C}$*
semilattice-assertional, there is a unique Boolean $G : \mathcal{B}^\frown \longrightarrow \mathcal{C}$ with $\Psi G = F$.
Furthermore, if F is strict, surjective on objects, cototal-preserving or such that each
$Summ(X) \longrightarrow Summ(XF)$ is surjective so too, respectively, is G.

Proof Let $\mathcal{B}^\frown$ have the same objects as $\mathcal{B}$ and define

15
$$\mathcal{B}^\frown(X,Y) = \{I(A) : \emptyset \neq A \subset \mathcal{B}(X,Y), \ A \ \text{finite}\};$$
identity morphisms: $I(id_X)$;
composition: $I(A)I(B) = I(AB)$.

(We shall write $I(\alpha)$ instead of $I(\{\alpha\})$.) It follows from **13**(4) that composition is well-
defined, so it is clear that $\mathcal{B}^\frown$ is a category. Define the functor $\Psi : \mathcal{B} \longrightarrow \mathcal{B}^\frown$ by

16
$$X\Psi = X, \ (X \xrightarrow{\alpha} Y)\Psi \ = \ X \xrightarrow{I(\alpha)} Y.$$

That Ψ is a functor is obvious. The zero object 0 of $\mathcal{B}$ is a zero object of $\mathcal{B}^\frown$ as well
since $X \xrightarrow{I(0)} Y$ provides a family of zero morphisms for $\mathcal{B}^\frown$.

Let $(X, P, i, \rho, Q, j, \theta)$ be a coproduct system in $\mathcal{B}$. We shall show that Ψ maps this to a coproduct system in $\mathcal{B}\hat{}$. Suppose $P \xrightarrow{\;I(A)\;} Y \xleftarrow{\;I(B)\;} Q$ in $\mathcal{B}\hat{}$. Then if $C = \{<\alpha, \beta> : \alpha \in A,\ \beta \in B\}$, C is finite and non-empty and $I(C)$ is determined by $I(A)$, $I(B)$ by **13**(5). We have $I(i)I(C) = I(iC) = I(A)$ and $I(j)I(C) = I(B)$. Suppose also $I(i)I(F) = I(A)$, $I(j)I(F) = I(B)$. By the definitions, $I(A_2) = I(A)$ if A_2 is defined as $\{\alpha : \exists \beta\ <\alpha, \beta> \in F\}$, and $I(B_2) = I(B)$ if $B_2 = \{\beta : \exists \alpha\ <\alpha, \beta> \in F\}$. By **13**(5) again, $I(C) = I(C_2)$ if $C_2 = \{<\alpha, \beta> : \alpha \in A_2,\ \beta \in B_2\}$. As $F \subset C_2$, $I(F) \subset I(C_2)$. Now let $\gamma \in C_2$, $\gamma = <\alpha, \beta>$. Then $\exists\ \alpha_1, \beta_1$ with $<\alpha, \beta_1>$, $<\alpha_1, \beta> \in F$. It follows that $<\alpha, 0> \in I(F)$, $<0, \beta> \in I(F)$ so $<\alpha, \beta> = <\alpha, 0> + <0, \beta> \in I(F)$. Thus $I(F) = I(C_2) = I(A)$. We have shown that $P \xrightarrow{\;I(i)\;} X \xleftarrow{\;I(j)\;} Q$ is a coproduct in $\mathcal{B}\hat{}$. As $I(i)I(\rho) = I(id_P) = id_P$ and $I(i)I(\theta) = I(0)$ is the zero morphism, $(X, P, I(i), I(\rho), Q, I(j), I(\theta))$ is a coproduct system in $\mathcal{B}\hat{}$.

To show that $\mathcal{B}\hat{}$ is a semiadditive category it is sufficient to show that $P \xleftarrow{\;I(\rho)\;} X \xrightarrow{\;I(\theta)\;} Q$ is a product in $\mathcal{B}\hat{}$. Given $P \xleftarrow{\;I(A)\;} W \xrightarrow{\;I(B)\;} Q$ define $C = \{\alpha i : \alpha \in A\} \cup \{\beta j : \beta \in B\}$. By **13**(6), $I(C) : W \longrightarrow X$ depends only on $I(A)$, $I(B)$. Then $I(C)I(\rho) = I(A)$ since $i\rho = id_P$, $i\theta = 0$ and $0 \in I(A)$, and $I(C)I(\theta) = I(B)$ similarly. Now suppose $I(F)I(\rho) = I(A)$ and $I(F)I(\theta) = I(B)$. As $\{\alpha : \alpha i \in I(C)\}$ is an ideal containing A, it contains $I(A)$. Thus $I(A)i \subset I(C)$ and $I(B)j \subset I(C)$ similarly. Then if $\gamma \in F$, $\gamma\rho \in I(F)I(\rho) = I(A)$ so $\gamma\rho i \in I(C)$ and $\gamma\theta j \in I(C)$ by the same method. We then see that $\gamma = \gamma\rho i + \gamma\theta j \in I(C)$ which establishes that $I(F) \subset I(C)$. Conversely, as $F = F\rho i + F\theta j$, $F\rho i \subset I(F)$ and $I(Ai) = I(F\rho i) \subset I(F)$. This means $Ai \subset I(F)$; $Bj \subset I(F)$ similarly, and so $I(C) \subset I(F)$ as needed.

To show $\mathcal{B}\hat{}$ is a semilattice-assertional category we must verify the three conditions of Definition 12. If $I(A_n) : X \longrightarrow Y$ in $\mathcal{B}\hat{}$, set $A = \{\alpha_1 in_1 : \alpha_1 \in A_1\} \cup \{\alpha_2 in_2 : \alpha_2 \in A_2\}$ so that $I(A) : X \longrightarrow Y + Y$ is the unique morphism which, followed by $I(\rho_n)$, gives $I(A_n)$. The morphism $\sigma = <id, id> : Y + Y \longrightarrow Y$ in $\mathcal{B}\hat{}$ is given as $I(<id, id>)$. Thus $I(A_1) + I(A_2) = I(A)\ I(\sigma) = I(A\sigma) = I(A_1 in_1 \sigma \cup A_2 in_2 \sigma) = I(A_1 \cup A_2)$. We have shown

$$17 \qquad\qquad I(A) + I(B) = I(A \cup B)$$

so it is clear that $\mathfrak{B}^\frown(X,Y)$ is a join-semilattice.

We use the finiteness of A in $I(A): X \longrightarrow Y$ to define $Ker(I(A))$ by

18 $$Ker(I(A)) \;=\; \bigcap_{\alpha \in A} Ker(\alpha).$$

For let $i: K \longrightarrow X \;=\; \bigcap_{\alpha \in A} Ker(\alpha)$ in $\mathfrak{B}$ so that $I(i): K \longrightarrow X$ is a summand in $\mathfrak{B}^\frown$. $I(i)I(A) = \{i\alpha : \alpha \in A\} = I(0)$ is the zero map. If $I(B): W \longrightarrow X$ with $I(BA) = I(0) = \{0\}$, $\beta\alpha = 0 \; \forall \alpha \in A \; \forall \beta \in B$ which implies $B = \{0\}$. This shows that kernels exist as summands in $\mathfrak{B}^\frown$.

Given $I(A): X \longrightarrow Y$ define

19 $$Ran(I(A)) \;=\; \bigcup_{\alpha \in A} Ran(\alpha)$$

$$Cok(I(A)) \;=\; (Ran(I(A))' \;=\; \bigcap_{\alpha \in A} Cok(\alpha).$$

For the coproduct system $(Y, C = Cok(I(A)), i, \rho, R = Ran(I(A)), j, \theta)$ in $\mathfrak{B}$, we must show $(Y, C, I(i), I(\rho), R, I(j), I(\theta))$ is a cokernel-range decomposition of $I(A)$ in $\mathfrak{B}^\frown$. We have $\alpha\rho = 0$ for all $\alpha \in A$ so $I(A)I(\rho) = \{0\}$. Now suppose
$$X \xrightarrow{\;I(A)\;} Y \xrightarrow{\;I(\theta)\;} I(R) \xrightarrow{\;I(B)\;} Z \;=\; \{0\}$$
so that, if $\beta \in B$, $\alpha\theta\beta = 0$ for all $\alpha \in A$. To show: For all $\beta \in B$ that $\beta = 0$. As R is the union of $j_\alpha: R_\alpha \longrightarrow R \;(\alpha \in A)$ in $Summ(R)$ it suffices to show, for fixed α, that $j_\alpha\beta = 0$. Consider a coproduct system $(R, C_\alpha \cap R, i_\alpha, \rho_\alpha, R_\alpha, j_\alpha, \theta_\alpha)$. Then $0 = \alpha\theta\beta = \alpha\theta(\rho_\alpha i_\alpha + \theta_\alpha j_\alpha)\beta \Rightarrow \alpha\theta\theta_\alpha j_\alpha\beta = 0$ (by 2). By considering the restrictions to the injections of the coproduct $R_\alpha \longrightarrow Y \longleftarrow R'_\alpha$, it is clear that $\theta\theta_\alpha$ is just the coproduct projection $Y \longrightarrow R_\alpha$. As $\alpha\theta\theta_\alpha$ is cototal, $j_\alpha\beta = 0$ as desired. This completes the argument that $\mathfrak{B}^\frown$ is semilattice-assertional.

Next we show that $\Psi: \mathfrak{B} \longrightarrow \mathfrak{B}^\frown$ is a completion as defined in 10. Ψ is, in fact, the identity on objects. By the constructions above, Ψ preserves coproduct systems, kernels and cokernels so is already a cototal-preserving strict Boolean functor (recall $[\alpha]Q = Ker(\alpha\theta)$ if $Q = Ker(\theta)$.) To show that $Summ(X) \longrightarrow Summ(X\Psi)$

is surjective it suffices, by Theorem 8.15, to show that if $J : X \longrightarrow X$ is a guard in $\mathcal{B}^{\wedge}$ then there exists a guard $p : X \longrightarrow X$ in $\mathcal{B}$ with $p\Psi = J$. Let $K \xrightarrow{I(i)} X \xleftarrow{I(j)} D$ be the kernel-domain decomposition of J. By the definition of a guard and the constructions already established, $J = I(<i,0>)$ (since $I(i)J = I(i)$, $I(j)J = \{0\}$) $= I(p)$ with $p = <i,0>$ a guard in $\mathcal{C}$.

Finally, we must establish the universal properties claimed for Ψ. Let $F : \mathcal{B} \longrightarrow \mathcal{C}$ be a Boolean functor with $\mathcal{C}$ semilattice-assertional. Define $G : \mathcal{B}^{\wedge} \longrightarrow \mathcal{C}$ by

20
$$XG = XF$$

$$(X \xrightarrow{I(A)} Y)G = \bigcup_{\alpha \in A} \alpha F .$$

To see that such G is well-defined, suppose $I(A) = I(B) : X \longrightarrow Y$ and consider $J = \{\alpha \in \mathcal{B}(X,Y) : \alpha F \leq \bigcup(\beta F : \beta \in B)\}$. Such J is an ideal containing B so $A \subset I(A) = I(B) \subset J$ and $\bigcup(\alpha F : \alpha \in A) \subset \bigcup(\beta F : \beta \in B)$, the reverse inclusion holding symmetrically. That G preserves identity morphisms is obvious. The proof that G preserves composition is given (using 7.8(2)) by

$$(I(A))G\, (I(B))G = (\bigcup_{\alpha \in A} \alpha F)(\bigcup_{\beta \in B} \beta F)$$

$$= \bigcup_{\alpha, \beta} (\alpha F)(\beta F) = \bigcup_{\alpha, \beta} (\alpha \beta)F$$

$$= (I(AB))G = (I(A)I(B))G.$$

That G preserves coproduct systems is clear from the constructions. Given $I(A) : X \longrightarrow Y$ in $\mathcal{B}^{\wedge}$ and $j : Q \longrightarrow YF$ in $Summ(YF)$, $j(\bigcup \alpha F) = 0 \Leftrightarrow$ each $j(\alpha F) = 0$ so $Ker((\bigcup \alpha F)G) = \bigcap Ker(\alpha F) = (Ker(I(A)))G$ since F preserves kernels and finite intersections. This clarifies that G is a Boolean functor. Exactly the same kind of proof shows that G preserves cokernels (and so is cototal-preserving) if F does. If F is strict and $XG = 0$ then $XF = 0$ so $X = 0$, and G is strict if F is . Clearly G is surjective on objects if F is. At long last, let $j : Q \longrightarrow XF$ be a summand and assume F induces isomorphisms $Summ(X) \cong Summ(XF)$. We must show that there is a summand $I(i) : P \longrightarrow X$ in $\mathfrak{B}\hat{\ }$ with $PG = Q \in$ $Summ(XF)$. To this end, choose $i : P \longrightarrow X$ with $PF = Q$.   □

21 EXAMPLE If $\mathfrak{B}$ is semilattice-assertional, the identity functor of $\mathfrak{B}$ is universal so $\mathfrak{B}\hat{\ } = \mathfrak{B}$. Note that $I(A) = I(\bigcup A)$.

22 EXAMPLE Let $\mathbf{Mfn}_{fin}$ be the subcategory of $\mathbf{Mfn}$ of all objects and maps $\alpha : X \longrightarrow Y$ with each $x\alpha$ a finite subset of Y. Then $\mathbf{Mfn}_{fin}$ is semilattice-assertional and $\mathbf{Pfn} \subset \mathbf{Mfn}_{fin}$ as well as $\mathbf{Mfn}_{fin} \subset \mathbf{Mfn}$ are Boolean extensions. We claim that $\mathbf{Mfn}_{fin} = (\mathbf{Pfn})\hat{\ }$. To see this, it is enough to check that for finite $A \subset \mathbf{Pfn}(X, Y)$,

$$J = \{\alpha \in \mathbf{Pfn}(X, Y) : \exists \text{ finite partition } P_1, ..., P_n$$
$$\text{of } Dom(\alpha) \; \forall i \; \exists a \in A \; \forall x \in P_i \; x\alpha = xa\}$$

is an ideal with $A \subset J \subset I(A)$, so that $J = I(A)$. From this it follows that if A, B are finite subsets of $\mathbf{Pfn}(X, Y)$ with $\bigcup A = \bigcup B \in \mathbf{Mfn}_{fin}(X, Y)$ then $A \subset I(B)$ so that $I(A) = I(B)$. Thus the induced Boolean functor $(\mathbf{Pfn})\hat{\ } \longrightarrow \mathbf{Mfn}_{fin}$ is an isomorphism.

23 EXAMPLE One might guess that the Boolean functor $F : \mathbf{Bag} \longrightarrow \mathbf{Mfn}$ defined by $XF = X$, $X(\alpha F) = \{y : \alpha_{xy} \neq 0\}$ is the universal semilattice completion of $\mathbf{Bag}$. To see that this is *not* so let $G : (\mathbf{Bag})\hat{\ } \longrightarrow \mathbf{Mfn}$ be the functor induced by F. Let $\mathbb{N}$ be the set of natural numbers and define $\alpha, \beta : \mathbb{N} \longrightarrow \mathbb{N}$ by $\alpha_{ny} = 1$, $\beta_{ny} = n + 1$. For $A, B \subset \mathbf{Bag}(Y, Z)$ it is easily verified that $I(A) = \{\gamma : \gamma \leq a_1 + \cdots + a_n \text{ for some } a_1, ..., a_n \in A\}$ where $\leq$ and $+$ are pointwise. Thus $I(\alpha)$ consists of the bounded matrices in $\mathbf{Bag}(\mathbb{N}, \mathbb{N})$ and so $\beta \notin I(\alpha)$. It follows that $I(\alpha) \neq I(\beta)$ but $G(I(\alpha)) = F(\alpha) = X \times X = F(\beta) = G(I(\beta))$ so G is not an isomorphism.

14   EQUATIONS FOR 3-VALUED IF-THEN-ELSE

The metatheory so far has emphasized formulas. The more general first-order theory of Boolean categories must consider statements about both morphisms and formulas together. In this section we consider the equational theory of *if-then-else* in the "3-valued case" in which the corresponding choice operator is deterministic but not necessarily idempotent as was previously true in Proposition **5.13**. Since "*if P then α else α = α*" is essentially the law of the excluded middle for P, we are therefore allowing such a law to fail, that is, "tests need not halt". This is realistic in any context in which a test can query the result of an arbitrary computable function.

After characterizing 3-valued *if-then-else* in Boolean categories we pave the way for the main result, Theorem **14.9** below, as succinctly as possible. The proofs, which are of a universal-algebraic nature, are in [Manes, 1992]; the gap to be bridged in this section is to elevate the results of that paper to the setting of preadditive Boolean categories with projection system. At this time, however, the main result applies only to the semilattice-assertional case.

1   DEFINITION   Let B be a Boolean algebra. The elements of B are "2-valued propositions". A 3-*valued proposition* on B is a pair $P = (P_F, P_T)$ with $P_F, P_T \in B$, $P_F P_T = 0$. [Note: supremum, infimim and complement in B will be written $P + Q$, PQ, P'; the symbols $\vee$, $\wedge$ will be given different meanings in **3**.] Intuitively, P is false if P_F, P is true if P_T and P diverges if $(P_F + P_T)'$.

2   NOTATION   Let $\mathcal{T} = \{0, 1, 2\}$ denote the set of fundamental truth values. Here

$0 = $ false, $1 = $ true, $2 = $ diverge.

Observe that a 3-valued proposition is essentially the same thing as a function P $: B \longrightarrow \mathcal{T}$ with $P_F = 0\, P^{-1}$, $P_T = 1\, P^{-1}$. Equivalently, we may think of P as a partial function $P : B \longrightarrow \{0,1\}$.

3   DEFINITION   For P, Q 3-valued propositions on B define

$$
\begin{aligned}
P \vee Q &= (P_F Q_F,\ P_T + P_F Q_T) \\
P^{\sim} &= (P_T, P_F) \\
P \wedge Q &= (P^{\sim} \vee Q^{\sim})^{\sim} &= (P_F + P_T Q_F,\ P_T Q_T) \\
0 &= (0, B) \\
1 &= (B, 0) \\
2 &= (0, 0) \\
PQR &= (P \wedge Q) \vee (P^{\sim} \wedge R).
\end{aligned}
$$

Here, $P \vee Q$ computes "P or Q" with short-circuit evaluation, running P first and diverging if P does, exiting true if P is true, but otherwise going on to run Q. Similarly for $P \wedge Q$. $P^{\sim}$ switches the truth values if P halts and otherwise diverges; this operator is perhaps better called "switch" than complement. The ternary operation PQR generalizes the Boolean *if P then Q else R* and can be used with the constants to generate the others via $P \vee Q = P1Q$, $P^{\sim} = P01$, $P \wedge Q = PQ0$. It must be emphasized that $P \vee Q$ and $P \wedge Q$ are not commutative and that permutations in expressions such as that for PQR produce different results.

Taking B to be the two-element Boolean algebra $\{0,1\}$, the set of 3-valued propositions on B may be identified with $\mathcal{T}$ via $0 \leftrightarrow (1,0)$, $1 \leftrightarrow (0,1)$, $2 \leftrightarrow (0,0)$. With these identifications, the operations on $\mathcal{T}$ may be described as follows:

$$
\begin{aligned}
x \vee y : \quad & 0 \vee y = y,\ \ 1 \vee y = 1,\ \ 2 \vee y = 2 \\
x^{\sim} : \quad & 0^{\sim} = 1,\ \ 1^{\sim} = 0,\ \ 2^{\sim} = 2
\end{aligned}
$$

$$x \wedge y : \quad 0 \wedge y = 0, \quad 1 \wedge y = y, \quad 2 \wedge y = 2$$
$$0 : \quad 0$$
$$1 : \quad 1$$
$$2 : \quad 2$$
$$xyz : \quad 0yz = z, \quad 1yz = y, \quad 2yz = 2 \, .$$

Then notice that the operations of **3** are just pointwise those of $\mathcal{T}$ when 3-valued propositions are regarded as $\mathcal{T}$–valued functions.

The languages C, Lisp and Prolog use the short-circuit operators above. Pascal, on the other hand, interprets "*P or Q*" by running both P, Q first and diverging if either does. This commutative version is expressible as $P(Q \vee Q^\sim)Q$. Ada provides keywords for both operators: *P or else Q* is $P \vee Q$ whereas *P or Q* is the commutative version.

The algebra of 2-valued propositions is axiomatized by the theory of abstract Boolean algebras. The earliest reference we know is [Huntington, 1904]. By contrast, the equational axiomatization of 0, 2, $(-)^\sim$, $\vee$ has taken much longer. Kleene noted these operations among the various "regular extensions" of the Boolean operations in [Kleene 1952]. [McCarthy 1963] explicitly emphasized the short-circuit operations in a programming setting and while he used them to present an equational theory for *if-then-else* he did not address equations in the operations themselves. Another 27 years passed until [Guzmán and Squier, 1990] provided the following definitions and completeness theorem.

4 DEFINITION A *C–algebra* is an algebra with constants 0, 2, unary operation $(-)^\sim$ and binary operation $\vee$ subject to the following equations (where we use the abbreviations $1 = 0^\sim$, $P \wedge Q = (P^\sim \vee Q^\sim)^\sim$:

$$P^{\sim\,\sim} = P$$
$$P \vee (Q \vee R) = (P \vee Q) \vee R$$
$$P \wedge (Q \vee R) = (P \wedge Q) \vee (P \wedge R)$$

$$(P \vee Q) \wedge R = (P \wedge R) \vee (P^\sim \wedge Q \wedge R)$$
$$P \vee (P \wedge Q) = P$$
$$(P \wedge Q) \vee (Q \wedge P) = (Q \wedge P) \vee (P \wedge Q)$$
$$2^\sim = 2$$
$$1 \wedge P = P.$$

For every Boolean algebra B, the set of all 3-valued propositions on B with the operations of **3** forms a C–algebra. We call these the *standard* C–algebras.

5 THEOREM   *The set of all equations in* $0, 2, (-)^\sim, \vee$ *satisfied by all standard C-algebras is precisely the set of all consequences of the eight equations defining a C-algebra in* **4**.   □

6 DEFINITION   In a Boolean category with projection system ρ, a *3–valued proposition on X* is a 3-valued proposition $P = (P_F, P_T)$ on $Summ(X)$. The *if-then-else operator induced by P*, written $if_P(-,-)$, is the choice operator $if_P(\alpha, \beta) = G < \alpha, \beta >$ where $G : X \longrightarrow X + X$ is defined in terms of the coproduct decomposition $X = P_T + P_F + (P_F \bigcup P_T)^\sim$ as $< i\, in_1, j\, in_2, 0 >$ where 0 is the ρ–null map whereas $i : P_T \longrightarrow X$, $j : P_F \longrightarrow X$ are the summand injections. It follows at once that $if_P(\alpha, \beta) = < i\alpha, j\beta, 0 >$ which we interpret as "α if P is true, β if P is false, 0 if P diverges".

We note that G is indeed deterministic. This follows at once from **12.12**.

7 THEOREM   [McCarthy 1963.] *The 2-sorted equational theory of 3-valued $if_P(\alpha, \beta)$ in Boolean categories with projection system is precisely the set of consequences of the C-algebra equations of* **4** *and the following equations:*

$$if_1(\alpha, \beta) = \alpha$$
$$if_0(\alpha, \beta) = \beta$$

$$if_{PQR}(\alpha,\beta) \;=\; if_P(if_Q(\alpha,\beta),\; if_R(\alpha,\beta))$$
$$if_P(if_P(\alpha,\beta),\; \gamma) \;=\; if_P(\alpha,\gamma) \;=\; if_P(\alpha,\; if_P(\beta,\gamma))$$
$$if_P(if_Q(\alpha,a),\; if_Q(b,\beta)) \;=\; if_Q(if_P(\alpha,b),\; if_P(a,\beta))$$
$$if_P(if_Q(\alpha,\beta),\; \gamma) \;=\; if_P(if_Q(if_P(\alpha,\alpha),\; if_P(\beta,\beta)),\; \gamma)$$
$$if_P(\alpha,if_Q(\beta,\gamma)) \;=\; if_P(\alpha,if_Q(if_P(\beta,\beta),\; if_P(\gamma,\gamma)))\;.$$

Proof As mentioned earlier, all equations in the C–algebra sort are a consequence of the Guzmán-Squier equations. Any equation in the morphism sort which holds in all Boolean categories with ρ will in particular hold in **Pfn** where the algorithm of [McCarthy 1963] reduces it to normal form. In McCarthy's (single-sorted) context, both terms in a valid equation must reduce to equal normal forms. In the 2-sorted context, proving that two normal forms are equal requires repeated use of universally-valid equations of the form $if_P(\alpha,\beta) = if_Q(\alpha,\beta)$ but these include the equations $PRS = QRS$ as a special instantiation and so, if true, are derivable from the Guzmán-Squier equations. Conversely, it is routine if tedious to show that the McCarthy equations hold in all Boolean categories with ρ.   □

While Theorem 7 provides a complete answer to the question of equations for *if-then-else* we would argue that this was not quite the right question to begin with! Analysis of a network of *if-then-else* statements requires an examination of each path through the network, whereas the language of *if-then-else* as presented so far is not sufficiently expressive to single out such paths. One can do better in a preadditive Boolean category where a straightforward generalization of 8.24 shows that the typical 3-valued *if-then-else* operator is

8          $$if_P(\alpha,\beta) \;=\; p_T\alpha + p_F\beta,\;\; p_T,\; p_F \text{ guards with } p_Tp_F = 0.$$

Here $p_T\alpha$, $p_F\beta$ are the two paths. A three-path network is $if_P(if_Q(\alpha,\beta),\gamma) = p_T(q_T\alpha + q_F\beta) + p_F\gamma = p_Tq_T\alpha + p_Tq_F\beta + p_F\gamma$.

At this writing we do not know a generating set of equations for the 2-sorted equational theory of *if-then-else* in preadditive Boolean categories in the style of the next theorem but conjecture (based on the results of [Manes 1985]) that it is the equations presented below for the semilattice-assertional case with "$\alpha + \alpha = \alpha$" deleted.

We conclude with the main result of this section:

9 THEOREM [Manes 1992] *Let C be a fixed C-algebra. The set of all C-algebra equations in $\emptyset$, $+$, $if_p(-,-)$ $(p \in P)$ satisfied by the standard models:*

> *X, Y objects of a semilattice-assertional category $\mathfrak{B}$,*
>
> *C represented as a C-subalgebra of the disjoint pairs in $Summ(X)$,*
>
> *$\emptyset$, $+$ the least element and semilattice join of $\mathfrak{B}(X,Y)$,*
>
> *$if_P(\alpha, \beta)$ $(P \in Summ(X)$, $\alpha, \beta : X \longrightarrow Y)$ as in 6,*

is precisely the set of consequences of the semilattice equations ($+$ is a monoid with unit $\emptyset$ and $\alpha + \alpha = \alpha$), two of the McCarthy equations namely

$$if_1(\alpha, \beta) = \alpha$$
$$if_{PQR}(\alpha, \beta) = if_P(if_Q(\alpha, \beta), if_R(\alpha, \beta))$$

and the new equations

10 $$if_2(\alpha, \beta) = \emptyset$$

and

11 $$if_{P_1}(f, \emptyset) \bigcup \cdots \bigcup if_{P_m}(f, \emptyset) = if_{q_1}(f, \emptyset) \bigcup \cdots \bigcup if_{q_n}(f, \emptyset)$$

whenever $p_1^\downarrow \vee \cdots \vee p_m^\downarrow = q_1^\downarrow \vee \cdots \vee q_n^\downarrow$ in the enveloping ada of C. $\square$

We refer the reader to [Manes 1992] for the theory of adas and the enveloping ada of a C-algebra, but note that it is an open question as to whether **11** can be derived from the other equations.

PART IV   DISTRIBUTIVE CATEGORIES

Boolean categories do not have enough structure to model data types. At the very least, finite products $X \times Y$ are needed to construct records and arrays. The recursive specification

$$L ::= A + A \times L$$

uses coproducts and products together to express "a non-empty list is either an atom or an atom followed by a non-empty list" (see [Manes and Arbib 1986, Chapters 10-12] for elementary development.) For purposes of lazy evaluation, one would hope that lists of length at most 2 are exposed by interpreting the specification as a fixed-point-equation and substituting once:

$$
\begin{aligned}
L &= A + A \times L \\
&= A + (A \times (A + A \times L)) \\
&\cong A + (A \times A) + (A + A \times L).
\end{aligned}
$$

The last step requires the distributive law $A \times (B + C) \cong (A \times B) + (A \times C)$. This law holds in any topos because the endofunctor $A \times (-)$ has a right adjoint and so must preserve coproducts. More generally, this law holds in any distributive category and in fact that is why those categories are given the name.

Products also play a major role in the semantics of imperative languages. Given n programming variables X_i taking values in V_i, the assignment $X_i := v$ can be viewed as an endomorphism ψ of the object of states $V_1 \times \cdots \times V_n$ namely, if we denote the jth product projection as $pr_j : V_1 \times \cdots \times V_n \longrightarrow V_j$, ψ is defined by

$$\psi \, pr_j \;=\; pr_j \qquad \text{if } j \neq i$$
$$\;=\; pr_i \, \widehat{v} \qquad \text{if } j = i$$

where $\widehat{v} = V_i \longrightarrow 1 \overset{v}{\longrightarrow} V_i$. Here 1 is the terminal object and we adopt the philosophy that the "values" $v \in V_i$ are adequately captured by morphisms from 1. The equalizer $eq(pr_j, pr_j \, \widehat{v})$ would seem to capture the test "$X_i = v$". This makes it reasonable to ask for a terminal object, binary products and equalizers and so, as is well-known [Mac Lane 1971, Section V.2], all finite limits are available. (For topos theorists, we note that the toposes in which every equalizer is a summand are precisely the toposes whose intrinsic intuitionistic logic is classical. More generally, by composing characteristic morphisms with double negation we see that there is always a largest summand contained in an equalizer. We wish to avoid such technicalities so as to continue to keep the list of categorical prerequisities required of the reader to a minimum. We have also not added the axiom "every equalizer is a summand" —or equivalently, by Proposition 10.21, that every surjective morphism be epimorphic— to the axioms for a distributive category in order to be consistent with the existing definiton. In applications which extend Boolean categories to data types, this is a very natural axiom to add as the example "$X_i = v$" above makes clear.)

In essence, a distributive category is a Boolean category with finite limits in which all morphisms are crisp. This suggests that we look at the crisp morphisms in a Boolean category as a candidate for a wide distributive subcategory for data types, but certain examples show that this subcategory is too large to have the intended semantic interpretation. In the frameworks of Section 1, the values that appear in assignments are atoms and so it is the atomic morphisms, those that map atoms to atoms, which form the best candidate. These are studied in Section 15. We also establish the result of [Huwig and Poigne 1990] —that there exists an endomorphism with no fixed point— for distributive categories as a corollary of the earlier result that no commutative idempotent choice is deterministic.

Section 16 deals with the converse problem. A given distributive category $\mathfrak{D}$, while Boolean, has no projection system so it is natural to seek a Boolean extension of $\mathfrak{D}$ with better properties. We introduce *monads* T in $\mathfrak{D}$ whose *Kleisli categories* $\mathfrak{D}_\mathsf{T}$ produce extensions $\mathfrak{D} \subset \mathfrak{D}_\mathsf{T}$ with the same objects. We characterize when such extensions are Boolean giving rise to the concept of a *Boolean monad*. We prove that there is always a Boolean monad whose Kleisli category is preadditive. This section provides a precise framework to compare Boolean categories to algebraic theory models.

ATOMIC MORPHISMS

Distributive subcategories make finite limit constructions available to the objects of a Boolean category. As discussed above, we shall interpret certain morphisms $v : 1 \longrightarrow V$ as values in the semantics of an assignment such as $X_i = v$. In basic frameworks such as those of Section 1, such 1 is a one-element set but, even so, not every morphism $1 \longrightarrow V$ is a value. What we have in mind is a genuine element of the set V, that is, an atomic summand of V. A natural way to abstract these examples is the concept of an *extensional* Boolean category, a strengthening of the atomic Boolean categories of Section 11. We will study these categories in the second half of this section. But first we must introduce distributive categories and set down their elementary properties.

1 DEFINITION (see [Cockett 1991, 1.5.2].) A category $\mathfrak{D}$ is *distributive* if it satisfies the following axioms.

    1. $\mathfrak{D}$ has an initial object 0 and a terminal object 1.

    2. Every pair (X, Y) of objects has a coproduct.

3. Every pair $X \xrightarrow{\alpha} Z \xleftarrow{\beta} Y$ has a pullback.

4. Every morphism is crisp.

5. Coproducts are disjoint, that is, if $P \xrightarrow{i} X \xleftarrow{j} Q$ is a coproduct, the square

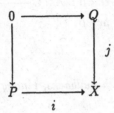

is a pullback .

2 PROPOSITION   *The following hold for a distributive category $\mathfrak{D}$.*

1. *$\mathfrak{D}$ is a Boolean category.*

2. *$\mathfrak{D}$ is finitely complete.*

3. *If X is not initial, there exists no morphism $X \longrightarrow 0$. In particular, unless all $\mathfrak{D}$-objects are initial, $\mathfrak{D}$ has no projection system.*

Proof   For the first statement, if T is a trivial object then $T \xrightarrow{id} T \xleftarrow{id} T$ is a coproduct so that the pullback of these morphisms is both $T \xleftarrow{id} T \xrightarrow{id} T$ (true in any category!) and $T \xleftarrow{} 0 \xrightarrow{} T$ (by disjointness of coproducts) so $T = 0$; the other Boolean category axioms are obvious.   Turning to the second statement, the product of X, Y with its two projections is obtained by pulling back   the unique morphisms to the terminal object, $X \longrightarrow 1 \longleftarrow Y$. The equalizer $i : E \longrightarrow X$ of α, β is obtained by pulling back

$$X \xrightarrow{[id_X, \alpha]} X \times Y \xleftarrow{[id_X, \beta]} X$$

to get two morphisms $E \longrightarrow X$ which are in fact equal because of the id_X in the first components above.   Since $\mathfrak{D}$ has finite products and equalizers, it has all finite limits. Finally, suppose there exists $X \longrightarrow 0$. Since this morphism is crisp, pulling back the coproduct $0\longrightarrow 0 \longleftarrow 0$ yields a coproduct $X \xrightarrow{\ t\ } X \xleftarrow{\ t\ } X$ so X is a trivial object and hence an initial object. $\square$

3 DEFINITION If $\alpha : A \longrightarrow B$, $\beta : C \longrightarrow D$ and the products $A \times C$, $B \times D$ exist, we define (dually to **2.16**) $\alpha \times \beta : A \times C \longrightarrow B \times D$ be the unique morphism ψ with $\psi \, pr_B = pr_A \, \alpha$, $\psi \, pr_D = pr_C \, \beta$.

4 LEMMA *In any category with pullbacks, binary products and binary coproducts, the following square is a pullback.*

$$
\begin{array}{ccc}
X \times Y & \xrightarrow{\ id_X \times in_Y\ } & X \times (Y+Z) \\
{\scriptstyle pr_Y}\big\downarrow & & \big\downarrow {\scriptstyle pr_{Y+Z}} \\
Y & \xrightarrow[\ in_Y\ ]{} & Y+Z
\end{array}
$$

Proof   Form the pullback

$$
\begin{array}{ccc}
P & \xrightarrow{\ \alpha\ } & X \times (Y+Z) \\
{\scriptstyle \beta}\big\downarrow & & \big\downarrow {\scriptstyle pr_{Y+Z}} \\
Y & \xrightarrow[\ in_Y\ ]{} & Y+Z
\end{array}
$$

For any $f : W \longrightarrow X$, $g : W \longrightarrow Y$ we have $[f, g \, in_Y] pr_{Y+Z} = g \, in_Y$ so that there exists unique $\psi : W \longrightarrow P$ with

$$
\begin{aligned}
\psi \alpha &= [f, g \, in_Y] \\
\psi \beta &= g \ .
\end{aligned}
$$

But then, $\psi(\alpha \, pr_X) = [f, g \, in_Y] \, pr_X = f$; and if $\varphi : W \longrightarrow P$ satisfies $\varphi(\alpha \, pr_X)$

$= f$, $\varphi\beta = g$ then $\varphi\alpha\, pr_{Y+Z} = \varphi\beta\, in_Y = g\, in_Y$ so $\varphi\alpha = [f,\, g\, in_Y]$ and $\varphi = \psi$. We have shown that

$$X\xleftarrow{\ pr_X\ }X\times(Y+Z)\xleftarrow{\ \alpha\ }P\xrightarrow{\qquad\quad\beta\qquad\quad}Y$$

is a product. Relative to this product, $pr_Y = \beta$; and, $\alpha\, pr_X = (\alpha\, pr_X)id_X$, $\alpha\, pr_{Y+Z} = \beta\, in_Y$ shows $\alpha = [id_X, in_Y]$. $\qquad\square$

5 PROPOSITION *In a distributive category*

$$(X\times Y)+(X\times Z)\xrightarrow{\ \ <id_X\times in_Y,\ id_X\times in_Z>\ \ }X\times(Y+Z)$$

is an isomorphism.

Proof Pull back the coproduct $Y\xrightarrow{\ in_Y\ }X+Z\xleftarrow{\ in_Z\ }Z$ under the crisp morphism $pr_{Y+Z}: X\times(Y+Z)\longrightarrow Y+Z$ and apply Lemma 4. $\qquad\square$

6 LEMMA *In a distributive category, given*

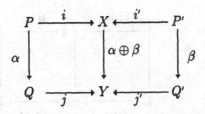

with both rows coproducts, both squares are necessarily pullbacks.

Proof By the commutativity of the diagram, $P\subset[\alpha\oplus\beta]Q$, $P'\subset[\alpha\oplus\beta]Q'$. As $\alpha\oplus\beta$ is crisp, $[\alpha\oplus\beta]Q = ([\alpha\oplus\beta]Q')' \subset P$ so $P = [\alpha\oplus\beta]Q$, $P' = [\alpha\oplus\beta]Q'$. $\qquad\square$

7   COROLLARY *In a distributive category* $\mathfrak{D}$, $1+1$ *is a summand classifier, that is, the passage* $Summ(X)\longrightarrow \mathfrak{D}(X,1+1)$, $P \mapsto \chi_P$ *defined by the diagram*

8

$$
\begin{array}{ccccc}
P & \longrightarrow & X & \longleftarrow & P' \\
\downarrow & & \downarrow{\scriptstyle \chi_P} & & \downarrow \\
1 & \xrightarrow{\;true\;} & 1+1 & \xleftarrow{\;false\;} & 1
\end{array}
$$

(with true, false a distinguished ordering of the coproduct injections) is bijective. □

It is a well-known maxim in theoretical science that run-of-the-mill completeness properties make it hard for a category to have the property that every endomorphism has a fixed point; see [Cockett 1990, p. 23 footnote 7], [Huwig and Poigne 1990], [Lawvere 1969], [Spencer 1990]. We now present such a theorem for distributive categories based on the theory of choice operators in section 2.

9   THEOREM *In a distributive category in which not every object is initial, the negation map* $\neg : 1+1 \longrightarrow 1+1$ *defined by*

$$
\begin{array}{ccccc}
1 & \xrightarrow{\;false\;} & 1+1 & \xleftarrow{\;true\;} & 1 \\
\downarrow & & \downarrow{\scriptstyle \neg} & & \downarrow \\
1 & \xrightarrow{\;true\;} & 1+1 & \xleftarrow{\;false\;} & 1
\end{array}
$$

has no fixed point, that is, no $\star : 1 \longrightarrow 1+1$ *exists with* $\star \neg = \star$.

Proof Suppose such $\star$ existed. Consider the diagram 8 with $X = 1$, $\star = \chi_P$. Because of the terminality of 1, $\star$ is a fanout as in 2.22, so that qua choice operator as in Proposition 2.23, $\star$ is an *if-then-else* operator. By Proposition **5.13**, $\star$ is a deterministic, idempotent choice. Now if $\star \neg = \star$, for $x,y : 1 \longrightarrow Z$ we have $x \star y = \star < x,y > = \star \neg < x,y > = \star < y,x > = y \star x$, so $\star$ is a commutative choice. By Proposition **5.19**, 1 is trivial. Thus for any X, there exists crisp $X \longrightarrow 1$ so X is trivial, hence initial. $\qquad\qquad\qquad\qquad\qquad\qquad\qquad\qquad\qquad\qquad\qquad\qquad$ $\square$

Let $\mathfrak{B}$ be a Boolean category. It is clear that any intersection of wide Boolean subcategories of $\mathfrak{B}$ is again such so it follows from **12.3**, **12.11** and **6.17** that the subcategory $\mathfrak{B}_{crisp} \subset \mathfrak{B}$ of crisp morphisms forms a wide Boolean subcategory. It is clear that if $\mathfrak{B}_{crisp}$ has a terminal object and pullbacks then $\mathfrak{B}_{crisp}$ is a distributive category. In the examples of Section 1, $\mathbf{Set} \subset \mathfrak{B}$ is a wide Boolean subcategory and $\mathbf{Set}$ is not only distributive but is a topos. It is this example we wish to emulate, that is, we wish to recapture $\mathbf{Set}$ from $\mathfrak{B}$ by abstract means. When $\mathfrak{B}$ is $\mathbf{Mfn}$ or $\mathbf{Pfn}$ then $\mathfrak{B}_{crisp} = \mathbf{Set}$ but, as we leave for you the reader to verify, the one-element set is not a terminal object of $\mathfrak{B}_{crisp}$ in general if $\mathfrak{B}$ is $\mathbf{Mat}_R$, Ω or $\mathbf{Pfn}_M$. On the other hand, the atoms of $Summ(X)$ in these examples are just the elements of X, and $\mathbf{Set}$ is identified as the *atomic morphisms* which map atoms to atoms. We shall shortly define *extensional* Boolean categories as a suitable class of $\mathfrak{B}$ for which the atomic morphisms yield a useful distributive subcategory.

10 DEFINITION Given an object X in a Boolean category $\mathfrak{B}$, let $|X|$ denote the set of atoms of $Summ(X)$. We write $x \in X$ as a synonym for $x \in |X|$. As before, we blur the distinction between a summand and a morphism representing it so that if an atom is represented by $x : W \longrightarrow X$ we also write $x \in X$. Say that $\alpha : X \longrightarrow Y$ is an *atomic* morphism if $x \in X \Rightarrow x\alpha \in Y$. It is obvious that the atomic morphisms constitute a subcategory of $\mathfrak{B}$ which will be denoted $\mathfrak{B}_{atomic}$.

11 DEFINITION A Boolean category $\mathfrak{B}$ is *extensional* if not every object is initial and if the following three properties hold.

1. (*Axiom of extent*) There exists an object 1 such that given
   $\alpha, \beta : X \longrightarrow Y$ with $\alpha \neq \beta$ there exists $x : 1 \longrightarrow X$ with x
   $\in X$ and with $x\alpha \neq x\beta$.

2. $\mathfrak{B}_{atomic}$ has finite limits.

3. $\mathfrak{B}$ has a projection system.

The object 1 (which is shown in the next proposition to be unique up to isomorphism) is called the *atomic generator* of $\mathfrak{B}$.

12 PROPOSITION *Let $\mathfrak{B}$ be an extensional Boolean category. The following hold.*

1. *Each Boolean algebra $Summ(X)$ is atomic.*

2. *If $i : A \longrightarrow B$ is an atom, $A \cong 1$. In particular, 1 is unique up to isomorphism.*

3. *$Summ(X)$ is the 2–element Boolean algebra if and only if $X \cong 1$.*

4. *Every atomic morphism is crisp.*

5. *Given $P \in Summ(X)$, $\alpha : X \longrightarrow Y$, $Q \in Summ(Y)$, $\{P\} \alpha \{Q\}$ if and only if for all $x \in P$, $\{x\} \alpha \{Q\}$.*

Proof Let ρ be a projection system for $\mathfrak{B}$ and denote the unique ρ–null morphism from X to Y by $0 : X \longrightarrow Y$. If $0 \neq P \in Summ(X)$ with ρ–guard $p : X \longrightarrow X$, $p \neq 0$ so there exists $x \in X$ with $xp \neq x0$. Since guards are ρ–nulling, $xp \neq 0$. As x is itself a summand it corresponds to a guard $r = 1 \xrightarrow{\;x\;} X \xrightarrow{\;\rho\;} 1$. Then $0 \neq xp = id_1 xp = (x\rho)xp = x(\rho x)p = xrp$. As x, being a summand, is ρ–nulling, $rp \neq 0$. Equivalently, $x \bigcap P \neq 0$ so that, as x is an atom, $x \in P$. This proves that $Summ(X)$ is an atomic Boolean algebra.

Suppose that $x : A \longrightarrow B$, $y : B \longrightarrow C$ are atoms. Thus A, B are not initial objects, and, by Lemma 5.5, $xy \in Summ(C)$. As $0 \neq xy \subset y$ and y is an atom, x is an isomorphism. To apply this principle, suppose $y : B \longrightarrow C$ is an atom. As $y \neq 0$ there exists an atom $x : 1 \longrightarrow B$ so the x is an isomorphism and the second statement is proved.

Similar reasoning proves the third statement. If $i : P \longrightarrow 1$ is a non-zero summand, let $x : 1 \longrightarrow P$ be an atom. Then $xix \subset x$ so xi is an isomorphism and i, being a monomorphism by 5.2 as well as a split epimorphism, is an isomorphism. Thus 0 and 1 are the only summands of 1. If X is also such that 0 and X are its only summands, let $x : 1 \longrightarrow X$ be an atom. Then as above x must be an isomorphism.

Next, let $\alpha : X \longrightarrow Y$ be atomic. We must show α is crisp. By Corollary 12.3, we must show that α is total and deterministic. If $Ker(\alpha) \neq 0$ there exists $x \in Ker(\alpha)$ whence $x\alpha$ is an atom, a contradiction as $x\alpha$ is null. Thus α is total. If $<\alpha> Q \subset [\alpha]Q$ is false, let $x \in <\alpha> Q$, $x \notin [\alpha]Q$. Then $x \notin (<\alpha> Q)' = [\alpha]Q' =$ whence $x\alpha \notin Q'$ so that $x\alpha \in Q$ and $x \in [\alpha]Q$, the desired contradiction.

Finally, we prove (5). The $\Rightarrow$ direction is obvious. For the converse, if $P \subset [\alpha]Q$ is false then there exists $x \in P$, $x \notin [\alpha]Q$. $\square$

13 PROPOSITION *If $\mathcal{B}$ is an extensional Boolean category then $\mathcal{B}_{atomic}$ is a wide Boolean subcategory of $\mathcal{B}$ and $\mathcal{B}_{atomic}$ is a distributive category whose terminal object coincides with the atomic generator of $\mathcal{B}$.*

Proof All summands are atomic morphisms by 5.5 and, in particular, all isomorphisms are atomic. Given $<\alpha, \beta> : X + Y \longrightarrow Z$ with α, β atomic, for $x \in X + Y$, $x \in X$ or $x \in Y$ so it is clear from the definition of $<\alpha, \beta>$ that $x <\alpha, \beta>$ is one of $x\alpha$, $x\beta$ and hence is an atom. Vacuously, $0 \longrightarrow X$ is atomic. This shows that $\mathcal{B}_{atomic}$ is closed under finite coproducts. Now consider the $\mathcal{B}$–pullback

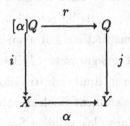

with α atomic. If $x \in [\alpha]Q$ then $xrj = xi\alpha$ is an atom of Y so yr is an atom of Q which shows that r is an atomic morphism. The diagram is then a pullback in $\mathcal{B}_{atomic}$ because if $\gamma : Z \longrightarrow [\alpha]Q$ is such that γi is atomic then γ is also. This shows that $\mathcal{B}_{atomic}$ is indeed a wide Boolean subcategory of $\mathcal{B}$. It is immediate from the definitions 1 and 11 and properties we have established for Boolean categories that $\mathcal{B}_{atomic}$ is a distributive category. Finally, let T be a terminal object of $\mathcal{B}_{atomic}$. By the previous proposition, $id_1 \in 1$ so that the unique morphism $1 \longrightarrow T$ is an atom. Since T has one element, $T \cong 1$.   □

14 PROPOSITION *Let $\mathcal{B}$ be an extensional Boolean category. Then the atoms functor $|-| : \mathcal{B}_{atomic} \longrightarrow Set$ is a strict, limit-preserving Boolean functor.*

Proof For $\alpha : X \longrightarrow Y$ in $\mathcal{B}_{atomic}$, $x \in |X| \Rightarrow x\alpha \in |Y|$ by the definition of an atomic morphism and this is exactly the condition needed for $|-|$ to be well-defined on morphisms; functoriality is then obvious. Since $id_1 \in 1$, every atomic morphism $1 \longrightarrow X$ is an atom so that $|-|$ is the representable functor $\mathcal{B}_{atomic}(1,-)$ and so it preserves all limits that exist in $\mathcal{B}_{atomic}$ (see [Mac Lane 1971, Thm. V.4.1].) The inexperienced reader need not be overpowered here since the basic idea is very straightforward. For example, $\mathcal{B}_{atomic}(1,-)$ preserves the product $X \times Y$ because a morphism $1 \longrightarrow X \times Y$ is tantamount to a pair of morphisms $(1 \longrightarrow X, 1 \longrightarrow Y)$.) In particular, then, $|-|$ preserves $[\alpha]Q$. Finally, if $X \neq 0$, there exists an atom $1 \longrightarrow X$ so $|X| \neq 0$.   □

Let us pause to take stock of what we have achieved with extensional Boolean categories. We offer $\mathcal{B}_{atomic}$ as a distributive subcategory of $\mathcal{B}$ which is useful for the semantics of some data type constructions not available in Boolean categories generally. The functor of Proposition **14** assigns sets of elements to data types in a manner consistent not only with finite limit constructions but also with the predicate transformer constructions of the ambient Boolean category. Indeed, the metatheorem of **11.7** guarantees that all **PBC**–formulas valid in **Set** are valid in $\mathcal{B}_{atomic}$ as well. Thus we have been reasonably successful so far.

The category $\mathcal{B}_{atomic}$ for extensional $\mathcal{B}$ is a distributive category satisfying the axiom of extent (with the terminal object as atomic generator) and having all morphisms atomic. In the next section we will show that, conversely, such distributive categories always have form $\mathcal{B}_{atomic}$ for preadditive extensional Boolean $\mathcal{B}$.

BOOLEAN MONADS

In this final section of the book we consider a class of Boolean extensions of a given Boolean category. While the main goal is to characterize the distributive categories arising as $\mathcal{B}_{atomic}$ for some extensional Boolean $\mathcal{B}$, the tools developed are of general interest.

1 DEFINITION   Let $\mathcal{K}$ be any category. A *monad* in $\mathcal{K}$ is a triple $(T, \eta, (-)^{\#})$ as follows. T is a *pre-functor*, that is, T assigns to each $\mathcal{K}$–object X a $\mathcal{K}$–object XT (but there is no mention of T acting on morphisms); η is a *pre-natural transformation* from *id* to T, that is, η assigns to each object X a morphism of form $X\eta : X \longrightarrow XT$; $(-)^{\#}$ assigns to each morphism $\alpha : X \longrightarrow YT$ a morphism $\alpha^{\#} : XT \longrightarrow YT$; and the following three axioms hold:

1a   For all $\alpha : X \longrightarrow YT$, $X\eta.\alpha^{\#} = \alpha$.

1b   For all X, $(X\eta)^{\#} = id_{XT}$.

1c   For all $\alpha : X \longrightarrow YT$, $\beta : Y \longrightarrow ZT$, $(\alpha\beta^{\#})^{\#} = \alpha^{\#}\beta^{\#}$.

2 DEFINITION   If $\mathbb{T} = (T, \eta, (-)^{\#})$ is a monad in $\mathcal{K}$, its *Kleisli category* [Kleisli 1965] is the category $\mathcal{K}_{\mathbb{T}}$ whose objects are those of $\mathcal{K}$, with morphisms $\mathcal{K}_{\mathbb{T}}(X, Y) = \mathcal{K}(X, YT)$, with identity morphisms $X\eta \in \mathcal{K}_{\mathbb{T}}(X, X)$, and with composition $\alpha \circ \beta$ for

$\alpha \in \mathcal{K}_{\mathrm{T}}(X,Y), \ \beta \in \mathcal{K}_{\mathrm{T}}(Y,Z)$ given by the $\mathcal{K}$–composition

$$\alpha \circ \beta = X \xrightarrow{\quad \alpha \quad} YT \xrightarrow{\quad \beta^{\#} \quad} ZT \ .$$

It is immediate from the axioms of 1 that $\mathcal{K}_{\mathrm{T}}$ is a category. Further, if we define $X^{\triangleleft} = X$ on objects and, on morphisms $\alpha : X \longrightarrow Y$,

$$\alpha^{\triangleleft} = X \xrightarrow{\quad \alpha \quad} Y \xrightarrow{\quad Y\eta \quad} YT$$

then $(-)^{\triangleleft} : \mathcal{K} \longrightarrow \mathcal{K}_{\mathrm{T}}$ is a functor. To prove this, $(id_X)^{\triangleleft} = X\eta$ is indeed the identity morphism in $\mathcal{K}_{\mathrm{T}}$ and, for $\alpha : X \longrightarrow Y, \ \beta : Y \longrightarrow Z$ in $\mathcal{K}$, $(\alpha\beta)^{\triangleleft} = \alpha\beta(Z\eta) = \alpha\beta^{\triangleleft} = \alpha(Y\eta(\beta^{\triangleleft})^{\#}) = \alpha^{\triangleleft}(\beta^{\triangleleft})^{\#} = \alpha^{\triangleleft} \circ \beta^{\triangleleft}$.

A morphism in K_{T} of form $\alpha^{\triangleleft}$ is said to be a *base morphism*.

3 DEFINITION If $\mathcal{B}$ is a Boolean category, a *Boolean monad* in $\mathcal{B}$ is a monad T in $\mathcal{B}$ such that $\mathcal{B}_{\mathrm{T}}$ is a Boolean extension via the inclusion functor $(-)^{\triangleleft} : \mathcal{B} \longrightarrow \mathcal{B}_{\mathrm{T}}$. (Here, we abuse language in a standard way. More precisely, $(-)^{\triangleleft}$ is a (necessarily strict) faithful Boolean functor —*Faithful* means that for $\alpha, \beta : X \longrightarrow Y$ with $\alpha \neq \beta$ then $\alpha^{\triangleleft} \neq \beta^{\triangleleft}$— so that $\mathcal{B}$ is isomorphic to its image and $\mathcal{B}_{\mathrm{T}}$ is a Boolean extension of this image.)

Virtually all of the examples of Section 1 arise through Boolean monads in **Set**. To see this, let's first make some general observations. First of all, the monad structure is determined by the category structure of $\mathcal{K}_{\mathrm{T}}$: $X\eta$ is the identity morphism of $\mathcal{K}_{\mathrm{T}}$ whereas, for $\beta : Y \longrightarrow ZT, \ \beta^{\#} = id_{YT} \circ \beta$. Morever, the fact that $\mathcal{K}_{\mathrm{T}}$ is a category gives the monad axioms:

$$(X\eta)^{\#} = id_{XT} \circ X\eta = id_{XT}$$
$$(X\eta)\alpha^{\#} = (X\eta) \circ \alpha = \alpha$$
$$(\alpha\beta^{\#})^{\#} = (\alpha \circ \beta)^{\#} = id_{XT} \circ (\alpha \circ \beta) = (id_{XT} \circ \alpha) \circ \beta = \alpha^{\#}\beta^{\#} \ .$$

We formalize with

4 OBSERVATION *Let* $\mathcal{K}, \mathcal{C}$ *be categories with the same objects. To show* $\mathcal{C} = K_{\mathbb{T}}$ *for some monad* $\mathbb{T}$ *it suffices to find a prefunctor* $T : \mathcal{K} \longrightarrow \mathcal{K}$ *with* $\mathcal{C}(X, Y) = \mathcal{K}(X, YT)$ *for all* X, Y *and such that the following identity holds:*

4a For $\alpha \in \mathcal{C}(X, Y)$, $\beta \in \mathcal{C}(Y, Z)$, $\alpha \circ \beta = \alpha(id_{YT} \circ \beta)$.

(Here we use $\circ$ for the composition of $\mathcal{C}$ and juxtaposition for the composition of $\mathcal{K}$; id_X refers to the identity morphism in $\mathcal{K}$ and, below, we will use I_X for the $\mathcal{C}$–identity.) *In particular,* **4a** *holds for any Kleisli category.*

Proof Given the prefunctor define $X\eta$ to be I_X and, for $\beta \in \mathcal{K}(Y, ZT)$, define $\beta^{\#} = id_{YT} \circ \beta$. That $\mathbb{T} = (T, \eta, (-)^{\#})$ is a monad was already shown above. We must still check that $K_{\mathbb{T}} = \mathcal{C}$. That the compositions are the same is exactly **4a**. To check that I_X is the $\mathcal{K}_{\mathbb{T}}$–identity, $I_X \alpha^{\#} = I_X(id_{XT} \circ \alpha) = I_X \circ \alpha = \alpha$ and $\alpha I_Y^{\#} = \alpha(Y\eta)^{\#} = \alpha\, id_Y = \alpha$. $\square$

While we will not indulge in such exotica here, examples of different Kleisli categories with the same prefunctor are known. Thus the axiom **4a** cannot be dispensed with.

5 EXAMPLE To represent $\mathbf{Mat}_R$ as $\mathbf{Set}_{\mathbb{T}}$ regard a matrix as a column-indexed family of row vectors. Thus XT is the set of summable X–indexed families in R. In the special case of $\mathbf{Mfn}$, $XT = 2^X$ whereas, for $\mathbf{Pfn}$, $XT = X + \{0\}$.

6 EXAMPLE To represent Ω as $\mathbf{Set}_{\mathbb{T}}$ is easy since the prefunctor $XT = X\Omega$ was used in the original definition 1.4.

7 EXAMPLE For $\mathbf{Pfn}_M$, $XT = (X \times M) + \{0\}$.

[Moggi 1991] interprets the morphism $\alpha : X \longrightarrow YT$ in $\mathcal{K}_\mathbb{T}(X,Y)$ as a program. [Manes 1985] interprets monads in **Set** as providing a general theory of nondeterminism; and, while they do not explicitly mention monads, [Main and Benson 1984] deal with certain matrix categories from a similar point of view.

Monads subsume algebraic theory models as we briefly discuss here. Denote the I–fold copower of an object A by $I \cdot A$. Consider a category $\mathcal{C}$ and an object D of $\mathcal{A}$ all of whose finite copowers exist. Let $\mathcal{A}$ denote the category whose objects are the natural numbers and with $\mathcal{A}(m,n) = \mathcal{C}(m \cdot D, n \cdot D)$, composition and identities being those of $\mathcal{C}$. As discussed in the introduction, such $\mathcal{A}$ is the typical algebraic theory. Suppose there exists an infinite cardinal number $\aleph$ such that for every set X with $Card(X) < \aleph$, $X \cdot D$ exists and $Card(\mathcal{A}(D, I \cdot D)) < \aleph$. Then if $\mathbf{Set}_\aleph$ is the full subcategory of **Set** of all sets of cardinality $< \aleph$, the prefunctor $XT = \mathcal{A}(D, X \cdot D)$ extends to a monad in $\mathbf{Set}_\aleph$ in a natural way, as we hope the reader will verify. Then $\mathcal{A}$ is the full subcategory of the Kleisli category whose objects are the natural numbers. In general, even if no such $\aleph$ exists, there is a category of algebras over $\mathcal{A}$ [Lawvere 1963]. The free algebra $F(X)$ generated by a set X exists. $\mathcal{A}$ is isomorphic to the full subcategory of all $F(n)$ for n a natural number.

We need some lemmas before we are able to characterize Boolean monads. The first two show that our definition of monad is coextensive with that of [Mac Lane 1971].

8 LEMMA   *Let $(T, \eta, (\text{-})^\#)$ be a monad in $\mathcal{K}$. Given $\alpha : X \longrightarrow Y$ define $\alpha T : XT \longrightarrow YT$ by*

8a. $$\alpha T = (X \xrightarrow{\ \alpha\ } Y \xrightarrow{\ Y\eta\ } YT)^\# .$$

Then the prefunctor T is in fact a functor and $\eta : id \longrightarrow T$ is a natural transformation. Further, if for each object X, $X\mu : XTT \longrightarrow XT$ is defined by

8b $$X\mu \;=\; (id_{XT})^{\#}$$

then $\mu : TT \longrightarrow T$ *is a natural transformation and* **8c, d** *below hold:*

8c For each X, $(X\eta)T.X\mu \;=\; id_{XT}$.

8d For each $\beta : XT \longrightarrow YT$, β *has form* $\alpha^{\#}$ *if and only if the following diagram commutes:*

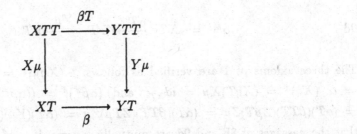

Proof $(id_X)T \;=\; (X\eta)^{\#} \;=\; id_{XT}$ and, for $\alpha : X \longrightarrow Y$, $\beta : Y \longrightarrow Z$, $(\alpha\beta)T \;=\; (\alpha\beta(Z\eta))^{\#} \;=\; (\alpha(Y\eta)(\beta(Z\eta))^{\#})^{\#} \;=\; (\alpha(Y\eta))^{\#}(\beta(Z\eta))^{\#} \;=\; (\alpha T)(\beta T)$, so T is functorial. For **8c**, $(X\eta T)X\mu \;=\; ((X\eta)(XT\eta))^{\#}(id_{XT})^{\#} \;=\; ((X\eta)(XT\eta)(id_{XT})^{\#})^{\#} \;=\; (X\eta)^{\#} \;=\; id_{XT}$. For **8d**, $(\beta T)(Y\mu) \;=\; (\beta(Y\eta))^{\#}(id_{YT})^{\#} \;=\; (\beta(Y\eta)(id_{YT})^{\#})^{\#} \;=\; \beta^{\#}$ whereas, if $\beta = \alpha^{\#}$, $(X\mu)\beta \;=\; (id_{XT})^{\#}\alpha^{\#} \;=\; (id_{XT}\,\alpha^{\#})^{\#} \;=\; \beta^{\#}$. Conversely, if the diagram commutes set $\alpha = (X\eta)\beta$ and use **8c** and the functoriality of T: $\beta = id_{XT}\beta \;=\; (X\eta T)(X\mu)\beta \;=\; (X\eta T)(\beta T)Y\mu \;=\; \alpha T\,(id_{YT})^{\#} \;=\; (\alpha(YT\eta))^{\#}(id_{YT})^{\#} \;=\; (\alpha(YT\eta)(id_{YT})^{\#})^{\#} \;=\; \alpha^{\#}$. Finally, μ is natural since this is just the special case of the diagram of **8d** with $\beta = \alpha T$ which *does* have form $\alpha^{\#}$. $\qquad\square$

9 **PROPOSITION** *Monads are coextensive with* (T, η, μ) *with* $T : \mathscr{K} \longrightarrow \mathscr{K}$ *a functor,* $\eta : id \longrightarrow T$ *and* $\mu : TT \longrightarrow T$ *natural transformations, subject to the equations* **abc** *expressed by the commutative diagrams*

$$
\begin{array}{ccccc}
T & \xrightarrow{\;\eta T\;} & TT & \xleftarrow{\;T\eta\;} & T \\
{\scriptstyle id}\downarrow & \text{(a)} & {\scriptstyle \mu}\downarrow & \text{(b)} & \downarrow{\scriptstyle id} \\
T & \xrightarrow[\;id\;]{} & T & \xleftarrow[\;id\;]{} & T
\end{array}
\qquad
\begin{array}{ccc}
TTT & \xrightarrow{\;\mu T\;} & TT \\
{\scriptstyle T\mu}\downarrow & \text{(c)} & \downarrow{\scriptstyle \mu} \\
TT & \xrightarrow[\;\mu\;]{} & T
\end{array}
$$

Proof If $(T,\eta,(-)^{\#})$ is a monad and μ is as in **8b** then **(a)** is given and the rest follows from Lemma 2. For the converse, define

9d $$ \alpha^{\#} \;=\; XT \xrightarrow{\;\alpha T\;} YTT \xrightarrow{\;Y\mu\;} YT \;. $$

The three axioms of **1** are verified as follows. $(X\eta)\alpha^{\#} = (X\eta)(\alpha T)Y\mu = \alpha(Y\eta)Y\mu$ $= \alpha$; $(X\eta)^{\#} = (X\eta T)X\mu = id_{XT}$; and $(\alpha\beta^{\#})^{\#} = ((\alpha\beta^{\#})T)Z\mu = ((\alpha(\beta T)Z\mu)T)Z\mu$ $= (\alpha T)(\beta TT)(Z\mu T)Z\mu = (\alpha T)(\beta TT)(ZT\mu)Z\mu = (\alpha T)(Y\mu)(\beta T)Z\mu = \alpha^{\#}\beta^{\#}$. To see that the passages of **8b** and **9d** are mutually inverse, if $(-)^{\#} \mapsto \mu \mapsto (-)^{\bigstar}$ then $\alpha^{\bigstar} = (\alpha T)Y\mu = (\alpha(YT\eta))^{\#}(id_{XT})^{\#} = (\alpha(YT\eta)(id_{XT})^{\#})^{\#} = \alpha^{\#}$ whereas if $\mu \mapsto (-)^{\#} \mapsto \nu$ then $X\nu = (id_{XT})^{\#} = (id_{XT}T)X\mu = X\mu$. $\qquad\square$

The (T,η,μ) form is often the most convenient in abstract discussions. On the other hand, to verify a specific example of a monad, the μ–form requires seven axioms, four of which require iterating T and one of these even requires TTT as opposed to the only three axioms of the original form where T need not be iterated.

10 LEMMA *Let $\mathcal{K}$ have finite coproducts and let $\mathbb{T} = (T,\eta,(-)^{\#})$ be any monad in $\mathcal{K}$. The following statements hold.*

    1. *$\mathcal{K}_{\mathbb{T}}$ has finite coproducts and $(-)^{\lhd} : \mathcal{K}\longrightarrow\mathcal{K}_{\mathbb{T}}$ preserves finite coproducts.*

    2. *Given $\mathcal{K}_{\mathbb{T}}$-morphisms $\alpha,\beta,\gamma,\delta$ as shown in (A) then (A) commutes in $\mathcal{K}_{\mathbb{T}}$ if and only if (B) commutes in $\mathcal{K}$ and (A) is a pullback in $\mathcal{K}_{\mathbb{T}}$ if and*

only if (**B**) *is a pullback in* $\mathcal{K}$.

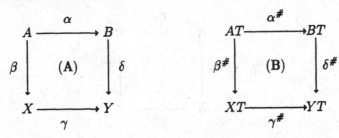

Proof If $P\xrightarrow{\ i\ }X\xleftarrow{\ j\ }Q$ is a coproduct in $\mathcal{K}$ and if $\alpha \in \mathcal{K}_\mathsf{T}(P,Y)$, $\beta \in \mathcal{K}_\mathsf{T}(Q,Y)$ then there exists a unique $\mathcal{K}$–morphism $\psi : X\longrightarrow YT$ with $i\psi = \alpha$, $j\psi = \beta$. But given $f : A\longrightarrow B$, $\gamma : B\longrightarrow CT$ we have, in any monad, the equality

$$11 \qquad f^{\vartriangleleft} \circ \gamma = f\gamma$$

(Check: $f^{\vartriangleleft} \circ \gamma = f(B\eta)\gamma^{\#} = f\gamma$.) Thus $i^{\vartriangleleft} \circ \psi = i\psi$, $j^{\vartriangleleft} \circ \psi = j\psi$ so it follows that

$$P\xrightarrow{\ i^{\vartriangleleft}\ }X\xleftarrow{\ j^{\vartriangleleft}\ }Q$$

is a coproduct in $\mathcal{K}_\mathsf{T}$. Further, if 0 is initial in $\mathcal{K}$ then $\mathcal{K}_\mathsf{T}(0,X) = \mathcal{K}(0,XT)$ has one element, so 0 is initial in $\mathcal{K}_\mathsf{T}$ as well. This proves the first statement.

For the commutativity assertion in the second statement, $\alpha \circ \delta = \beta \circ \gamma \Leftrightarrow \alpha\delta^{\#} = \beta\gamma^{\#} \Leftrightarrow (\alpha\delta^{\#})^{\#} = (\beta\gamma^{\#})^{\#}$ (by axiom 1a) $\Leftrightarrow \alpha^{\#}\delta^{\#} = \beta^{\#}\delta^{\#}$. The remainder of the proof is safely left to the reader. $\qquad\square$

12 LEMMA *Let* $j : R\longrightarrow X$ *be a summand in a Boolean category* $\mathcal{B}$ *and let* T *be a Boolean monad in* $\mathcal{B}$. *The following statements hold.*

1. $jT : RT\longrightarrow XT$ *is a monomorphism in* $\mathcal{B}$.

2. *If* $X\eta$ *factors through* jT, j *is an isomorphism in* $\mathcal{K}$.

Proof For the first statement, $(-)^\lhd : \mathcal{B} \longrightarrow \mathcal{B}_\mathbb{T}$ preserves $[j]R$ so

$$
\begin{array}{ccc}
R & \xrightarrow{\;R\eta\;} & R \\
\scriptstyle R\eta \downarrow & & \downarrow \scriptstyle j^\lhd \\
R & \xrightarrow{\;j^\lhd\;} & X
\end{array}
$$

is a pullback in $\mathcal{B}_\mathbb{T}$. By Lemma 10(2),

$$
\begin{array}{ccc}
RT & \xrightarrow{\;id\;} & RT \\
\scriptstyle id \downarrow & & \downarrow \scriptstyle jT \\
RT & \xrightarrow{\;jT\;} & XT
\end{array}
$$

is a pullback in $\mathcal{B}$ and this is equivalent to the statement that jT is a monomorphism.

For the second statement, suppose $\epsilon : X \longrightarrow RT$ with $X\eta = \epsilon(jT)$. Since η is natural, $j(X\eta) = (R\eta)(jT)$. Thus

$$
R \xrightarrow{R\eta} RT \xrightarrow{jT} XT \xrightarrow{\epsilon^\#} RT \xrightarrow{jT} XT
$$

$$
= R \xrightarrow{\;j\;} X \xrightarrow{X\eta} XT \xrightarrow{\epsilon^\#} RT \xrightarrow{jT} XT
$$

$$
= R \xrightarrow{\;j\;} X \xrightarrow{\;\epsilon\;} RT \xrightarrow{jT} XT
$$

$$
= R \xrightarrow{\;j\;} X \xrightarrow{X\eta} XT
$$

$$
= R \xrightarrow{R\eta} RT \xrightarrow{jT} XT
$$

As jT is a monomorphism, $(R\eta)(jT)\epsilon^\# = R\eta$. Since $(jT)\epsilon^\#$ is of form $\gamma^\#$ (for $\gamma = j^\lhd \epsilon^\#$), and $\gamma^\# = ((R\eta)\gamma^\#)^\#$, it follows $(jT)\epsilon^\# = (R\eta)^\# = id_{RT}$. On the other hand, $(X\eta)\epsilon^\#(jT) = \epsilon(jT) = X\eta$ and $\epsilon^\#(jT) = \delta^\#$ (for $\delta = \epsilon(jT)$), similar reasoning shows $\epsilon^\#(jT) = id_{XT}$. In $\mathcal{B}_\mathbb{T}$ we can show $j^\lhd \circ \epsilon = I_R$, $\epsilon \circ j^\lhd = I_X$, so $j^\lhd$, ϵ are inverse isomorphisms in $\mathcal{B}_{\mathbb{T}}$. Since $(-)^{\triangleleft} : \mathcal{B} \longrightarrow \mathcal{B}_{\mathbb{T}}$ is a Boolean extension, ϵ is a base isomorphism and so preserves an inverse to the $\mathcal{B}$-isomorphism j as desired. $\square$

13 THEOREM *Let $\mathcal{B}$ be a Boolean category and let $\mathbb{T} = (T, \eta, (-)^{\#})$ be a Boolean monad in $\mathcal{B}$. Then the following hold.*

1. *For all X, $X\eta$ is a monomorphism in $\mathcal{B}$.*

2. *Every isomorphism in $\mathcal{B}_{\mathbb{T}}$ is a base morphism (and hence an isomorphism in $\mathcal{B}$.)*

3. *If $i : P \longrightarrow X \in Summ(X)$, the following square is a pullback in $\mathcal{B}$:*

$$
\begin{array}{ccc}
P & \xrightarrow{\;P\eta\;} & PT \\
{\scriptstyle i}\downarrow & \textbf{(A)} & \downarrow{\scriptstyle iT} \\
X & \xrightarrow{\;X\eta\;} & XT
\end{array}
$$

4. *For $\alpha : X \longrightarrow Y$, $j : Q \longrightarrow Y \in Summ(Y)$, if* **(B)** *is a pullback in $\mathcal{B}$ with $i : P \longrightarrow X \in Summ(X)$, then* **(C)** *is a pullback.*

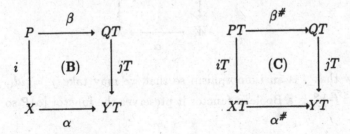

5. *T preserves $\mathcal{B}$-pullbacks of form $[\alpha]Q$.*

6. *For every summand $i : P \longrightarrow X$, the following square is a $\mathcal{B}$-pullback:*

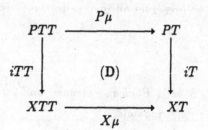

Proof Condition (2) obtains directly from the definition of a Boolean extension. Given $f, g : X \longrightarrow Y$ with $f(Y\eta) = g(Y\eta)$, by the naturality of η established in Lemma 8 we have $f^{\triangleleft} = (X\eta)(f^{\triangleleft})^{\#} = (X\eta)(fT) = f(X\eta) = g(X\eta) = \ldots = g^{\triangleleft}$ so that, by Definition **3**, $f = g$. This shows $Y\eta$ is a monomorphism. Turning to (3), the square (**C**) commutes by the naturality of η. Let $X \xleftarrow{\ \alpha\ } W \xrightarrow{\ \beta\ } PT$ satisfy $\alpha(X\eta) = \beta(iT)$. We must show that there exists $\psi : W \longrightarrow P$ with $\psi i = \alpha$, $\psi(P\eta) = \beta$ (uniqueness being clear since i is a monomorphism.) It is in fact enough to find $\psi i = \alpha$ since then $\psi(P\eta)(iT) = \psi i(X\eta) = \alpha(X\eta) = \beta(iT)$ whence $\psi(P\eta) = \beta$ because iT is mono by 12(1). Form the pullback for $[\alpha]P$:

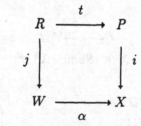

We will show that j is an isomorphism so that we may take $j = id_W$ whence t is the desired ψ. As $(-)^{\triangleleft}$ is a Boolean functor it preserves the functor $[\alpha]P$ so that, by **10**(2),

$$
\begin{array}{ccc}
RT & \xrightarrow{\ tT\ } & PT \\[2pt]
{\scriptstyle jT}\big\downarrow & & \big\downarrow{\scriptstyle iT} \\[4pt]
WT & \xrightarrow[\ \alpha T\ ]{} & XT
\end{array}
$$

is a pullback in $\mathfrak{B}$. In particular we have verified (5). Since $WT \xleftarrow{\ W\eta\ } W \xrightarrow{\ \beta\ } PT$

satisfy $(W\eta)\alpha T = \alpha(X\eta) = \beta(iT)$, $W\eta$ factors through jT so that j is indeed an isomorphism by Lemma 12(2).

Now the fourth statement. Since all $\mathfrak{B}_{\mathbb{T}}$-isomorphisms are base the $\mathfrak{B}_{\mathbb{T}}$-summands are just the morphisms of form $k^{\triangleleft}$ for $k : R \longrightarrow X$ a summand in $\mathfrak{B}$. As $\mathfrak{B}_{\mathbb{T}}$ is Boolean, given $(\mathbf{B})$ we may form $[\alpha]Q$ in $\mathfrak{B}_{\mathbb{T}}$ to get a $\mathfrak{B}_{\mathbb{T}}$-pullback of form

$$
\begin{array}{ccc}
R & \xrightarrow{\;\gamma\;} & Q \\
k^{\triangleleft} \downarrow & & \downarrow j^{\triangleleft} \\
X & \xrightarrow{\;\alpha\;} & Y
\end{array}
$$

with $k : R \longrightarrow X$ a summand. Consider the $\mathfrak{B}$-diagram

$$
\begin{array}{ccccc}
R & \xrightarrow{\;R\eta\;} & RT & \xrightarrow{\;\gamma^{\#}\;} & QT \\
k \downarrow & (\mathbf{E}) & kT \downarrow & (\mathbf{F}) & \downarrow jT \\
X & \xrightarrow{\;X\eta\;} & XT & \xrightarrow{\;\alpha^{\#}\;} & YT
\end{array}
$$

Then $(\mathbf{E})$ is a pullback by the proof we have just given whence $(\mathbf{F})$ is a pullback by Lemma 10(2). By pullback pasting 5.20, the perimeter is a pullback and must be isomorphic to $(\mathbf{B})$ so that $P = R$ in $Summ(X)$ whence $(\mathbf{C})$ is isomorphic to $(\mathbf{F})$ and so is a pullback.

(6) follows from (4) since the following square is a pullback (check!).

$$
\begin{array}{ccc}
PT & \xrightarrow{\;id\;} & PT \\
iT \downarrow & & \downarrow iT \\
XT & \xrightarrow{\;id\;} & XT
\end{array}
$$

$\square$

Theorem **13** has the following converse.

14 THEOREM *Let $\mathfrak{B}$ be a Boolean category and let $\mathbb{T} = (T, \eta, (-)^{\#})$ be a monad in $\mathfrak{B}$ satisfying conditions $(1, 2, 3, 4)$ of theorem **13**. Suppose $\mathfrak{B}, \mathbb{T}$ satisfies either*

1. *If $i : P \longrightarrow X$ is a summand in $\mathfrak{B}$, so is $iT : PT \longrightarrow XT$,*

or

2. *$\mathbb{T}$ satisfies **13(5)** (i.e. T preserves pullbacks of form $[\alpha]Q$) and every equalizer in $\mathfrak{B}$ is a summand.*

Then $\mathbb{T}$ is a Boolean monad.

Proof First of all, $(-)^{\triangleleft} : \mathfrak{B} \longrightarrow \mathfrak{B}_{\mathbb{T}}$ is faithful as follows immediately from the hypothesis **13(1)**. By Lemma **10**, $\mathfrak{B}_{\mathbb{T}}$ has finite coproducts and $(-)^{\triangleleft}$ preserves them. Further, by hypothesis **13(2)**, every $\mathfrak{B}_{\mathbb{T}}$-summand of x has a representative of form $i^{\triangleleft}$ for $i : P \longrightarrow X$ a $\mathfrak{B}$-summand.

We pause to prove that $(2) \Rightarrow (1)$ so that (1) holds regardless. By **5.14**, if $F : X \longrightarrow X + X$ is the fanout of P,

$$
\begin{array}{ccc}
P & \xrightarrow{\ \ i\ \ } & X \\
{\scriptstyle i}\big\downarrow & & \big\downarrow{\scriptstyle F} \\
X & \xrightarrow[\ in_1\ ]{} & X + X
\end{array}
$$

is a pullback. As T preserves $[F]in_1$ by hypothesis (2),

$$
\begin{array}{ccc}
PT & \xrightarrow{\ \ iT\ \ } & XT \\
{\scriptstyle iT}\big\downarrow & & \big\downarrow{\scriptstyle FT} \\
XT & \xrightarrow[\ in_1 T\ ]{} & X + X
\end{array}
$$

is a pullback, so $iT = eq(in_1T, FT)$. But we assume that every equalizer is a summand, so (1) is shown.

Now consider a $\mathcal{B}$–morphism $\alpha : X \longrightarrow YT$ and summand $j : Q \longrightarrow Y$. By (1), the pullback **13(A)** exists as $[\alpha](QT)$ and $i : P \longrightarrow X$ is indeed a summand. Thus **13(B)** is a pullback in $\mathcal{B}$ by hypothesis or, equivalently by Lemma 10,

$$
\begin{array}{ccc}
P & \xrightarrow{\ \beta\ } & Q \\
{\scriptstyle i}\,^\triangleleft \big\downarrow & & \big\downarrow\,{\scriptstyle j}\,^\triangleleft \\
X & \xrightarrow[\ \alpha\ ]{} & Y
\end{array}
$$

is a pullback in $\mathcal{B}_\mathbb{T}$ so that $P = [\alpha]Q$ exists in $\mathcal{B}_\mathbb{T}$.

To see $(-)^\triangleleft : \mathcal{B} \longrightarrow \mathcal{B}_\mathbb{T}$ preserves $[\alpha]Q$, let

$$
\begin{array}{ccc}
P & \xrightarrow{\ \beta\ } & Q \\
{\scriptstyle i}\big\downarrow & & \big\downarrow{\scriptstyle j} \\
X & \xrightarrow[\ \alpha\ ]{} & Y
\end{array}
$$

be the pullback square for $[\alpha]Q$ in $\mathcal{B}$. Applying hypothesis **13(3)**, paste the pullback

$$
\begin{array}{ccc}
Q & \xrightarrow{\ Q\eta\ } & QT \\
{\scriptstyle j}\big\downarrow & & \big\downarrow{\scriptstyle jT} \\
Y & \xrightarrow[\ Y\eta\ ]{} & YT
\end{array}
$$

on the right to get the perimeter pullback $\beta^\triangleleft(jT) = i\alpha^\triangleleft$ which is an instance of **13(4B)** so that **13(4C)** and Lemma **10** give the desired pullback

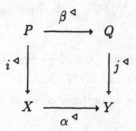

The remaining details that $(-)^{\triangleleft} : \mathcal{B} \longrightarrow \mathcal{B}_{\mathbb{T}}$ is a Boolean extension are trivial. $\square$

We now apply Theorem **14** to create a general class of Boolean monads which generalize Ω with all $\Omega_n = \emptyset$ if $n \neq 0$.

15 PROPOSITION *Let $\mathcal{B}$ be any Boolean category and let A be an object of $\mathcal{B}$. Define $\mathbb{T}_A = (T, \eta, (-)^{\#})$ by $XT = X + A$, $X\eta = in_X$, $\alpha^{\#} = {<}\alpha, in_A{>}$. Then $\mathbb{T}_A$ is a Boolean monad in $\mathcal{B}$.*

Proof It is trivial to check that $\mathbb{T}_A$ is a monad —note that $(\alpha\beta^{\#})^{\#} = \alpha^{\#}\beta^{\#} = {<}\alpha{<}\beta, in_A{>}, in_A{>}$.

In any category with binary coproducts, if $P \xrightarrow{\ i\ } X \xleftarrow{\ j\ } Q$ is a coproduct then so is $P + A \xrightarrow{i \oplus id} X + A \xleftarrow{j \oplus id} Q + A$. Thus **14**(1) holds and so, by Theorem **15** we have only to show that $\mathbb{T}_A$ satisfies conditions (1,2,3,4) of **13**. We have that $X\eta$ is a monomorphism by Lemma **5.2**.

For **13**(2) we will prove the stronger statement that any split monomorphism in the Kleisli category is base. Let $\alpha : X \longrightarrow Y + A$, $\beta : Y \longrightarrow X + A$ with $\alpha \circ \beta = I_X$, that is, with $\alpha\beta^{\#} = in_X$. Construct the pullbacks $P = [\alpha]Y$, $Q = [\alpha]A$ as shown.

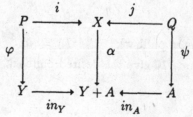

so that i, j are summands. By the disjointness of coproducts **5.2**,

$$
\begin{array}{ccc}
0 & \longrightarrow & X \\
\downarrow & & \downarrow {in_X} \\
A & \underset{in_A}{\longrightarrow} & X + A
\end{array}
$$

is a pullback. As $\psi\, in_A = \psi\, in_A < \beta, in_A > \; = \; \psi\, in_A \beta^{\#} = j\alpha\beta^{\#} = j\, in_X$, $Q = 0$ by the pullback property, so $P = Q' = X$ and $\alpha = \varphi\, in_Y$ is base.

Let $i : P \longrightarrow X \in Summ(X)$. To show **13(3)** we must demonstrate that

$$
\begin{array}{ccc}
P & \overset{in_P}{\longrightarrow} & P + A \\
i \downarrow & & \downarrow {i \oplus id_A} \\
X & \underset{in_X}{\longrightarrow} & X + A
\end{array}
$$

is a pullback. This is shown by the calculation $[in_X](P + A) = (P + P') \bigcap (P + A)$ $= (P \bigcap (P + A)) \bigcup (P' \bigcap (P + A)) = P$.

For **13(4)**, let $i : P \longrightarrow X \in Summ(X)$, $j : Q \longrightarrow Y \in Summ(Y)$ and suppose given a pullback

$$
\begin{array}{ccc}
P & \overset{\beta}{\longrightarrow} & Q + A \\
i \downarrow & & \downarrow {j \oplus id_A} \\
X & \underset{\alpha}{\longrightarrow} & Y + A
\end{array}
$$

It is easily checked that $jT = (j^{\triangleleft})^{\#} = j \oplus id_A$, so we must show that

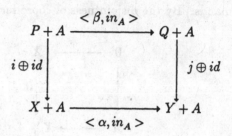

is a pullback. By **10.1(8)**, $[<\alpha, in_A>](Q+A) = [\alpha](Q+A) + [in_A](Q+A)$. Now $[\alpha](Q+A) = P$ by hypothesis and, applying the same reasoning as just used above, $[in_A](Q+A) = [in_A]Q + [in_A]A = 0 + A = A$. $\qquad\qquad\qquad\Box$

We conclude with the promised converse to Proposition **15.13**.

16 PROPOSITION *Let $\mathfrak{D}$ be a distributive category in which all morphisms are atomic and possessing an atomic generator (15.11) G such that whenever $X \neq 0$ there exists an atom $x : G \longrightarrow X$. Then there exists a Boolean monad $\mathbb{T} = (T, \eta, (-)^\#)$ in $\mathfrak{D}$ such that $\mathfrak{D}_\mathbb{T}$ is an extensional Boolean category with zero morphisms such that $(\mathfrak{D}_\mathbb{T})_{atomic} = \mathfrak{D}_{tot} = \mathfrak{D}$.*

Proof If 1 (the terminal object of $\mathfrak{D}$) is initial then all objects are, so that the identity monad $XT = X$, $X\eta = id_X$, $\alpha^\# = \alpha$ will do. Otherwise, there exists an atom $x : G \longrightarrow 1$. If x is not an isomorphism, x' is not the zero summand and so there is an atom $y : G \longrightarrow 1$ which factors through x'. As such, $x \bigcap y = 0$ so that $x \neq y$, and this contradicts the terminality of 1. Thus the atomic generator must be terminal.

Let $\mathbb{T}$ be the Boolean monad $\mathbb{T}_1$ of Theorem **15**. That 0 is a zero object in $\mathfrak{D}_\mathbb{T}$ is obvious so $\mathfrak{D}_\mathbb{T}$ has a unique projection system, which is the third axiom of Definition **15.11**. We next shall show that 1 is an atomic generator for $\mathfrak{D}_\mathbb{T}$. By the proof of **15** we know that the pullback square for $Ker(\alpha) = [\alpha]0$ in $\mathfrak{D}_\mathbb{T}$ is constructed as the following pullback square in $\mathfrak{D}$:

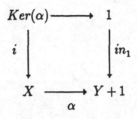

Now let $\alpha, \beta : X \longrightarrow Y + 1$ with $\alpha \neq \beta$. If it is false that $Dom(\alpha) \subset Dom(\beta)$ then there exists $x \in Dom(\alpha)$, with $x \notin Dom(\beta)$ (recall that $x \in X$ means $x : 1 \longrightarrow X$ is an atom in $\mathfrak{D}$) in which case $x\alpha$ factors through $in_Y : Y \longrightarrow Y + 1$ whereas $y\alpha$ factors through in_1 so that $x\alpha \neq x\beta$. Similarly, if $Dom(\beta) \subset Dom(\alpha)$ is false. Otherwise $Dom(\alpha) = D = Dom(\beta)$. There exists pullbacks

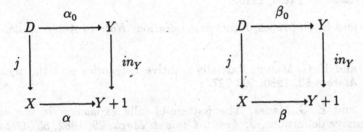

Since $Ker(\alpha) = Ker(\beta)$ and α, β necessarily agree on this common summand as just discussed above, $\alpha_0 \neq \beta_0$ so, as 1 is an atomic generator in $\mathfrak{D}$, there exists $x \in D$ with $x\alpha_0 \neq x\beta_0$ and hence with $x\alpha \neq x\beta$.

As every $\mathfrak{D}$-morphism is atomic, $\mathfrak{D} \subset (\mathfrak{D}_\top)_{atomic}$. Conversely, each atomic morphism in $\mathfrak{D}_\top$ is total (by the proof of 15.12(5)), and it is clear from the discussion of kernels and domains above that total $\Leftrightarrow$ base. The remaining details are then easily left to the reader.   □

BIBLIOGRAPHY

M. A. Arbib and E. G. Manes, *Arrows, Structures, and Functors: The Categorical Imperative*, Academic Press, 1975.

M. A. Arbib and E. G. Manes, Functorial iteration, *Notices Amer. Math. Soc.* **25**, 1978, A-381.

M. A. Arbib and E. G. Manes, Partially-additive categories and the semantics of flow diagrams, *J. Algebra* **62**, 1980, 203-227.

M. A. Arbib and E. G. Manes, The pattern-of-calls expansion is the canonical fixed point for recursive definitions, *J. Assoc. Comput. Mach.* **29**, 1982, 557-602.

A. Asperti and G. Longo, *Categories, Types and Structures: An Introduction to Category Theory for the Working Computer Scientist*, MIT Press, 1991.

M. Barr and C. Wells, *Category Theory for Computing Science*, Prentice-Hall, 1990.

D. B. Benson, Counting paths: nondeterminism as linear algebra, *IEEE Trans. Software Engin.* **SE-10**, 1984, 785-794.

S. L. Bloom (ed.), *Calvin C. Elgot, Selected Papers*, Springer-Verlag, 1982.

S. L. Bloom, Elgot's analysis of monadic computation, *Fundamenta Informaticae* **2**, 1982a, 171-186.

S.L. Bloom, C.C. Elgot and J.B. Wright, Solutions of the iteration equation and extensions of the scalar iteration operation, *SIAM J. Comput.* **9**, 1980, 25-45.

S. L. Bloom and Z. Ésik, Floyd-Hoare logic in iteration theories, Technical Report #8801, Stevens Institute of Technology, Castle Point, Hoboken, New Jersey 07030, USA, Jan. 1988.

S.L. Bloom and Z. Ésik, Matrix and matricial iteration theories of regular sets; condensed version Equational axioms for regular sets, Dept. Computer Science, Stevens Institute of Technology, Hoboken, NJ 07030, USA, 1991, preprints.

S. L. Bloom, Z. Ésik and D. Taubner, Iteration theories of synchronization trees, technical report TUM-I9014, Mathematisches Institut und Technische Universität München, 1990.

S. L. Bloom, S. Ginali and J. Rutledge, Scalar and vector iteration, *J. Comput. Sys. Sci.* 14, 1977, 251-256.

A. Carboni and R. F. C. Walters, Cartesian Bicategories I, *J. Pure Appl. Alg.* 49, 1987, 11-32.

J. R. B. Cockett, Introduction to distributive categories, Macquarie University Computing Report No. 90—0052C, April, 1990.

J. R. B. Cockett, Conditional control is not quite categorical control, Macquariet University Computing Report No. 91-0063C, January, 1991.

J. R. B. Cockett and T. Fukushima, About CHARITY, preprint, Nov. 1991.

J. H. Conway, *Regular Algebra and Finite Machines*, Chapman and Hall, London, 1971.

P.-L. Curien and A. Obtulowicz, Partiality, cartesian closedness, and toposes, *Information and Computation* 80, 1989, 50-95.

E. W. Dijkstra, *A Discipline of Programming*, Prentice Hall, 1976.

E. W. Dijkstra and C. S. Scholten, *Predicate Calculus and Program Semantics*, Springer-Verlag, 1990.

R. Di Paola and A. Heller, Dominical categories: Recursion theory without elements, *J. Symb. Logic* 52, 1987, 594-635.

S. Eilenberg, *Automata, Languages and Machines. Vol. A.*, Academic Press, 1974.

S. Eilenberg and S. Mac Lane, General theory of natural equivalences, *Trans. Amer. Math. Soc.* 58, 1945, 231-294.

C. C. Elgot, Monadic computation and iterative algebraic theories, in H.E. Rose and J. C. Shepherson (eds.), *Proceedings of Logic Colloquium '73*, North-Holland, 1975, 175-230.

C. C. Elgot, S. L. Bloom and R. Tindell, On the algebraic structure of rooted trees, *J. Comput. Sys. Sci.* 16, 1978, 362-399.

Z. Ésik, Identities in iterative and rational theories, *Computational Linguistics* 14, 1980, 183-207.
Z. Ésik, Algebras of iteration theories, *J. Comput. Sys. Sci.* 27, 1983, 291-303.

Z. Ésik, Independence of the equational axioms for iteration theories, *J. Comp. Sys. Sci.* 36, 1988, 66-76.

M. J. Fischer and R. E. Ladner, Propositional dynamic logic of regular programs, *J. Comp. Sys. Sci.* **18**, 1979, 286-294.

P. Freyd, *Abelian Categories*, Harper and Row, 1964.

J. A. Goguen, Abstract errors for abstract data types, in *Formal Description of Programming Concepts*, North-Holland, 1978, 491-525.

M. J. C. Gordon, *The Denotational Description of Programming Languages, An Introduction*, Springer-Verlag, 1979.

F. Guzmán and C. Squier, The algebra of conditional logic, *Algebra Universalis* **27**, 1990, 88-110.

D. Harel, A. R. Meyer and V. R. Pratt, Computability and completeness in logics of Programs, *Proc. 9th ACM Symposium on the Theory of Computing*, 1977, 261-268.

C. A. R. Hoare, An axiomatic basis for computer programming, *Comm. Assoc. Comput. Mach.* **12**, 1969, 576-580, 583.

E. V. Huntington, Sets of independent postulates for the algebra of logic, *Trans. Amer. Math. Soc.*, **5**, 1904, 288-309.

H. Huwig and A. Poigne, A note on the inconsistencies caused by fixpoints in a cartesian closed category, *Theoretical Comput. Sci.* **73**, 1990, 101-112.

P. T. Johnstone, *Topos Theory*, Academic Press, 1977.

S. Kasangian, A. Labella and A. Pettorossi, Observers, experiments, and agents: a comprehensive approach to parallelism, *in Semantics of Systems of Concurrent Processes*, Lecture Notes in Computer Science **469**, Springer-Verlag, 1990, 375-406.

S. C. Kleene, *Introduction to Metamathematics*, Van Nostrand, 1952.

H. Kleisli, Every standard construction is induced by a pair of adjoint functors, *Proc. Amer. Math. Soc.* **16**, 1965, 544-546.

S. Koppelberg, *Handbook of Boolean Algebras, Vol. 1*, North-Holland, 1989.

D. Kozen, A representation theorem for models of *-free PDL, in J.W. de Bakker and J. Van Leeuwen (eds.), *Automata, Languages and Programming, ICALP '80*, Lecture Notes in Computer Science 85, Springer-Verlag, 1980, 351-362.

D. Kozen, On induction vs. *-continuity, in E. Engeler (ed.), *Logics of Programs*, Lecture Notes in Computer Science **131**, 1981, 167-176.

D. Kozen, *A completeness theorem for Kleene algebras and the algebra of regular events*, Technical Report TR 90-1123, Dept. Computer Science, Cornell University, Ithaca, NY 14853-7501, USA, 1990, preprint.

J. Lambek and P. J. Scott, *Introduction to Higher Order Categorical Logic*, Cambridge University Press, 1986.

F. W. Lawvere, *Functorial Semantics of Algebraic Theories*, dissertation, Department of Mathematics, Columbia University, 1963.

F. W. Lawvere, An elementary theory of the category of sets, *Proc. Nat. Acad. Sci. USA* 52, 1964, 1506-1511.

F. W. Lawvere, The category of categories as a foundation for mathematics, in *Proceedings of the Conference on Categorical Algebra at La Jolla*, Springer-Verlag, 1966, 1-21.

F. W. Lawvere, Diagonal arguments and cartesian closed categories, in *Category Theory, Homology Theory and their Applications, II*, Lecture Notes in Mathematics 92, Springer-Verlag, 1969, 134-145.

G. Longo and E. Moggi, Cartesian closed categories and partial morphisms for effective type structures, *Lecture Notes in Computer Science* 173, 1984, 235-255.

S. Mac Lane, *Categories for the Working Mathematician*, Springer-Verlag, 1971.

M. G. Main and D. B. Benson, Functional behaviour of nondeterministic and concurrent programs, *Information and Control* 62, 1984, 144-189.

M. G. Main and D. L. Black, Semantic models for total correctness and fairness, Department of Computer Science technical report CU-CS-417-88, University of Colorado, Boulder, March, 1989.

E. G. Manes, A class of fuzzy theories, *J. Math. Anal. Appl.* 85, 1982, 409-451.

E. G. Manes, Guard modules, *Algebra Universalis* 21, 1985, 103-110.

E. G. Manes, Assertional Categories, in M. Main (ed.), Mathematical Foundation of Programming Language Semantics, *Lecture Notes in Computer Science* 298, Springer-Verlag, 1988, 85-120.

E. G. Manes, Adas and the equational theory of if-then-else, *Algebra Universalis*, 1992, to appear.

E. G. Manes and M. A. Arbib, *Algebraic Approaches to Program Semantics*, Springer-Verlag, 1986.

E. G. Manes and D. B. Benson, The inverse semigroup of a sum-ordered semiring, *Semigroup Forum* 31, 1985, 129-152.

C. E. Martin, C. A. R. Hoare and He Jifeng, Pre-adjunctions in order enriched categories, *Mathematical Structures in Computer Science* 1, 1991, 141-158.

J. McCarthy, A basis for a mathematical theory of computation, in P. Braffort and D.

Hirschberg (eds.), *Computer Programming and Formal Systems*, North-Holland, 1963.

B. Mitchell, *Theory of Categories*, Academic Press, 1965.

E. Moggi, Notions of computation and monads, *Information and Computation* **93**, 1991, 55-92.

V. R. Pratt, Semantical considerations on Floyd-Hoare logic, *Proc. 17th IEEE Symposium on the Foundations of Computer Science*, 1976, 109-121.

V. R. Pratt, Dynamic algebras and the nature of induction, *Proc. 12th ACM Symp. Theory. Comput.*, 1980, 22-28.

E. Robinson and G. Rosolini, Categories of partial maps, *Inform. Computation* **79**, 1988, 95-130.

D.E. Rydeheard and R.M. Burstall, *Computational Category Theory*, Prentice-Hall, 1988.

K. Segerburg, A completeness theorem in the modal logic of programs, *Notices Amer. Math. Soc.* **24**, 1977, A-522.

D. Spencer, A Survey of categorical computation: fixed points, partiality, combinators, ... control?, *Bull. EATCS* **43**, 1990, 285-312.

Gh. Stefănescu, On flowchart theories: Part I. The deterministic case, *J. Comput. Sys. Sci.* **35**, 1987, 163-191.

J. E. Stoy, *The Scott-Strachey Approach to Programming Language Theory*, M. I. T. Press, 1977.

M. Tierney, Sheaf theory and the continuum hypothesis, in F. W. Lawvere (ed.), *Toposes, Algebraic Geometry and Logic*, Lecture Notes in Mathematics **274**, Springer-Verlag, 1972, 13-42.

N. Yoneda, On the homology theory of modules, *J. Fac. Sci. Tokyo, Sec. I.*, **7**, 1954, 193-227.

INDEX

Printed in the United States
By Bookmasters